The VisiCalc Applications Book

Jack Grushcow

Reston Publishing Company, Inc.
A Prentice-Hall Company
Reston, Virginia 22090

*This book is dedicated to
Anne and Joseph Abrams*

Library of Congress Cataloging in Publication Data
Grushcow, Jack.
   The VisiCalc applications book.

   1.VisiCalc (Computer program) I. Title.
QA76.6.G787 1982   001.64'25   82-15114
ISBN 0-8359-8390-0
ISBN 0-8359-8389-7 (pbk.)

©1983 by Jack Grushcow
All rights reserved. No part of this publication may be reproduced, stored in a retrieval system, or transmitted in any form or by any means, electronic, mechanical, photocopying, recording or otherwise, without the prior written permission of the publishers, with the exception that the packed model listings may be entered, stored and executed in a computer system, but they may not be reproduced for publication or sold for profit.

Disclaimer of Warranties and Limitation of Liabilities
   The author has taken due care in preparing this book and the packed models in it, including research, development, and testing to ascertain their effectiveness. The author and the publishers make no expressed or implied warranty of any kind with regard to these programs or the supplementary documentation in this book. In no event shall the author or the publishers be liable for the incidental or consequential damages in connection with or arising out of the furnishing, performance, or use of any of these models.

All rights reserved. No part of this book may be reproduced in any way, or by any means, without permission in writing from the publisher.

10   9   8   7   6   5   4   3

Printed in the United States of America

CONTENTS

Preface, v
Acknowledgments, vii
Why and How to Use this Book, viii

PART I   LEARNING TO USE VISICALC, 1

Chapter 1   VisiCalc: The Revolution Begins, 3
Chapter 2   The Preliminaries, 7
Chapter 3   Exploring the Electronic Sheet, 17
Chapter 4   Balancing Your Checkbook with VisiCalc, 25
Chapter 5   Housekeeping on the Electronic Sheet, 33
Chapter 6   The Replicate Command: VisiCalc Shorthand, 41
Chapter 7   Modifying an Existing Model: Two for the Price of One, 55
Chapter 8   Manipulating the Electronic Sheet, 69
Chapter 9   Learning How to Use the Models in this Book, 83

PART II   APPLICATIONS AND MODELS, 93

Chapter 10   Credit Control, 95
Chapter 11   Financial Statement Analysis, 119
Chapter 12   Forecasting, 151
Chapter 13   Budgeting, 171
Chapter 14   Cash Management, 201
Chapter 15   Portfolio Management, 217
Appendix, 247
Index, 273

Preface

The VisiCalc Applications Book is written for both novice and advanced VisiCalc users. It is designed to help you apply VisiCalc to your own day-to-day business problems. As much effort is spent explaining *why* you should use VisiCalc for a specific business solution as is spent showing you *how*.

Potential purchasers of VisiCalc can use this book to discover what the electronic spread sheet is capable of doing for them.

The book is divided into two sections. The first is a hands-on tutorial, which begins by introducing the basic VisiCalc commands. You learn each command as it is needed in the context of building different models. The tutorial slowly moves on to the more advanced areas of spread sheet design and modification. This insures that all readers understand how to use VisiCalc before moving on to the applications section.

The second section is devoted to the design of spread sheets that will improve the profitability and efficiency of your business. An overview of these application areas appears below.

- Credit Control   In times of high interest rates, speeding up collections is crucial. The models developed in this chapter help you collect faster and allow you to separate your good credit customers from bad. By using these spread sheets, you will know exactly how much it is costing you to offer credit each month. You will also get an aged analysis of your outstanding receivables.

- Financial Statement Analysis   This model lets the potential investor, trade creditor, or manager measure a company's performance using a series of key financial ratios. These ratios tell the story of a company's liquidity, efficiency, profitability, and long-term solvency.
- Forecasting   The models developed in this chapter make up a two-step forecasting system. The first model is used to help you develop your sales forecast. The second model then uses this forecast to project your income statement into the future. This lets you measure the effect that the projected sales will have on your future profits.
- Budgeting   Both manufacturer's and retailer's budgets are built in this chapter. The manufacturer's budgets are designed to control labor and material costs. The retailer's budgets are designed to guard against shrinking profit margins.
- Cash Management   These models are designed to help both large companies and small businesses reduce borrowing costs and to make better use of short-term funds.
- Portfolio Management   Tax reporting, monitoring cash flow from investments, analyzing portfolio composition, and recording transactions are performed by the models developed in this chapter.

The keystrokes necessary to build each of the models in the book are provided for you. You can also order your own copy of these models stored on a floppy disk, saving you the work of keying the models in yourself. The order form can be found immediately preceding the Appendix.

This book teaches business management principles at the same time as it shows you how to apply VisiCalc. No VisiCalc model, or any other management tool, can help you if you don't know how and where to use it.

This book, and the models it contains, were designed to make your business run more efficiently and profitably. If it helps you reach these goals, its purpose will have been well served.

Acknowledgments

I would like to thank some of the people who helped *The VisiCalc Applications Book* see the light of day.

First and foremost, my thanks to Sandy, who has worked many long hours with me to put this book together. Her hard work, attention to detail, and moral support were crucial in helping this project come together.

I am indebted to the Tandy Corporation, which has generously lent me one of its excellent Model II microcomputers for this project. Thanks especially to Dave Gunzel and Heinz Stier of Radio Shack.

Bill Campbell and Karen Edwards from the local Radio Shack Computer Center contributed generously their time, energy, and ideas. They were both a source of inspiration.

Thanks to Geoff Swannell, corporate planner at B.C. Resources and friend, who spent time leading me through the sometimes confusing maze of corporate finance.

To my friend Tom Shiffman, entrepreneur extraordinaire, for his comments about life in the retail business.

To Chris Evans, investment department, National Trust, and Phil Swift, corporate planning, B.C. Timber, for their comments.

Each of these people has helped improve this book.

Any errors or omissions remain, as always, the sole responsibility of the author.

Why and How to Use this Book

> I think that it may be true that fortune is the ruler of half of our actions, but she allows the other half or thereabouts to be governed by us.
>
> Machiavelli
> (1469-1527)

WHY

At the time that Machiavelli made this observation, man thought that the earth was the center of the solar system. Columbus was still on his voyage of discovery and Guttenberg had only recently finished building his press. Back in this medieval era Machiavelli believed man could control a good part of his destiny.

We are just beginning the decade of the 1980's. Telephones can instantly connect us to any part of the world. Television signals bounce off orbiting satellites before they appear in our living rooms. We are in a time when many of us can have our own computer—a machine that extends the reach of our minds in the same way the space shuttle has extended the reach of our senses.

How much of our fate are we now able to control?

This book is about how you can use your personal computer to wrestle with fate and reduce its impact on the way you live and do business. It can mark the beginning of your participation in the most challenging era since the industrial revolution. And you don't have to be a computer expert to join.

This book is about learning to use VisiCalc, the first computer tool to be made available for everyone. It's a tool that lets you harness the vast power of the personal computer and apply it to solve your day-to-day problems.

By reading the first part of this book you can learn to use VisiCalc in several hours. Next, six applications chapters will show you how VisiCalc can be used to help your business and your private finances run more efficiently. That means more profits, with more time left over to enjoy them.

HOW

The VisiCalc Applications Book has been designed in a modular way so that each reader can easily get to the information needed. The time you take to read this section will be saved many times over. Read the first sentence in the following paragraphs. When you find a description that fits, the paragraph will tell you how to proceed.

1. You have heard a lot about microcomputers and VisiCalc and you want to know what all the noise is about. Read Chapter 1 in Part I entitled "VisiCalc: The Revolution Begins" to get an overview of VisiCalc. Select one or two of the applications chapters contained in Part II that interest you and read through them. Concentrate on the models section at the end of each chapter, as this will illustrate how VisiCalc is applied to specific problems. To really get an appreciation of what VisiCalc is all about, you should go to a computer store and ask for a demonstration. Watching it work is half the fun.

2. You are thinking of buying a microcomputer and want to know what VisiCalc can do for you. The first chapter, "VisiCalc: The Revolution Begins" gives you a general appreciation of what VisiCalc is all about. After reading Chapter 1, turn to Part II and read through the applications. Skim the first part of these chapters and examine the models section contained at the end of each chapter. The models section explains what VisiCalc can do

x Why and How to Use this Book

for you in each of the application areas. To complete the picture you should see VisiCalc demonstrated at your local computer store.

3. You recently bought a microcomputer, you are a new VisiCalc user and want to know how to get the most out of VisiCalc. You should read the book from cover to cover. Start with Part I and go through the lessons step-by-step. It's a "hands-on" learning guide. You will sit in front of your computer and follow the lessons at your own speed. After you know how to use VisiCalc, you can go to the specific applications chapters in Part II.

4. You own a microcomputer and have used VisiCalc a bit. Read Chapters 1 and 2 to get an overview of VisiCalc and see how to translate the various keystrokes for use on your micro. Skim the other chapters in Part I until you get to the final chapter in the section entitled "How to Use the Models in this Book." Read this chapter carefully and do the exercise. Once you understand this chapter you can proceed to Part II and the applications chapters that interest you.

5. You own a microcomputer, are an experienced VisiCalc user, and want to use the models contained in the book. Read Chapter 9 entitled "How to Use the Models in this Book." Be sure to do the cash flow exercise. Once you understand this chapter you can proceed to Part II and the applications chapters that interest you.

The author would like to hear about your experiences with using the models in this book. Comments would be appreciated and can be sent in care of the author to:

> Reston Publishing Company, Inc.
> 11480 Sunset Hills Road
> Reston, Virginia 22090

Part 1

Learning to Use VisiCalc

Chapter 1

VisiCalc®:
The Revolution Begins

The invention of the electronic spread sheet is for microcomputers what the invention of the light bulb was for electricity. A tremendous source of raw power is transformed into a tool which we can all use and from which we can all benefit.

The creation of VisiCalc and the legion of similar products that will follow signal the deliverance of computer technology from the mysterious back rooms of the digital wizards into the offices, schools, and homes of North America and Europe. The 1980s will see the development of many new software products that will convert small computers into powerful tools specifically designed to solve many of our everyday problems.

This book is divided into two parts. The first part is an introduction to using VisiCalc. It is a "hands-on" instruction manual which has been designed so that you learn to use VisiCalc as you solve specific problems. By learning to apply VisiCalc to familiar problems, we have found that people learn faster and remember more of what they learn. This manual was developed as the result of extensive field experience. It has been distilled from teaching VisiCalc to different groups ranging from students to engineers.

VisiCalc® is a registered trademark of VisiCorp. Personal Software, Inc.

The second part of the book is devoted to specific VisiCalc applications. These VisiCalc spread sheets are designed to increase the efficiency and profitability of your business. Once you know how to build VisiCalc models, the next step is to see where and how specific models can be used in a business environment. Knowing how to use VisiCalc is like knowing how to cook. Most of us can cook, and some can cook better than others, but almost everyone can improve by examining the suggestions of James Beard or Craig Claiborne. The application chapters are designed to broaden your VisiCalc horizons and to furnish you with a series of models that you will be able to use for many of your business challenges.

There are six applications chapters. Each chapter is divided into two sections. The first section acts as a general introduction to the application area. The introductions are designed to place the models that follow in a meaningful framework. The idea is to insure that the reader is familiar enough with the individual subject to use the models with an appreciation of their limitations as well as their benefits.

The second section of each application chapters deals with the actual VisiCalc models. First, the keystrokes necessary to create the models can be found in the appendix. Each application chapter's title appears, followed by the model names and appropriate keystrokes necessary to build each one. Next, an actual example is loaded into the spread sheet. This allows you to learn how to customize the book's models so that they fit your own particular situation.

Since some of the models developed in the applications chapters are large, they will require some time and effort to key them into the VisiCalc sheet. For the readers that would like to be able to load the models directly from disk (we will discuss how this is done shortly), they can be purchased in disk form. To order your own copy of the applications models, see the order form immediately preceding the Appendix.

A general introduction begins each applications chapter and is meant to act only as an introduction. It would be impossible to examine each subject in detail in this book. Each applications chapter ends with a bibliography which contains further suggested reading. This allows you to explore the subject in more depth should you so desire.

Just what is this electronic sheet, and how can it help solve your problems while it saves you time and money? VisiCalc magically creates the perfect sheet of paper. Using it, you can make changes quickly and easily. It calculates results in less time than it takes for you to reach for your pencil sharpener, and recalculates using new data just as quickly. It grows and shrinks in size so that it can accommodate either a hundred rows and columns or only a few. It lets you see how increases in your production costs, changing consumer demand for your goods and services, new government regulations, and many other "What if?" situations affect your business. These are just some of the features that we will enjoy discovering in the first part of the VisiCalc Applications Book.

The idea of the electronic sheet began with the observation that much of our day-to-day work requires calculations. Whether we are figuring out payroll, how much new stock we need to order, or our bank balance, the process is usually the same. We roll up our sleeves, get the pencil and paper, and begin scratching away.

The thing to note about these calculations is that the data, the numbers on which you are basing your calculations, will constantly change as your business conditions change. However, the way you use this data to calculate payroll, determine how much stock you need to order, or find your bank balance, remains the same. You perform the same calculations over and over again with new data. This translates into hundreds of tasks that are time consuming, error prone, and tedious.

The inventors of VisiCalc made another key observation: Much of this type of work is organized into rows and columns. Look at any of the order forms, ledgers, or time sheets that clutter your office. You will see that a grid of rows and columns appears on many of your own work sheets.

The spectrum of VisiCalc applications is amazingly diverse. Complex budgets, sales forecasting, analyzing financial statements, football pool accounting, managing inventory, tracking team bowling performance, and managing personal investments represent only a few samples taken from the universe of VisiCalc applications. This book will teach you how to create your own unique VisiCalc models.

Chapter 2

The Preliminaries

This book has been designed for owners of the Apple, IBM, and Radio Shack personal computers. The vast majority of VisiCalc instructions are identical, regardless of the computer you own. For this reason, a single manual can be used to teach VisiCalc on the various machines. There are, however, some differences involved in using VisiCalc on the various computers. In fact, for the purposes of our introduction to VisiCalc, there are five main differences encountered when using VisiCalc on the various machines. These have to do with the keys that move the cursor, the amount of the electronic sheet that can be displayed on the screen at one time, the key that is used to cause a back space, the key used to enter information into the VisiCalc sheet, and the use of the repeat key. Do not worry if all these terms are not familiar, as they will be explained in detail as we discuss each difference separately.

Before we examine the differences, turn to the computer section at the end of this chapter. Take a moment to examine the keyboard picture of the micro you own, have access to, or just plain covet. We will refer to this diagram at several points throughout this section so you should know where to find the diagram of your particular micro.

The first difference we will discuss involves how you move the cursor on the VisiCalc screen. Throughout this book we will adopt a convention that any characters displayed in boldface are to be typed into the VisiCalc program. The VisiCalc commands that you will be instructed to enter will be the same, regardless of the computer you are using. The differences will be the key you have to use on your micro to produce the required characters. We use the four arrows ▲ ▼ ◄ ► to indicate cursor motion in one of the four directions. For example, if we said "enter these keystrokes: ►►▼", you would type the keys on your computer that would cause the cursor to move two spaces to the right and one space down. Turn to the picture of your micro at the end of this chapter. Below the picture you will find point 1. Read it now to see which keys you will use to cause the cursor to move in each of the four directions. Do this before you read any further.

For those of you who own an Apple, you should now know that since your keyboard only has two directional arrows, ► and ◄, you need to use the space bar to go from horizontal to vertical mode. The owners of the Radio Shack Model II, III, and IBM computers can use the four keys indicated to get direct motion in each of the four directions. After reading point 1 on your specific micro, you should know which keys to enter when the ▲ ▼ ◄ ► keys are requested.

The second difference among the computers is that they may have screens of different widths. Screen widths for the micros discussed in this book can range from 40 to 80 characters. In order to illustrate what a screen should look like at various points in the book, we will use pictures of the VisiCalc screen so that you can compare your model to ours. Unfortunately, the VisiCalc screen will look different depending on the width of your computer display. The wider screens will display more columns at one time than the narrower screens. Whenever we show a picture of the screen we will show an 80-column display. This allows us to see more of the VisiCalc sheet. When we use a picture we introduce it with a sentence like, "Your screen should look like the picture below." If your screen is less than 80 columns wide, then your screen will only show part of what appears in the picture. This will become clear when we start using the screen pictures. At that time we will learn how to look at the part of the VisiCalc sheet that is hidden from view.

The third difference among the computers is which key you must depress to cause a back space to occur. This key will come in handy when we need to correct typing errors. Turn again to the diagram of your micro and see which key to enter when the *BS* key is specified.

You should now know which key your micro uses when we call for a *BS* to be entered.

The next difference between the various systems is the key required to enter data into the VisiCalc model. Turn to the diagram of your micro and notice which key to press when we say type Ⓔ.

The final difference has to do with the repeat key. Turn once again to your micro's keyboard and read point 2.

To make sure that you know how to use your own specific keyboard, ask yourself which keys you would use to type the following characters: ◀ ▶ ▼ ▲ Ⓔ *BS* ▶▶▶▶▶▶▶. Hint: In the last group of " ▶ " characters, use the repeating effect.

This covers the main differences that we will need to be concerned with in the introduction to VisiCalc section. We now have a common way to refer to the different keyboards on the Radio Shack, Apple, and IBM computers.

We can now take our first look at VisiCalc. At this point, you should get your VisiCalc users guide. Read the introduction section at the beginning of the manual if you have not done so already. This will show you how to load the VisiCalc program and how to make back-up copies of your master VisiCalc disk. These instructions will apply to your own particular brand of microcomputer.

Once you have read the introduction, go to your computer and follow the instructions for making a back-up copy of your master VisiCalc disk. You will use this back-up disk throughout the introduction section of this book.

Not all versions of VisiCalc allow back-up copies of the master disk to be made. If this is the case with your version of VisiCalc, be sure to handle your master disk with special care. You should initialize a storage disk to use throughout this book to store our sample models.

Before proceeding beyond this point, you should

1. Know which keys on your microcomputer represent the special characters discussed in this chapter.
2. Know how to load VisiCalc.
3. Have a back-up copy made of your VisiCalc disk. If this is not possible, then initialize a new storage disk.

COMPUTER SECTION

TRS-80 MODEL II

1. Your keyboard has the four directional keys indicated.
2. The repeat key shown above needs to be used with the key you

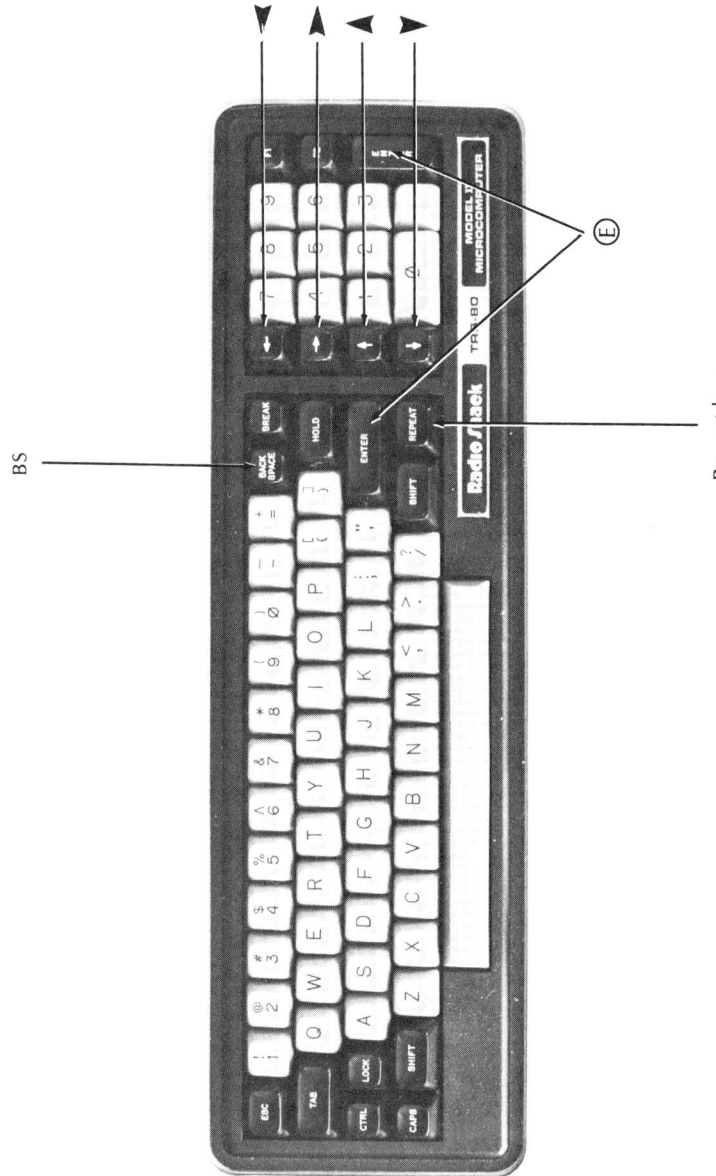

Figure 2-1 TRS-80 Model II

want repeated. You hold down the repeat key and enter the key you want repeated, keeping both keys depressed at the same time.

TRS-80 MODEL III

1. Your keyboard has the four directional keys indicated.
2. Your computer keyboard has keys that repeat automatically. All you have to do is hold a key down for a few seconds and it will automatically begin repeating.

APPLE II

1. Your keyboard has only the two directional keys shown. When you first load VisiCalc, these keys will allow you to move the cursor to the left or right. If you want to change the direction that these arrows let you move, you need to enter the space bar. When you do this the ▶ will cause the cursor to move down while the ◀ will cause the cursor to move up. To change direction you enter the space bar again.

    In the upper right-hand corner of your VisiCalc screen you will see the letter "C" followed by either "!" or "-". These characters tell you whether your two directional arrows will move horizontally, "-", or vertically, "!". By using the space bar you switch back and forth from horizontal to vertical motion.

    Suppose you have just loaded your VisiCalc program and you are told to enter the keystrokes ▶▶▼. You would enter ▶▶ "space bar" ▶. The space bar lets you change from horizontal to vertical mode. Use the directional indicator to keep track of what mode you are in. We will illustrate how this works shortly.
2. The repeat key shown above needs to be used with the key you want repeated. You hold down the repeat key and enter the key you want repeated, keeping both keys depressed at the same time.

IBM PERSONAL COMPUTER

1. Your keyboard has a dual purpose numerical keypad. By depressing the "NUM LOCK" key, you can use the four keys indi-

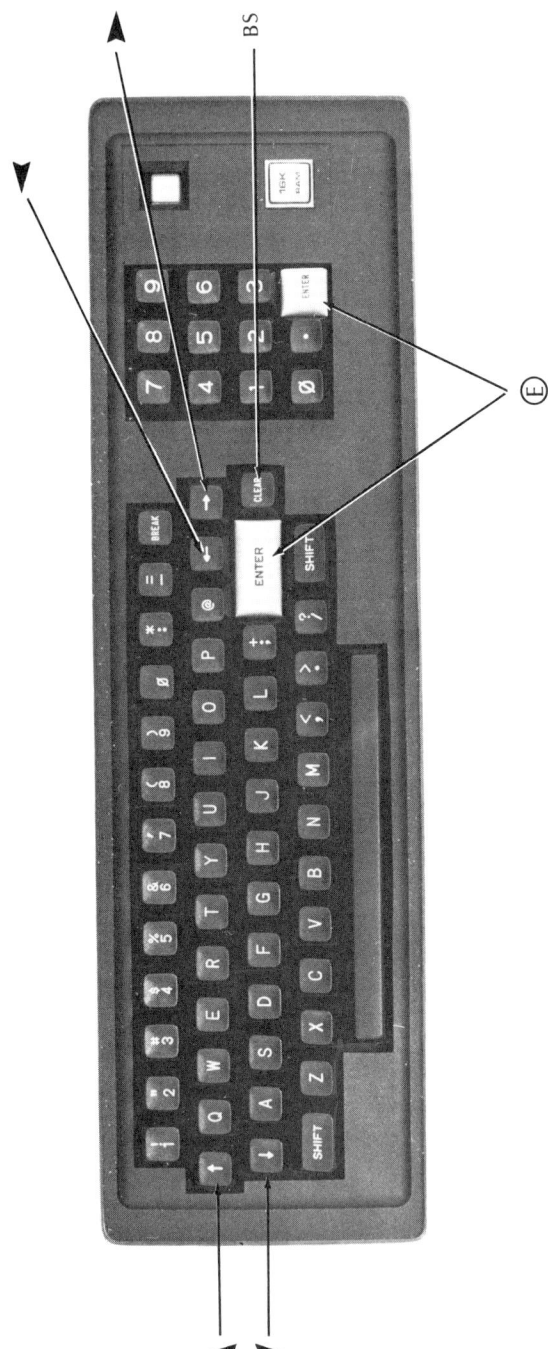

Figure 2-2 TRS-80 Model III

Figure 2-3 Apple II

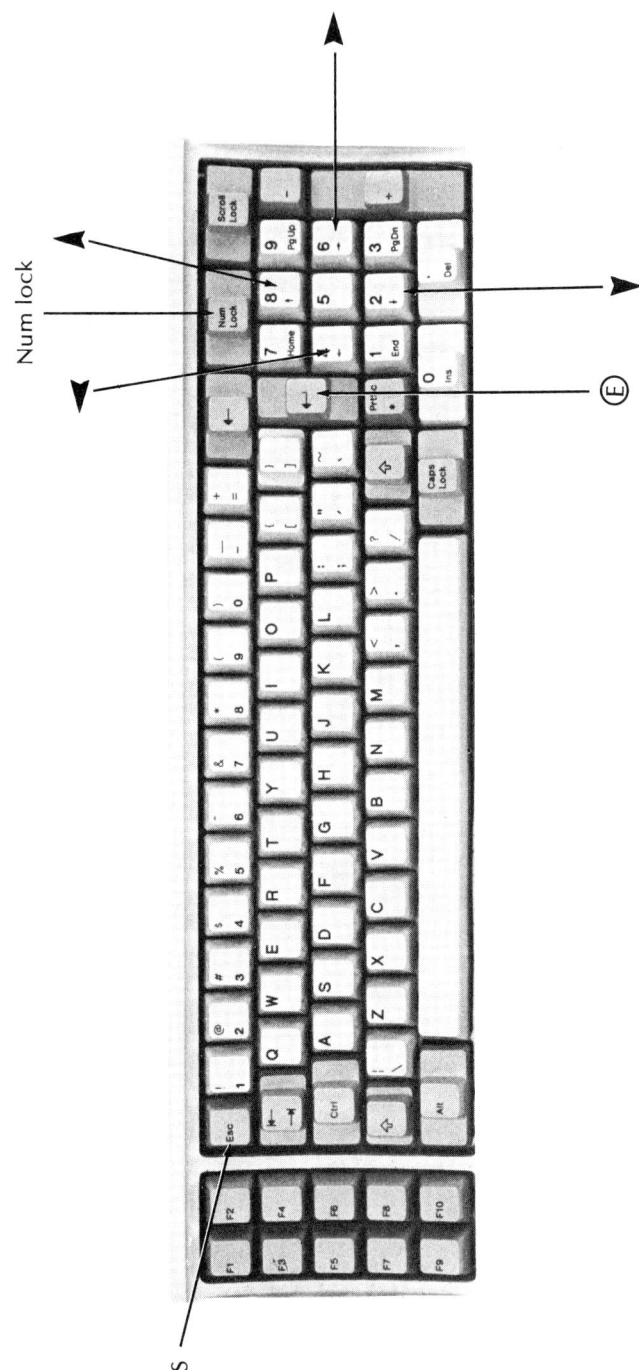

Figure 2-4 IBM Personal Computer

cated to move the cursor in any direction. By releasing the "NUM LOCK" key, these directional keys revert to numeric keys.
2. Your computer keyboard has keys that repeat automatically. All you have to do is hold a key down for a few seconds and it will automatically begin repeating.

Chapter 3

Exploring the Electronic Sheet

We will now spend some time getting a general feel for the VisiCalc sheet. Following the instructions for your computer, load your working copy of VisiCalc. Once the program is loaded you should see a screen that looks like Fig. 3-1.

In the upper portion of the screen you will see a line displaying the letters A through H. If your computer display has fewer than 80 columns, your screen will be displaying fewer letters across the top of the screen. To compare your screen to the one in the picture, begin at the left and move to the right comparing column for column. When you get to the right edge of your own display, the comparison will be complete. We will learn how to look at the concealed portion of your screen shortly.

Across the top of the screen you will see "Software Arts, Inc.," displayed along with the year and the version number of your VisiCalc Program. The year and the version number that are shown on your screen will be different from the ones in the picture. This is as it should be. The various versions will differ from one machine to another.

In the upper right-hand corner you will see the letter "C" and this may or may not be followed by a dash, "-". The dash is called the directional indicator. If your computer has all four directional keys you will not see a dash displayed beside the "C". IBM and Radio Shack Model II and III owners can skip the next paragraph because it explains what the dash is all about. If your screen displays the dash, read on.

18 Learning to Use VisiCalc

Figure 3-1

If you have only two directional arrows on your keyboard, you already know that you need to use the space bar to go from horizontal to vertical mode. The directional indicator lets you know what mode you are currently in. If the dash is shown, the arrows can move you either to the left or right. If the exclamation point is displayed, the two arrows will move you up or down. Depress the space bar several times. Each time you press the bar the directional indicator flips back and forth between the horizontal and vertical positions.

The letter "C" refers to the order of recalculation. This indicates whether VisiCalc will calculate the spread sheet across the rows or down the columns. We will always recalculate our models in column order.

The number that appears below the "C" is the memory indicator. This number tells you how much room is left in the computer's memory. Since VisiCalc models can grow to be quite large, it is possible to run out of computer memory. The memory indicator keeps you informed of how much space you have left. The number displayed is in thousands of characters, so if the number 25 appears below the "C" you have room to store 25,000 more characters of information on your VisiCalc sheet. When you first load VisiCalc this number will tell you how much memory your computer has. As the model grows this number will shrink as memory is used. It always shows the amount of memory still remaining.

A broad white bar appears across the top of the VisiCalc screen. This bar is actually composed of two separate lines. Model III owners have the same two lines at the top of their screens, but they are not shown in white. The top line is called the Entry Contents line and the bottom one is called the Prompt line. The Prompt line displays the "Software Arts, Inc." message.

Another line appears below the Prompt line, sandwiched between the Prompt line and the top of the VisiCalc sheet. This is the Edit line. As we begin to enter data into the electronic sheet we will use this line as a kind of examination area. It is here that we can make any corrections that are required to the information before we enter it into the sheet.

The entire upper section that is made up of these three special lines is called the Control Panel. This area acts as a central control through which we will communicate with VisiCalc. The various functions of the Control Panel will become clear as we begin to use VisiCalc.

To be sure that you know what the control panel on your computer looks like you can refer to your pocket reference card that comes with your VisiCalc documentation. The reference card has a labeled illustration of your control panel.

Below the Control Panel you will see a row of letters beginning with "A". These letters are used to name the columns of the VisiCalc sheet. Down the left side of the screen are the numbers starting from 1. These numbers are used to identify the rows of the VisiCalc sheet. Together they form a grid of letters and numbers that are used to locate the various "intersections" on the VisiCalc street map. If you want to refer to a particular location on the sheet, you can do so by specifying a coordinate such as A1. This means that you are referring to the position that is in column A and row 1. Similarly, the address of the position that is two columns over and on the same line as A1 would be C1. Using this convention any location on the VisiCalc sheet can be specified.

If you look at location A1, you will notice a white rectangle. This is called the cursor. The cursor acts as our guide to the electronic sheet. If we could physically write on the VisiCalc sheet, the cursor would be our pen. It gives us a way to reach any location on the sheet, and provides the means to enter information into the various locations or cells.

Let us begin using the VisiCalc sheet by learning to move the cursor around the screen. Type the ► character on your keyboard. You will notice that the cursor has moved one space to the right. You are now in location B1. Look at the left-hand corner of the Entry Contents line. You will notice that the current position of the cursor is displayed at the left-hand edge of the line. Enter the ◄ character to move the cursor back to A1. The entry location has changed to reflect the current cursor position. One way to find out your current cursor position is to look at the Entry line.

Enter the keystrokes ►►. The cursor obediently moves two spaces to the right. The Entry line changes to report that your current position is C1. Now enter ▼ (remember that if you have a keyboard that does not have four directional arrows, you will have to hit the space bar first to switch from horizontal to vertical direction). The cursor will now move down one row and you will be in position C2. If you are not sure where you are, simply look at "central control." It reports your current position as C2.

Take a few minutes to move the cursor around the screen. The status area always keeps you posted on your current position. Try moving the cursor from right to left as well as up and down.

Move the cursor back to A1. If you have entered some characters onto the screen accidentally, do not worry. You can wipe the screen clear by typing **/CY.** In either case, you should be looking at a blank screen with your cursor at A1.

Keep in mind throughout this section that you can not harm the VisiCalc program regardless of the characters you type in at the keyboard. Short of actually doing physical harm to the machine, there is no way to upset the VisiCalc program. Think of your screen as a superblackboard. Anything that you scribble on it can easily be wiped away. No matter how big the mess you can always start over again with a clean sheet.

So far we have only sampled a small area of the electronic sheet. What we can see on our screen at any one time is only the tip of the iceberg, the upper left portion of the iceberg, in fact. The electronic sheet extends far to the right and below our current cursor position.

Just how much space does VisiCalc give us? We can use the cursor to find out. Begin typing ► and continue to do so until the cursor "bumps" into the right edge of the screen. This will take a minute or two. As you continue typing ►, you will notice that the letters across the top of the screen begin to change. You are actually moving to a different section of the sheet. The letters of the alphabet are moving across the top of your screen informing you that you are moving farther into the VisiCalc sheet. The ability of the cursor to push its way past the end of the screen and beyond is called scrolling. By moving the cursor to the right you are moving your VisiCalc viewing window along with you.

As you continue tapping away at the ► key you may begin to get a bit impatient. A convenient alternative to constantly pecking away at the ► key is to use the repeat capability on your keyboard. If you have a repeat key (Model II and Apple II), hold it down and enter ▶. If your keyboard repeats automatically (Model III and IBM), simply enter ▶ and keep this key depressed. The cursor will motor happily along on its own.

Continue pressing the keys down and you will see that you go past all the letters until you reach Z. Since we have run past the 26 letters of the alphabet, the columns now need two letters in order to have a unique name. If you continue holding down the keys you will eventually get to the column named BK. This is the end of the line. The cursor can move no further to the right. There are 63 columns on the VisiCalc sheet, and you have finally bumped into the right-hand edge of the sheet.

If you now enter ▼ along with the repeat key, you will begin going down the rows of the electronic sheet. As you bump into the bottom edge of the screen, the row numbers will scroll along on your left. Eventually you will reach the last row which is row number 254. The Entry line informs you that you are now in position BK254, which is the lower right-hand edge of the screen—a long way from our starting location at A1.

Pause for a moment and consider what we have just done. The majority of the electronic sheet is hiding behind your small video display. You can only see a small piece of it at a time. By moving the cursor you can scroll to any section of the screen that you desire. It is as if you are wearing a horse's blinders which allow you to only see one piece of the whole sheet at any given time. Moving your cursor is like moving your blinders around—you can only see one section of the sheet at a time. The narrower your screen, the smaller the section of the sheet you can see at one time.

We now have a way to compare narrower screens to the illustrations in the book. Compare your own screen to the picture from left to right. When you get to the edge of your screen and you want to check the next few columns against the picture, move the cursor to the right to scroll the next few columns into view. This way you can check all of your columns against the pictures.

The cursor is still at BK254. Do we have to sit around with our fingers glued to the keyboard to get back to our starting point at A1? Even using the repeat key it would take a while. Fortunately, there is a better way. VisiCalc provides an express route to any location on the sheet that you care to reach.

Type > and look at the Prompt line. That is the middle line that makes up the status area. The message "GO TO: COORDINATE" is displayed. VisiCalc is using the Prompt line to ask you for information. When you typed >, you informed VisiCalc that you wanted to move directly to a specific location, bypassing all the intermediate locations.

VisiCalc is asking for the location you want to select as your destination. Type **A1 Ⓔ,** and watch as we are transported back to our initial starting point. That is a much quicker way to get around on the VisiCalc sheet.

Notice that we had to follow the keystrokes A1 with Ⓔ. This special Ⓔ key is used anytime we want VisiCalc to process a request. For example, we could have entered AA1, A111, or AA111 to VisiCalc's request for a destination. Each of these addresses represents a valid location on the VisiCalc sheet. The only way VisiCalc can distinguish one of these responses from the other is to rely on us to signal when we are finished entering the address. The special Ⓔ key is used for this purpose. It says, in effect, "message complete." Whenever you press this key, VisiCalc will process your current request.

Take a few minutes to send the cursor around to various parts of the sheet. Try entering in a location like AAA1 or 23I and see what happens. Even though these are not valid locations, VisiCalc is very forgiving and responds by simply ignoring your request to move to a nonexistent location. After you get the feel for how to move the cursor directly from cell to cell, return to A1.

This brings us to the end of our initial chapter on the use of VisiCalc. Each of the first nine chapters is like a course in a gourmet meal; one chapter prepares you for the next while never leaving you too full to enjoy what is still to come.

We learn best when physically and emotionally rested. As we assimilate new concepts and ideas we begin to tire, and as a result the learning process becomes more difficult. We have tried to make each chapter easy to digest. We suggest that after you complete a chapter you take a break. This will give you time to assimilate the information covered in the chapter.

In order to encourage you to take "the pause that refreshes," each chapter ends with a point form review of the major ideas that were covered. After you have completed a chapter you can turn off your computer, sink into a comfortable chair, and take some time to review the major topics of the chapter. You will find that VisiCalc is easy to learn, but stopping from time to time and reviewing our progress will help you to absorb the VisiCalc basics much easier. By taking a break between chapters, you will find the learning more enjoyable, and at the same time, you will retain more of what you learn.

Below you will find the first of our chapter summaries. These summaries will be useful in several ways. In addition to reviewing the information contained in the chapters, they help you pick up where you left off if several days have passed since you last used the book. The summaries also allow readers to scan the chapter contents to see if the material contains matter of interest to them.

SUMMARY

- We began our look at the electronic sheet by introducing the memory indicator and the recalculation order indicator.
- We saw that the electronic sheet is divided into a grid section and a status section.
- The grid section is composed of many cells. Each cell is identified with a unique address, composed of a column letter and a row number and makes the screen look a bit like a street map.
- We introduced the status area which is the communications link through which we interact with the VisiCalc program.
- The status area is actually composed of three different lines. They are the Entry Contents, Prompt, and Edit lines. Each uses its own set of functions to keep us informed of the current status of the electronic sheet.
- You can move the cursor to any location on the grid using any of the direction keys, and you can also use the direction keys in combination with your microcomputer's repeat capability.
- We discovered that the cursor can be used to scroll across the screen, and we learned that we could only see a small portion of the screen at any one time.
- Upon discovering the true size of the screen during our travels to BK254, we learned how to use direct cursor movement: the ">" command.
- Using direct cursor movement introduced us to our first VisiCalc prompt, and we had to use the Ⓔ key to indicate to VisiCalc that we had completed entering our destination address.

We can now begin to learn how to enter information into the electronic sheet, and we will also build our first VisiCalc model.

Chapter 4

Balancing Your Checkbook with VisiCalc

If you have taken a break from the computer, reload your VisiCalc program. We will now construct a VisiCalc model that will balance a checkbook. The purpose of the examples developed in this section of the book is to learn the VisiCalc commands in the context of building various models. We have started with simple models intentionally so that you can concentrate on using VisiCalc.

We know how to move our cursor from one location to another on the electronic sheet. The next step will be to fill some of these cells with useful information.

What kind of information can we store in the VisiCalc sheet? All the information we can enter into the VisiCalc sheet can be divided into one of two groups: labels or values. Labels are composed of letters, characters, and other symbols that are used to describe the data that have been entered into the sheet. Labels are used to provide descriptive information or to enhance the appearance of our VisiCalc sheet. Values, on the other hand, are numbers that can be used in calculations. A value can also include a formula or a function that results in a number.

Since this example is about balancing a checkbook, we will begin building our spread sheet by entering an appropriate title at the top of the electronic sheet. Move the cursor to C1, and type **CHECK**. Notice the status area. As soon as you typed the first letter C in CHECK the word "Label" appeared in the Prompt line. This indicates that VisiCalc recognizes that you are entering a label in the cell at C1. At the same time as the label appears, the letters that you type into the cell at C1 are displayed on the Edit line. As long as the contents of the cell appear on the Edit line, you can alter the information before you actually enter it into the cell. To illustrate this, use the *BS* key to back over the label. Enter **BS** key five times. You will see the letters K, C, E, H, and C disappear one at a time as you hit the *BS* key. Notice that the letters disappear in location C1 as well as on the Edit line. After you have entered the *BS* key five times, there should not be any letters showing at C1. Now enter **BS** key one more time. The word "Label" has disappeared from the Prompt line. You have used the *BS* key to back out of entering a label in location C1 of the sheet.

Let us actually enter the label **CHECK** in position C1. This time, after typing the last letter of the label, type ▶. Now CHECK has disappeared from the Edit line. VisiCalc has entered the label CHECK in location C1. By moving the cursor over to the next cell you have signaled to VisiCalc that you are happy with the contents of the Edit line and you want it to be stored in C1. Your cursor is now at D1, and you have just written your first label onto the electronic sheet. To be sure, enter ◀ to move back to C1. The status area now shows that you are at location C1, and (L) and CHECK appear on the Entry Contents line. VisiCalc is reporting that you are in location C1 and that this location contains the label CHECK. VisiCalc displays (L) to indicate that a label is stored in a cell.

To add the next word in the title, enter ▶, which will move you to D1. Now enter the label BOOK in this location by typing **BOOK** Ⓔ while your cursor is at D1. Notice that after you type the last letter of the label—K—the label still appears on the Edit line. This is the same type of situation we encountered when we used direct cursor movement. In that example, we needed to tell VisiCalc that we had finished typing in our response to the "GO TO: COORDINATE" prompt. VisiCalc is waiting for us to indicate that we have finished entering the label. We signaled this last time by moving the cursor to the right. Let us use the Ⓔ key this time. Type Ⓔ and watch the status area. VisiCalc has transferred the label from the Edit line into the Entry Contents line. This indicates that the label has been stored in D1. We have used the Ⓔ key to signal that the label should be entered into the model as is, and we do not need to make any editing changes to it.

Our electronic checkbook should have a place reserved for the owner's name as well as a place to record the date on which the check data was last entered. To enter labels for this information, first type >**A2** Ⓔ to move the cursor to A2. Now type **NAME:** and ▼**DATE:** Ⓔ. Now we need to enter the name and date in the designated cells.

Enter ►▲ to move the cursor to the cell that we want to hold the name. Let us assume that this spread sheet will keep track of John Acorn's checkbook information. Enter his name at B2. Be sure to type **JOHN ACORN** then Ⓔ with your cursor at B2. With your cursor at B3, enter the date as follows: **JUL 31.**

Move your cursor to B2 and take a look at the Contents line and location B2. The label is too long to fit into the cell. The letters that are displayed at B2 are JOHN ACOR—the last letter, N, has been cut off. Only the first nine letters in the name are shown. If you look at the Entry line, however, you can see the entire name. What makes this happen? The Entry line can always be relied on to display the entire contents of each cell, regardless of how much information is stored in the cell. You can think of the Entry Contents line as a window on the cell. Even though we cannot see the full label when we look at the specific location, we can see the entire contents of any cell by simply moving the cursor to the cell in question and reading the Entry line. This feature is especially helpful if you have lots of words like Consolidation or Disbursement in your row and column titles. There is a way to make the cells wider so that you can see more of their contents, and we will learn how to do that a bit later.

Our electronic checkbook will be divided into five columns. These columns will record the date that the check was made out, who the check was payable to, the amount of each check, the amount of the deposit, and in the final column, we will record the account balance.

To improve the readability of the sheet, let us leave a line between the label DATE: and the names of the columns. To enter the names of the five columns enter the following keystrokes:>**A5** Ⓔ **DATE►PAY TO ►AMOUNT►DEPOSIT►BALANCE** Ⓔ. We have now written column headings across the top of our checkbook.

So far we have only entered labels on the electronic sheet. The first number we want to enter on the electronic sheet will be the opening account balance. Let us assume that John's opening account balance is $2,100. Move the cursor to E6 and type **2100** Ⓔ. Notice how the response on the Prompt line differs when you enter a number as opposed to a label. VisiCalc responds with the word "Value" on the Prompt line to signify that we have entered a numeric value in the location at E6. As in the case of the label we can use the *BS* key to back up and correct any errors in the value while it is still on the Edit line.

Now we can start to enter the checks that have been written during the month in question.

Suppose that on July 2 he wrote a check to cover rent, and the amount of the check was $450. To enter the check information into our

sheet we would enter the following keystrokes:>A7 Ⓔ JULY 2▶RENT
▶450 Ⓔ. The information has been entered in each of the appropriate columns.

The next step is to use VisiCalc to help us calculate the new account balance. Now you will begin to see why VisiCalc is such an amazing tool. Enter ▶▶ to move the cursor to E7 since this is where the new balance will be displayed. We want this cell to contain the difference between the $2,100 opening balance and the $450 rent check. Try typing in **2100-450** Ⓔ. The Entry line shows 2100-450; however, the cell contains the number 1650, which is the new bank balance.

When you store a formula in a cell VisiCalc will calculate the formula and display the result. The Entry Contents line, however, will always display the formula exactly as you entered it.

Let us continue this example by entering more of the checks that were written by Mr. Acorn in July. On July 5 he paid $250 to have the brakes on his car fixed. Enter this information using the following keystrokes:>A8 Ⓔ **JULY 5▶CAR REPAIR▶250** Ⓔ.

As we did with the last check, we will need to calculate the new account balance. This time, however, we will use a slightly different approach. We want to know the difference between our current balance of $1,650 and the amount of our latest check, the $250 for the car. We could simply enter 1650-250 in location E8 as we did last time and let VisiCalc calculate the answer. A better way would be to ask VisiCalc to subtract the contents of location C8 from the contents of location E7.

What makes this approach better? We should realize that in order for the checkbook model to be really useful it should work for different checks. If we keep entering the actual check amounts every time we need to calculate the new account balance we will be painting ourselves into a corner. Every time we add a new check or enter someone else's check information we will have to retype the old account balance and the check amount. When we use a formula we only need to enter the check amount in one place, and the new balance will automatically be calculated. This is referred to as using a cell reference in a formula.

One of the most powerful features of VisiCalc is that it allows you to perform calculations using numbers found in other parts of the sheet. Let us see how this works. With the cursor at E8 type **+E7-C8** Ⓔ. The correct new balance of 1400 is displayed, and this time the Entry line reveals that the formula +E7-C8 is stored in position E8.

The concept of using cell references is important enough to bear repeating. When VisiCalc goes to evaluate the formula +E7-C8 it substitutes the values currently in locations E7 and C8 into the formula first and then displays the result. In the current case the formula becomes 1650-250. Should we decide to change the amount of the car repair check the balance will be immediately altered. We will explore how this works in a moment.

You may be curious about why we had to enter the location E7 as +E7. Since we want to store a formula in location E8, we want VisiCalc to recognize it as a value so that a calculation will be performed. If we typed in the formula as E7-C8, VisiCalc would see the leading "E" in the formula as a letter and store the formula as a label. In order to tell VisiCalc that we are actually entering a value, we begin with a "+" symbol. As a result, the formula must be entered as +E7-C8.

Try changing the amount of the car repair check from $250 to $199.95. To do this move the cursor to C8 and type **199.95** Ⓔ. The current account balance instantly changes to reflect the new check amount! This instant recalculation feature is one of VisiCalc's key strengths.

In general, it is better to use formulas instead of typing in actual numbers. Should you need to change any of the numbers on the sheet (and it is a safe bet that you will have to, given how quickly things change), using formulas can save you from having to change a number in each location it appears.

To illustrate this point let us look back on how we handled the rent check. Suppose the rent check was entered incorrectly as $450, and the actual amount of Acorn's check was really $470. To correct this error you would have to change 450 to 470 at C7 as well as alter the formula in location E7. This formula would now have to be 2100-470 instead of 2100-450. Imagine how much work you would have to do if the model required this number in 20 different places! By defining general relationships using formulas, you end up with a more useful, flexible, and powerful model.

If we needed to correct the car repair check, all we need to do is alter the check amount that appears in C8. The new balance is automatically adjusted.

To continue with our example we need to enter the other checks that have been written on this account during the month. We will enter these other transactions one line at a time using the following keystrokes:

>A9 Ⓔ ►JULY 7►AMEX CARD►325.89►►+E8-C9 Ⓔ
>A10 Ⓔ ►JULY 15►CASH►100►►+E9-C10 Ⓔ

Suppose that Acorn is paid monthly and he earns $1500/month. We can record his deposit as follows: **>A11** Ⓔ **JULY 25 ►PAY ► ►1500 ►+E10+D11** Ⓔ. Notice that because we are making a deposit we add the contents of location D11, our deposit, to the account balance to get the new account balance.

To complete the electronic checkbook, let us calculate the total checks and deposits written in July. We will leave a line and enter the label "TOTALS" at A13. Use the following keystrokes:**>A13** Ⓔ **TOTALS** Ⓔ.

30 Learning to Use VisiCalc

We need to decide what formula to use to calculate the total checks written and the total deposits made during the month. Looking at the screen we can see that we will need to total the checks that are stored in locations C7, C8, C9, and C10. Move the cursor to C13 as this is where we want the total for the checks to appear. To store the formula, enter the following keystrokes with your cursor at C13: **+C7+C8+C9+C10 ▶**. By moving the cursor to the right after you enter the formula you store the formula in C13, and at the same time, you position the cursor over location D13. This is the location we want to use to store the deposit total. In this case the formula we use is simply "+D11", since we only have the one deposit. With your cursor at D13, enter +**D11** Ⓔ.

Move the cursor back to A1 and look at the electronic sheet. Your screen should now look like Fig. 4-1.

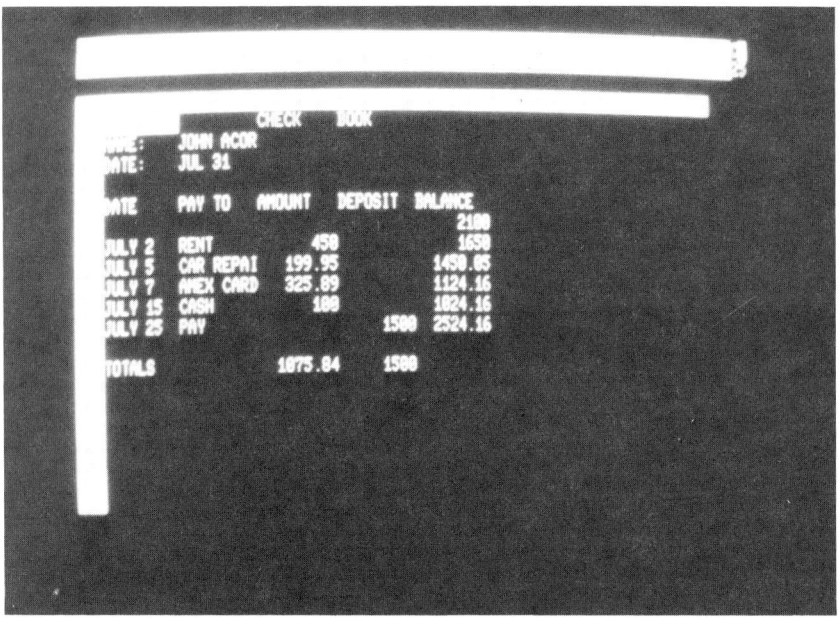

Figure 4-1

Let us save this model on our disk using the name "CHECKS." To save the VisiCalc model, type in the following keystrokes:/**SSCHECKS** Ⓔ. The light on your disk drive will go on and you will hear some whirring and clacking. We have just made a permanent copy of our VisiCalc spread sheet. This copy has been stored on the disk and can be loaded back into our VisiCalc screen whenever we want to use it again. By entering "**/SS**" in front of the model name, you instruct VisiCalc to save your current sheet under the name you supply. Similarly, "**/SL**" before a model name instructs VisiCalc to load the model.

Below, you will find a review of the material we have covered in this chapter.

SUMMARY

- We discussed how to enter values and labels onto the VisiCalc sheet. This led to the construction of our first model, the electronic checkbook.
- The Edit line allows us to change a value or label before we enter it into the electronic sheet through the use of the *BS* key.
- The Prompt line is where VisiCalc can request more information such as in the case of the "GO TO: COORDINATE" prompt when VisiCalc needs to know which location we want to reach.
- The Entry line shows us exactly what was entered in the location defined by the current cursor position, even if it is too wide to be displayed at the cell.
- We performed our first calculation with VisiCalc using actual numbers and later substituted cell locations and formulas to get a more general solution.
- We noted that using cell references in formulas allowed us to easily change the values in our spread sheet.
- The use of cell references led to understanding the benefits of the VisiCalc automatic recalculation feature. For example, when we changed the amount of a check the new account balance was immediately displayed.

This concludes our quick review of the chapter. We are now ready to expand our knowledge of VisiCalc further.

If you are ready for the next course, return to the computer and load the VisiCalc program. In the next section you will learn how to control the way data is displayed in each VisiCalc cell.

Chapter 5

Housekeeping on the Electronic Sheet

To load the checkbook model, type **/SLCHECKS Ⓔ**. You should now be looking at the same screen we saved in the previous exercise. If you examine the checkbook model for detail, you may notice several things about its appearance that could be improved.

The most obvious problem with the model as it now stands is that the columns of numbers do not line up on the electronic sheet. This results in a sloppy looking page. VisiCalc has several ways to fix this problem and they all come under the general description of format commands. Format commands control how values and labels are displayed in each cell.

We will start by changing the format of a specific number on the VisiCalc screen. The first thing we do is position the cursor over the entry we want to alter. Let us begin by moving to C7, which holds the amount of our rent check. We now have to signal VisiCalc that we want to perform a task other than moving the cursor or entering data. We do this with the use of the special character "/". Like the conductor whose crisp baton tap brings the entire orchestra to attention, typing the "/" character will cause VisiCalc to respond with a list of available commands which can be performed at your request. Enter the / key now.

Each of the commands that appear on the Prompt line will be discussed in turn. The one we are interested in now is the F (Format) command.

34 Learning to Use VisiCalc

With your cursor at C7, type **F**. The Prompt line should be displaying the letters and symbols D G I L R $ *. Each letter or symbol represents a different type of format. VisiCalc uses these formats to display labels and values in different ways. Any of these formats can be selected at this point by typing in the character in the list that represents our format choice.

Select the $ format by entering the $ character. Notice what happens to the amount of our rent check. What was previously displayed on the sheet as 450 now appears as 450.00. We recognize this as the standard format for amounts expressed in dollars and cents. VisiCalc has inserted the two trailing zeros and the decimal point for us.

Enter ▼ to move the cursor to C8 and type **/F$** to change the format of the car repair check. This time nothing happens, because we entered the amount of the check as 199.95, and this already is in the $ format.

Each format specification that you apply in this way is in effect for the specific cell which is highlighted by the cursor. You can enter different numbers in location C8, but they will all be displayed in this format until you alter the format. For example, with your cursor still at C8 enter the number 200 by typing **200 Ⓔ**. Since you have already set this cell up to display numbers in $ format, the final two zeros and the decimal point are automatically added for you. Now change this entry back to 199.95. With the cursor still in the same position try entering the keystrokes **/FI**. The number 199.95 is now displayed as 200. The I (Integer) format rounds the number currently highlighted by the cursor to the nearest integer. Move the cursor down one line to location C9, and change this location to integer format as well. After you have done this, look at the Entry line in the status area. VisiCalc remembers the entry at this position exactly as you typed it: "325.89", even though it is currently being displayed as the integer 326. The Entry line actually reads "C9 /FI (V) 325.89". This informs you that the cursor is currently at location C9, which contains the value 325.89 and is being displayed under an integer format.

If you move the cursor up one line to the car repair cell, you will notice again that the Entry line reveals the number 199.95 as you originally typed it. This is true even though the cell currently displays 200. This happens because VisiCalc stores the numbers exactly as you enter them and uses them as is for the purposes of calculation. In the case of the car repair bill, VisiCalc knows that the number to be used for calculations is 199.95, but responds to your format request by displaying the real number 199.95 in the integer form 200.

The F command gives you the option of displaying a number in a more visually desirable way. The contents of the cell, however, remain as originally entered. The format commands produce purely cosmetic changes in the appearance of the sheet.

It seems logical that in our current example we would want all values displayed in $ format. One way to accomplish this would be to move the cursor around to each location that contains a number and to enter the keystrokes /F$ to format each location as desired. Try this in your current location. The cursor should still be highlighting the number 200 at position C8. Type **/F$** to display 199.95 as before.

If you are wondering, "If this is supposed to be the computer age, why should I have to push the cursor around to each location and enter /F$ in each position?" you would be right to suspect that there is an easier way. Remember, VisiCalc is there to make life simpler, not more complex.

Enter the keystrokes **/GF$** and notice what happens. The columns line up as neatly as the pinstripes on a lawyer's suit. All numbers are now displayed in identical format except for your Amex card payment, which still appears as the integer number 326. Why was this one entry unaffected?

The G in /GF$ stands for Global. This tells VisiCalc that you want the following command to apply to the entire sheet, not just a single location. So we have requested that all values on the sheet be displayed in $ format.

What about the mystery at location C9? Position your cursor at this cell, and you will notice that the format /FI is still in effect. The Global format command changes the format of any location that you have not formatted individually. Because we entered /FI at C9 the value is still displayed in integer format. The Global format change had no effect on this location. This allows you to exercise total control over how data is displayed at each location. At the same time, the Global option can be used to quickly format all other cell entries.

The /FD (Default) command resets the current location of the cursor to the Global format currently in effect. With your cursor at C9, enter **/FD**. The /FI specification on the Entry line disappears, and 326 is now displayed as 325.89. We now have all our numbers lining up perfectly. The Default command removed the integer format and applied the /GF$ specification to this location.

Thus, there are two ways to use the format command. By typing /F followed by the desired format you can control the format of an individual entry. The format for this cell can only be changed by entering another specific format at the same location, effectively overwriting the previous format.

The Global format, on the other hand, changes the format of all cells that have not previously been given a format of their own. If you recall, we used the specific /F$ format for location C7 and C8. Since this $ format is the same as the one we used in the Global format, the amounts 450.00

and 199.95 appear in the format we want. To verify this, move the cursor first to C7 and then to C8 and notice that the Entry line shows that the specific format /F$ is in effect for these cells. With your cursor at C7, enter **/FD.** There is no change in the way the amount of the rent check is displayed. This is because the specific format was the same as the Global format. However, the /F$ entry for this location disappears signifying that C7 no longer has a specific format attached to it. Now move your cursor to C8, and enter **/FD.** This removes the specific format for this cell as well.

Now that we have completed our initial task of straightening out the columns of numbers, it would be nice to have the column headings line up above these neatly organized numbers. We will now examine how the /FR and /FL commands can do this for us.

The R and L format options refer to Right and Left justification, respectively. The justification specifies which end of the cell you would like the data to be placed against. Move the cursor to C5 so that the column heading AMOUNT is highlighted by the cursor. Enter the keystrokes **/FR,** and you will notice that the title bumps up against the right side of the cell. Enter the keystrokes **/FL,** and you will see the label go back up against the left side of the cell.

When you enter numbers onto the VisiCalc sheet they are always right justified. This is to insure that there is as much space as possible available to display numbers. Labels, on the other hand, are always left justified to allow for as much room as possible for displaying letters.

If you look at the screen, you will see that the headings do not line up over the columns of numbers the way you might like them to. You can remedy this by entering the following keystrokes: **/FR▶/FR▶/FR.** Now the three column headings, AMOUNT, DEPOSIT, and BALANCE, all line up over the numbers. You can use the /FR and /FL commands on either values or labels. Your screen should look like the picture in Fig. 5-1.

Save the checkbook model by entering the following keystrokes: **/SSCHECKS Ⓔ.** This new version of the checkbook model will be permanently saved on your disk with all the format changes we have just made.

We will now illustrate the format option called the Bar Graph format command. First, let us clear the screen using the /C (Clear Screen) command. This command erases all entries that have been made on the electronic screen. This includes all values, numbers, and format specifications. Type **/C,** and you will notice that the prompt "CLEAR : Type Y to confirm" appears. Since this command can wipe out hours of hard work in the twinkling of an eye, VisiCalc is asking you to enter the letter Y to indicate that Yes, you really do want to erase the entire contents of the screen and go back to square one. Since we have already made a perma-

Housekeeping on the Electronic Sheet 37

Figure 5-1

nent copy of the current model on our disk, we can safely answer "Y" to the prompt. Do that now and watch the screen wipe itself clean. Should you ever enter the /C command by mistake, you can stop the screen from erasing itself by entering any other key but "Y" in answer to the prompt.

We now have a new screen to work with. Enter the following keystrokes: **1▼2▼3▼4▼5 Ⓔ**. You can see the numbers 1 to 5 in column A. Now enter the following keystrokes: **/F*▲/F*▲/F*▲/F*▲/F***. You have now selected the Bar Graph format for the numbers in column A. This format displays the number of stars that correspond to the integer portion of the number displayed in the cell. The number is not rounded; the fractional portion is simply ignored. To illustrate this, move the cursor to A5 and enter the number 5.9 in this location. You will see that only five stars are displayed. This format is especially useful when you have data that requires a graphic presentation.

The last format option to be discussed is the /G (General) format. This is the format that is in effect each time you load VisiCalc or begin with a new sheet using the /CY command. Enter **/CY** to reset the screen. The General format always tries to display as many significant figures as possible for any value you enter. Of course the number of digits that can be represented is restricted by the width of the cell. If the number is too big to fit in the cell, VisiCalc will use scientific notation and again try to display as many significant figures as possible. These numbers are right justified, and a leading blank is placed in the leftmost column. Labels entered under /G format are automatically left justified.

You may now wish to spend a few minutes on the screen experimenting with different formats and how they affect values and labels. Remember, this is just a scratch pad, so scribble away. You will learn faster if you do not worry too much about making mistakes. The best way to learn is to type numbers like 112334423232 or .001023 and see what happens. Try different formats with the Global options, and just plain fool around for a while.

When you are finished, clear the screen (provided you do not want to save what you have done) and take some time to go over the following review section.

SUMMARY

-We began this section on housekeeping by trying to see how we could fix up the slightly ragged appearance of our checkbook model.

-The "/" character was introduced as the way we get the VisiCalc program to perform specific tasks other than moving the cursor or entering data into the sheet—our conductor's baton.

-When we entered the F (Format) command after the "/" character, VisiCalc responds by displaying all the various format options available on the Prompt line. The various formats appear below.

D (Default) format: Causes all entries without their own specific format to obey the Global format currently in effect.

G (General) format: Displays the most significant digits possible using scientific notation if necessary. This is the format in effect each time you load or reset the VisiCalc screen.

I (Integer) format: Displays values as whole numbers, rounding the fractional portion of any entries.

L (Left) justify: This format command causes the entry to be pushed up against the left boundary of the cell.

R (Right) justify: Causes the entry to be placed against the right side of the cell.

Housekeeping on the Electronic Sheet 39

$ format: The format we selected for our checkbook example. All numbers are displayed showing a decimal point with two trailing digits, which can be interpreted as dollars and cents.

* Bar Graph format: Causes a number of asterisks to be displayed representing each number under this format. The fractional portion of the number is ignored.

-Once a format is entered for a specific cell it remains in effect until another format is used while the cursor is highlighting the cell, effectively overwriting the previous format.

-We observed that the cell contents are stored exactly as entered. The Entry line reveals the actual contents of the location, regardless of the way it is displayed through the format command.

-The G (Global) prefix was used to apply format specifications to the entire sheet.

-We observed that the Global option alters all formats except those in locations that already have been assigned a specific format.

-Finally, before we actually illustrated the use of the * and G (General) formats, we showed how the screen could be wiped clean with the C (Clear) command followed by a "Y" response to the verification prompt.

You now know how to use the various types of format options VisiCalc has to offer. You may now want to take a break before continuing with the next section which deals with the Replicate command.

Chapter 6

The Replicate Command: VisiCalc Shorthand

In this section we will discuss in detail an extremely powerful VisiCalc command called the Replicate command. You evoke this command using the /R keystrokes. When we use this command we are asking VisiCalc to make a replica of a value or label stored in one location and reproduce it in another.

In many business problems certain elements repeat themselves. For example, rent has to be paid at regular intervals, as do loans, payroll, utilities, and many other business costs. For these types of recurring values, the Replicate command can save hundreds of keystrokes.

Our example in this section will show how VisiCalc can be used to construct a cash flow spread sheet. A cash flow is used to track the flow of money into and out of a business, revealing how much money, if any, remains at the end of each month. By using a cash flow in your own business you will be able to assess future cash needs as well as examine how well you are progressing towards your operating goals. Along the way we will pay special attention to discovering how the Replicate command can be used to save time and to improve accuracy in constructing spread sheets.

Our sample company is a one-man computer consulting firm which goes by the name of Applied Systems. Ted Prior is the self-employed computer systems analyst who owns the company. He works out of a one-man office which offers shared secretarial service. He has several clients who pay him by the month to write computer programs for them.

At the beginning of the year Ted decides that he wants to know how much money he stands to make in the coming year. Since he is always afraid of running out of clients, he also hopes that the model will give him plenty of warning of when his various contracts are terminating so he can spend more time prospecting new clients.

We will put together a cash flow model to help him solve both of these problems. You may not be a free-lance systems analyst, but you should still build the model as we go along. In the next chapter we will also show how this model can be quickly modified to suit other types of businesses. More important, the exercise will show you how to use the Replicate command, which is an extremely useful VisiCalc command.

Begin by loading your VisiCalc program. You should be looking at a blank VisiCalc screen.

We will start by entering a title for our model. Move the cursor to A2 and enter **APPLIED▶SYSTEMS▶CASH▶FLOW Ⓔ**. We have left the first line blank to improve readability.

Leave another line by moving the cursor to A4. We want to know what the cash flow will be over the entire year. That means we will need to use 12 columns so that we can store each month's information in its own column. Leave the first column blank for now. We will use it later to label our rows of numbers. Therefore, we will begin entering the names of the months in column B. With the cursor at B4 enter the following keystrokes: **JAN▶FEB▶MAR▶APR▶MAY▶JUN▶JUL▶AUG▶SEP▶OCT▶NOV▶DEC Ⓔ**. Your cursor should now be at M4, and you should have entered the abbreviated month names across row 4. Enter>**A3 Ⓔ** to move the cursor directly back to A3.

We will now add a border below the title to set our screen off even more. This is a commonly used technique to improve general screen presentation.

We will use the "=" sign as our border element. Enter "========= to fill this cell with equal signs. Enter▶"=========Ⓔ to fill the next cell with the same characters. Earlier, we noticed that we had to precede a formula with a plus sign to tell VisiCalc that we were entering a value, not a label in a cell. The equal sign is preceded with a quote for a similar reason. By beginning an entry with a quote VisiCalc will treat what follows as a label, regardless of the numbers or characters you enter. You can see that we are building up a line of equal signs to act as a border. Since we want this border row to extend across the top of the whole model we need to continue this process until we reach the final column which contains the label for December. That journey would require a lot of keystrokes! As you may have suspected, this is our first chance to use the Replicate command.

The Replicate Command: VisiCalc Shorthand 43

We want to copy the equal signs already contained in location B3 into the locations C3,D3,E3,F3...M3. Take a minute to think about this. We have entered a label at B3. It is identical to the label we want to see in each cell of this row, up to the column containing the last month of our model. We want to copy the label located in B3 into each position in row 3 from column C through M.

With your cursor still at B3, evoke the Replicate command by entering /**R.** The Prompt line displays "REPLICATE: SOURCE RANGE OR ENTER". Two pieces of information need to be supplied each time we use the Replicate command: (1) what do we want copied, and (2) where do we want it copied to. This first prompt is asking us for the source range. The source range refers to the cell or group of cells we want copied. We can respond to this prompt by entering a range of locations or by entering Ⓔ. The Ⓔ key is used to indicate that we want to use a single location, not a range, as the source of the copy. The source range in this case is taken to be the contents of the cell highlighted by the current cursor position.

If you examine the Edit line, you will see B3 displayed. The Edit line informs you that VisiCalc considers the current cursor position, B3, to be the first cell in a range of source cells. Enter Ⓔ to inform VisiCalc that you want to copy only the contents of B3. The Edit line now shows B3...B3:, indicating that the source range is made up of the single location B3.

The Prompt line is now asking: "REPLICATE: TARGET RANGE". Now that you have specified what you want copied, you need to indicate where you want this data copied to. We want to copy this label into all the locations from C3 through M3. Enter **C3.** . The "." is used to inform VisiCalc that the coordinate is only the first location of a range and that another location will follow to complete the target range description. The Edit line now looks like this: B3...B3:C3... . VisiCalc is now only missing the last part of the target range. Enter **M3** Ⓔ and watch what happens.

A line of equal signs springs across the row. How far does this border line extend? Move the cursor to the right of the screen by using the ▶ key. Continue until you reach the end of the line of equal signs. Notice that it ends just where we specified, at column M. We have just used the Replicate command to save a lot of keystrokes.

We saw that the Edit line used some special characters to communicate information about the Replicate command to us. The "..." or ellipsis is used to indicate a range of locations. The colon is used to separate the source from the target range. When we see B3...B3:C3...M3, we can recognize this as saying, copy the contents of location B3 into each cell starting at C3 and continuing through to M3.

Let us begin Ted's cash flow by entering his monthly cash outlays on the VisiCalc sheet. The first cost that comes to mind is Ted's office rent.

He pays $350 per month for his modest office. Since he meets with his clients at their offices, he does not need to spend a lot of money on his surroundings. The rent also entitles him to several hours of secretarial time each week. We can enter the rent as follows:>A5 Ⓔ RENT▶350 Ⓔ. Assuming that the rent will not change for the rest of the year, let us replicate this amount across all the months of the year. Enter the following keystrokes to accomplish this: /R Ⓔ C5.M5 Ⓔ. Watch as the value 350 is copied into each location we specified. Check this by moving the cursor across the "RENT" row until you get to column M, the month of December.

As you look at the VisiCalc sheet you will notice that the numbers are right justified and the month titles are left justified. The screen looks ragged. We need to right justify the month names so they line up with the column of numbers.

Move your cursor to B4 and enter /FR. The month name JAN becomes right justified. To do this for the remaining eleven months, enter the following keystrokes: ▶/FR▶/FR▶/FR▶/FR▶/FR▶/FR▶/FR ▶/FR▶/FR▶/FR/FR. Now all the month names line up with the columns of numbers.

Let us continue with expenses by entering the amount of money Ted spends on renting a parking spot. He pays a parking rental of $30 a month and the payments are made in $90 lumps each quarter. To enter this information, position the cursor at location A6. Enter the following keystrokes: **PARKING▶▶▶90▶▶▶90 ▶▶▶90 ▶▶▶90 Ⓔ**. We have now entered the parking rental for the year.

Ted has two other major expenses: the telephone and occasional secretarial costs.

The telephone rental is a constant $28/month, but the long distance charges vary. Ted knows from experience that on the average his total telephone bill is about twice his rental. Ted says that you notice those types of things when you are a programmer. He dismisses it as an occupational hazard.

We can enter his telephone costs into our model as follows:>A7 Ⓔ **PHONE▶28*2** Ⓔ /R Ⓔ C7.M7 Ⓔ. This time we entered the formula 28*2, where the * symbol stands for multiplication.

When we enter a formula like the one for the telephone bill, VisiCalc automatically calculates the result and displays it. If you examine the Entry line contents for any cell in the telephone expense row you will see that VisiCalc has saved the telephone cost exactly as it was entered as the formula 28*2.

Periodically, Ted experiences a work crunch and uses more secretarial time than his allowed monthly maximum. This happens when he has to prepare a progress report for a client or deliver a proposal for a new project. He knows roughly when during the year he will need to do this extra work. We can enter this cost data as follows:**>A8 (E) SECRETAR-IAL>150>100>>100>>>75 >>>100>150>150 (E)**. Since this is a projected cash flow, Ted is taking his best guess at when he will need to buy secretarial time and how much time he will require.

This type of uncertainty is encountered by all of us. The future can not be known in advance, yet decisions still need to be made. One of the great benefits that you gain from using VisiCalc is that the models you construct can be extremely flexible. As we learn more about a given situation we can quickly refine the estimates our model will use. This new data instantly updates the model. We will see many examples of this flexibility throughout the book. What we need to learn is how to build our spread sheets with flexibility in mind so our model is every bit as powerful as it can be.

We have now entered all of Ted's major expenses. Let us look at the sheet so far. When you place your cursor at A1 your screen should look like the picture in Fig. 6-1 below.

What will happen to our model if the office rent is raised to $400 in April? The obvious way to adjust the rent would be to move the cursor to position E5, enter the new amount of 400, and repeat this process for each

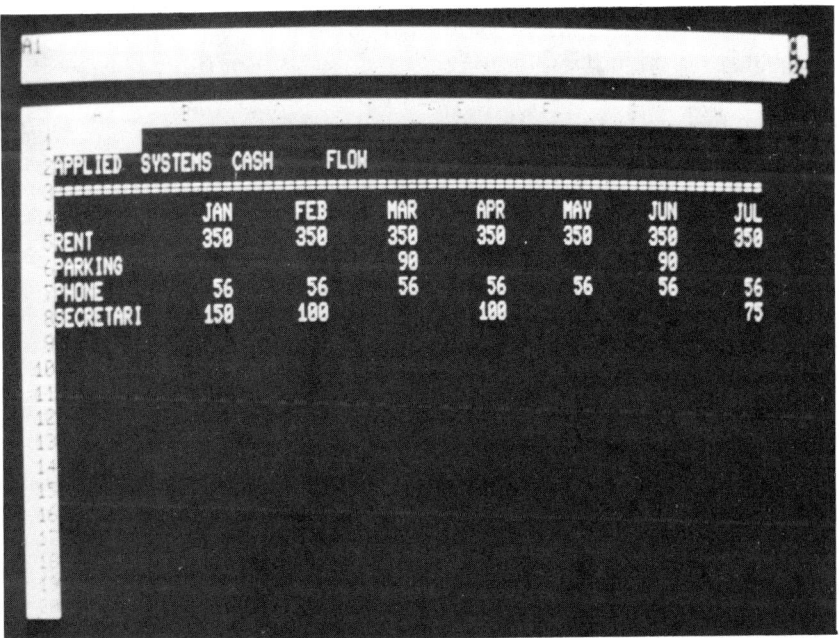

Figure 6-1

of the remaining months. You could also enter the new amount at E5 and use the Replicate command to copy this amount into each of the remaining positions. The Replicate command will overwrite the contents of any cell in the target range.

There is a better way.

It would be nice if we could set up the sheet so that each cell borrowed its contents from the cell before it. That way if we made a change in one location all the locations following it would instantly reflect this change. We want the sheet to behave like a line of dominoes—by knocking down one domino all the ones after it fall as well. We will find many examples where this set-up will be useful, as in any sheet that may have to reflect an increase in monthly salary, changes in a loan payment, increased utility costs, or any other expense that once changed remains changed. Let us see how we can define our cells so that we can easily handle these changes.

Move the cursor to C5. We want this cell to store whatever happens to be in B5. This is the first in our line of dominoes. To set this up, enter the keystrokes **+B5** Ⓔ. Remember that we need to enter the + symbol to inform VisiCalc that we are entering a value not a label. We have just stored the contents of B5 in C5. The Entry line for C5 displays the formula +B5. The rent displayed is still 350. Move the cursor over one cell to D5 and enter **+C5** Ⓔ. We have now stored the contents of C5 in D5. Thus, the entry in D5 depends on what is stored in C5 while the entry in C5 depends on what is stored in B5. Our line of dominoes is now three cells long.

Move the cursor back to B5 and enter the amount **400** in this location. Be sure to follow this number with the Ⓔ key to actually store the new rent figure. You will also see this amount appear in locations C5 and D5 as well. By entering an amount in one cell it is immediately transferred to all the cells that follow. To prove this, move the cursor to C5 and enter the value **500** Ⓔ in this location. You will see that the contents of B5 are unaffected while the contents of D5, the next location over, reflect this new value. We have set the cells up so that the change flows to the right. This is most often the direction used since models measure time from left to right.

Now that we know how to construct a more flexible expense line, do we need to type in a formula in each location on the rent line? No. Again, we will use the Replicate command, but this time the procedure will be used a bit differently because we are copying a formula that contains a variable.

First, we need to restore the formula that was stored in C5. With your cursor at C5, enter **+B5** ➤ and now enter the following keystrokes: **/R** Ⓔ **E5.M5** Ⓔ. Look at the Prompt line: It shows "Replicate: N=No

The Replicate Command: VisiCalc Shorthand   47

Change R=Relative". The Edit line looks like this: "D5:E5...M5:+C5". The formula +C5 is highlighted.

VisiCalc is responding to your request to copy the contents of location D5, which is the formula +C5. There are two ways VisiCalc copies formulas. It either makes the coordinates relative to the cell it is copied into, or it copies the formula exactly as it appears with no change. This is much easier to see than to describe. Enter **N** to signify that you want "No Change" and watch what happens.

The formula +C5 has been copied into all the cells in the row up until column M. Move the cursor across this row, and by looking at the entry line, you will see that the formula +C5 appears in each cell. Now move the cursor back to C5 and enter the number **600** Ⓔ. The whole row has filled with the value 600—so far so good. Move the cursor over to D5 and enter **700** Ⓔ. Only the value in this location is affected. This is not what we had in mind since our dominoes have not fallen. We want each location to echo the value stored in the cell to its immediate left.

Since we copied the formula without any changes, each entry in this row will contain whatever number we enter in location C5. This is because we entered +C5 in each of the locations. Let us go back to the drawing board and see if we can get the desired effect.

Move the cursor back to C5. Replace 600 with the formula **+B5** Ⓔ. This time we will request a relative copy. Enter these keystrokes: **/R** Ⓔ **D5.M5** Ⓔ **R**. Now move the cursor along this row and examine the Entry line contents as you go. VisiCalc has altered the formula in each location. Beginning at cell C5 you should see the following formulas appear in the Entry line as you move the cursor to the right: +B5 +C5 +D5 +E5 and so on until you reach +L5 in column M. Now the contents of each cell on this line depend on the contents of the previous cell.

When we specify the relative option the source formula is copied relative to the target cell. Actually, a relative copy occurs in several steps. First, the source formula is incremented by one location. Then this modified formula is stored in the first location at the target range. Next, this new formula is itself incremented by one and stored in the next cell of the target range. This process continues one step at a time until the entire target range is filled. In our current example the initial formula +B5 is incremented to +C5 and then stored in location D5. Next, this new formula is incremented to +D5 and stored in location E5. This process continues until the entire target range is filled. We will be developing more examples using the Replicate command with both the R and N options.

Let us make sure that the rent line will behave exactly as we want it to. Move the cursor to various positions in the line and enter different

rent values. You will see that all the values to the right of this new entry instantly reflect the new rents.

Once you are satisfied that this line behaves as it should, return Ted's rent to $350 a month. Note that you may have to re-enter the appropriate formulas in some of the cells that you used to enter new rent amounts. It may be quicker to replicate the entire line depending on how many cells you have altered.

We have now completed a list of all the major expenses that Ted expects to encounter in the coming year. Now let us calculate what the total cash outlay for each month will be.

Start by drawing a border below the final expense line. This time we will use a line of dashes. Move to A9 and enter "--------- Ⓔ, that is nine dashes in all, to totally fill location A9. Replicate this formula using these keystrokes: /R Ⓔ B9.M9 Ⓔ. Now enter the label: **TOTAL EXPENSES** Ⓔ in A10. We are now ready to total all the expenses we have listed for each month.

In our previous example of the checkbook we had to add up a column of numbers. Our approach was to enter a formula that listed all the cells we wanted to add up. The formula we are referring to looked like this: +C7+C8+C9+C10, and it was used to total the checks that were written. You can see that if you had a lot of numbers to total, this method would become extremely tedious. Once again, VisiCalc has a convenient short cut to offer us.

We want to total up all the values in a month to get the total expenses for that month. We can use a VisiCalc built-in function called the SUM function to accomplish this.

A built-in function performs a calculation on a list of values which you supply. This calculation depends on which specific VisiCalc function you select. Each VisiCalc function is preceded by the "@" character.

With the cursor at B10, enter the following keystrokes: **@SUM(B5.B8)**. We are asking for the sum of the expenses for the month of January. We want to sum up all the values in this column. Type Ⓔ and look at your current cursor location. The amount displayed is Ted's total cash outlay for the month: 556.

Try changing the rent figure to 500 for January. The total expenses immediately reflect this change in the rental cost. The number on the total line should read 706. Change the rent back to 350 again.

We need to know the total expenses for each month. That means we will have to enter the @SUM function for each month across the total expense row. We can use the Replicate command with the relative option.

With the cursor at B10 enter the following keystrokes: **/R** Ⓔ **C10.M10** Ⓔ. We have specified the source and the target range. The Edit line displays: "B10:C10...M10:@SUM(B5". The first coordinate in the sum function, B5, is highlighted and the Prompt line wants to know if we want this coordinate to be relative or not. Let us imagine for a moment that we are moving the cursor across the total line. What would we want the formulas that appear in the Entry line to look like as we move the cursor? Since we want to sum each column individually we would want to see the formulas @SUM(B5...B8), @SUM(C5...C8), @SUM(D5...D8), @SUM (E5...E8), and so on. Each column needs to have its own particular range so that the correct total is calculated for that month of expenses. As a result we want the initial coordinate of the sum function, B5, to change for each column as the formula is replicated. We select the R option. Enter **R** if you have not already done so.

The Edit line now reads "B10:C10...M10:@SUM(B5...B8". The final location of the sum function, B8, is now highlighted, and VisiCalc is again prompting for your choice of either Relative or No Change. Again, we select relative since both the beginning and ending locations for the sum function need to change relative to the column into which they are copied. Enter **R** in answer to this prompt.

Once your final selection has been made, VisiCalc proceeds to copy this formula into each of the specified locations. As quickly as the formulas appear, the total expenses for each month are displayed.

Move your cursor across this TOTAL EXPENSE row. Notice how the coordinates of the sum function change for each column as we wanted them to. Note also that each month has the correct total showing for expenses.

We have now helped Ted start figuring out his cash position. We know where the cash is going; now, where is it coming from?

Applied Systems is under contract to three different companies. Ted is designing and programming computer applications for each of the companies. One of his clients is the Freeman Trucking Company. Ted is involved in designing and programming a system that will help this trucking company minimize their delivery routes. He is paid a retainer of $1,100/month, and the contract is for a 12-month period.

His second client is the TransPacific Fish Company. This fish distributor must maintain tight control over their inventory at all times. Their reputation for supplying fresh fish is crucial to their continued success. Ted is designing a system that will organize customer orders by the type of fish they require. This will enable the TransPacific buyers to purchase only the types and amounts of fish they need. Ted's contract calls for the job to be completed in eight months with a fixed price of $10,000. Ted will bill this client $1,000/month for the eight months he works on the project. The remaining $2,000 has been paid in the form of an advance.

Both of these projects are scheduled to begin in January.

Ted's final client is the engineering firm of Brown and Brown. This company employs 18 engineers of different skill and experience levels.

As the year begins Ted is in the last six months of a contract to produce a customer billing system. The billing system tracks the staff assigned to a specific project, totals their biweekly billing, and reports on whether the project is proceeding within budget. Ted bills Brown and Brown using an hourly rate of $30, and his monthly invoice is usually around $1,500.

We can now begin to enter Ted's sources of income into our VisiCalc cash flow sheet.

Let us use a border to separate the TOTAL EXPENSE line from the income portion of our cash flow. Move the cursor to A11 and enter the following keystrokes: **"--------- Ⓔ /R Ⓔ B11.M11 Ⓔ**. You should now have a line of dashes both above and below the TOTAL EXPENSES line. We can now enter Ted's projected billings.

Move the cursor to A12. We will use this line to record our expected cash flow from Freeman Trucking. Enter the following keystrokes: **FREEMAN▶1100 Ⓔ /R Ⓔ C12.M12 Ⓔ**. Next, we can record the income from Ted's other two clients as follows:**▶A13 Ⓔ TRANSPACIFIC▶3000 ▶1000 Ⓔ /R Ⓔ D13.I13 Ⓔ**.

Remember that in the TransPacific case he receives an advance as well as his first monthly check in January. For the rest of the months he receives $1,000/month. Enter the final income source as follows:**▶A14 Ⓔ BROWN & BROWN▶1500 Ⓔ /R Ⓔ C14.G14 Ⓔ**.

This completes the entry of all the income sources. We will now calculate the total income earned during each month as we did for the expenses.

Move the cursor to A15. We will use a slightly different method to draw a border of dashes across this row. Enter **/R,** but this time use your **BS** key to erase the first entry on the Edit line. The request to specify the source range is still present on the Prompt line. Using the directional arrows move your cursor up four lines so that the dashes at A11 are highlighted, and watch the Edit line as you go. The location of the cursor appears on the Edit line as the first location of the source range. When you are required to enter a location for a source of entry range you can simply move the cursor to the desired location and use the enter key to enter the coordinate. With the cursor at A11 the Edit line should now look like this "A11". Enter Ⓔ and the Edit line looks like this: "A11...A11:". You have used your cursor to directly specify the source range you want.

The cursor moves back to A15 on its own. You want to copy the line of dashes across this row. The target range will be A15 ...M15. With the cursor at A15 enter **A15. .** You have now specified that your current cursor position, A15, is to be used as the initial coordinate of the target range. The Edit line now looks like this: "A11:A15...". Now, instead of moving

The Replicate Command: VisiCalc Shorthand 51

the cursor all the way across this row to column M it is faster and easier to enter the desired location directly as we have done before. Enter **M15** Ⓔ and watch as the line of dashes appears across the row.

We have just illustrated a very convenient way to give VisiCalc the coordinates it needs to perform certain tasks. Instead of looking at the sheet and wondering if the location we want is D7 or D8, we can simply move the cursor to that location and enter it. This way you will not make a mistake by incorrectly reading a coordinate and using this wrong address in a formula.

We can now complete the income section of this model by totaling up the expenses for all the months.

With the cursor at A16 enter the following: **TOTAL INCOME** ►**@SUM(**. At this point you can also use direct cursor movement to supply the coordinates of the range for the Sum function. The range over which to add the expenses is from B12 to B14. Move the cursor up to B12 and type **..** Now move the cursor to B14 and type **)** Ⓔ. The total revenue for January, 5600, appears in B16. Notice that once the Sum function has been entered, VisiCalc sends your cursor back to the location where you began to enter the @SUM function.

Let us replicate the Sum function across the TOTAL INCOME row. Try to do this yourself before you read further.

Did it work? You should have done the following:/**R** Ⓔ **C16.M16** Ⓔ **RR**. Remember that you have to select the Relative option since the @SUM function will differ in each column. You could have moved the cursor to enter the desired coordinates directly, but the results will still be the same.

To complete this model we need to show what Ted's net cash position will be at the end of each month. Leave a line and move the cursor to A18. Enter the label **NET CASH FLOW** Ⓔ. This will be the difference between the total expenses for the month and the total income.

Let us use the cursor to select the locations we need in this calculation. Move the cursor to B18 and enter **+**. We have informed VisiCalc that we want to enter a formula in this location. Move the cursor to B16 which contains the total income for January. The Edit line should show +B16. Now enter **–**, to signify that we want to subtract a value from location B16. Move the cursor to B10, which contains the total expenses for January, and type Ⓔ. You have now told VisiCalc that your formula is complete. The difference between these two numbers, 5044, should appear highlighted at B18.

We can replicate this formula across the row using the following

52 Learning to Use VisiCalc

keystrokes: /R Ⓔ C18.M18 Ⓔ RR. We again need to select the R option because the formula needs to change relative to the column into which it is copied.

As a final touch we should display the screen values in $ format. The following keystrokes accomplish this: /GF$.

Move the cursor back to A1. Your screen should now look like the picture in Fig. 6-2 below.

	JAN	FEB	MAR	APR	MAY	JUN	JUL
APPLIED SYSTEMS CASH FLOW							
RENT	350.00	350.00	350.00	350.00	350.00	350.00	350.00
PARKING			90.00			90.00	
PHONE	56.00	56.00	56.00	56.00	56.00	56.00	56.00
SECRETARI	150.00	100.00		100.00			75.00
TOTAL EXP	556.00	506.00	496.00	506.00	406.00	496.00	481.00
FREEMAN	1100.00	1100.00	1100.00	1100.00	1100.00	1100.00	1100.00
TRANSPACI	3000.00	1000.00	1000.00	1000.00	1000.00	1000.00	1000.00
BROWN & B	1500.00	1500.00	1500.00	1500.00	1500.00	1500.00	
TOTAL INC	5600.00	3600.00	3600.00	3600.00	3600.00	3600.00	2100.00
NET CASH	5044.00	3094.00	3104.00	3094.00	3194.00	3104.00	1619.00

Figure 6-2

Let us save this sheet under the name CASH. The following keystrokes will do the trick: /SSCASH Ⓔ.

We have covered many VisiCalc features in this section. This would be a good time to get away from the machine for a while and to let some of the things that we have covered sink in.

The main points covered in this section appear below. Reviewing them will help you solidify your understanding of these VisiCalc features.

SUMMARY

-We used a sample cash flow model to illustrate some of the ways the Replicate command can be used.

The Replicate Command: VisiCalc Shorthand

- In each Replicate command at least two pieces of information need to be supplied: (1) what do you want to copy, and (2) where do you want it copied to.
- VisiCalc defines the cell or cells you wish to copy as the source range and their destination as the target range.
- The colon is used to separate the source from the target range on the Edit line, while the ellipsis is used to designate a range of coordinates.
- If you select the N or No Change option when copying a formula, the formula is copied into the target range exactly as it is stored in the source cell.
- If you select the R or Relative option when copying a formula, the formula is copied relative to the target range so the coordinate locations in the formula actually change as the copy proceeds.
- We used the R option to create a flexible line of expenses that could respond to change easily. This row of cells behaved like dominoes.
- The coordinates of the source or target range can be entered by moving the cursor to the desired location and typing in the Ⓔ key. This often makes entry of coordinates easier and less prone to error.
- We used the Sum function to calculate the total expenses and income for each month.
- When we used the Replicate command on the Sum function, we had to specify that both the beginning and ending coordinates of the sum range were relative.
- We could enter the range of the Sum function by either moving the cursor to the desired coordinates or by typing in the locations into the Edit line directly.

Chapter 7

Modifying an Existing Model: Two for the Price of One

There is nothing permanent except change.

-Heraclitus
(540-475 B.C.)

In order for your VisiCalc models to continue to serve you, they will have to be modified periodically so that they accurately represent current business conditions.

In this section we will discuss how two different types of changes will affect our VisiCalc models. First, we will want to modify our VisiCalc models so that they represent a more accurate, complete picture of the problem we are attempting to solve. This is the process of ongoing modification and enhancement. It occurs as new ideas strike us, or as the problem we are examining changes in some way. It is as if we are renovating a house by adding a new room. The purpose of the house remains the same, but we have increased its usefulness. The second type of changes our models will experience are due to changing data. Our business conditions are always changing and so will the contents of our spread sheets. These changes can be compared to a house that has a new family move in. Structurally the house remains the same, but the people who live there have changed.

The cash flow model that we have built for Applied Systems essentially accomplishes everything that we set out to do. It reveals how well Ted is doing on a month-to-month basis, and it also points out that towards the end of the year he had better find some new accounts.

What often happens in many computer applications is that once the job is complete the customer begins to realize how many other features can be added to both improve and enhance the original application. This is VisiCalc's forte. It lets you experiment with your models until they evolve into a form that gives you exactly what you want. We are about to discover that Ted's cash flow model can be improved upon, and we can thank VisiCalc for making the suggestions.

If you have had some time to relax since you entered the cash flow model, you should now be fresh and ready for the next helping of VisiCalc.

Load the VisiCalc program. Next, load the cash flow spread sheet model using the following commands: **/SLCASH Ⓔ**.

Looking at the model as it currently stands, several areas that could be improved come to mind. For example, it would be nice to keep a running total of the company's cumulative cash position in addition to the month-to-month information we now have. This would let us see how much retained income the company earns as the year progresses. Let us add this new feature to our model.

We will use the row below NET CASH to keep track of accumulated cash. Move the cursor to A19 and enter the label **ACCUMULATED CASH Ⓔ**.

Location B19 will contain the accumulated cash for the first month. This is equal to the amount of money that was earned during the month: $5,044. We could enter 5044 directly in B19, but this would reduce the generality of our model. Instead, we will store the formula +B18 here since we know that B18 holds the earnings for January. If we decide to change any of the expense or income figures for January, the changes will automatically be reflected in the accumulated cash. Enter **+B18 Ⓔ** in B19.

For the month of February we have to take the accumulated cash from January and add it to February's earnings. We do this by storing the formula +B19+C18 in location C19. Enter **+B19+C18 Ⓔ** here and try to replicate it so that it calculates the accumulated cash for every month of the year. Each month will have to add the previous month's accumulated cash to the current month's earnings. That means the formula in column D should be +C19+D18, for column E it should be +D19+E18, and so on. Can you use the Replicate command correctly? Go ahead and try before reading on.

With your cursor at C19 you should have entered **/R Ⓔ D19.M19 Ⓔ RR**. Now move the cursor across the row to confirm that the correct formula has been stored in each of the locations in this row. By moving

Modifying an Existing Model: Two for the Price of One 57

the cursor over to December you can see the total accumulated cash for the year is $26,143.

This new addition to our model lets us see the consistent growth of cash throughout the year. Seeing all this cash on hand suggests that we should put some of it to work by depositing it in an interest-bearing account.

You can see that VisiCalc encourages you to expand, change, and improve your models. Often one enhancement reveals new information which again suggests a further enhancement. Most VisiCalc users find their models are continually evolving into forms that better suit their needs.

Let us assume that once Ted sees this excess cash he will decide to place 70 percent of his cumulative earnings in a savings account. He wants to keep the other 30 percent on hand to cover unexpected expenses, as well as for other investments. Each month the money he deposits in savings will earn interest over the next 30 days. The following month we will have to add this interest to the last month's accumulated cash and the current month's income to get the new accumulated cash.

The formula we use to calculate interest is

Interest earned =(Deposit amount*% annual rate)/12

Since we want to know how much interest was earned each month, we need to divide the annual interest by 12 to arrive at the monthly interest figure.

There is 5044*.7=3530.80 available for deposit in the savings account at the start of February. We should make the 70 percent contribution level variable since it will be interesting to see how changes in this figure will affect our annual retained earnings. Notice that we try to make the model as flexible as possible. There is no telling what you will learn if you start altering the variables in your model. To set this up we will use a specific cell to store the contribution percentage and reference this cell in the appropriate calculations. This is a particularly useful technique which is used to increase a model's flexibility. We will use this same technique to make the interest rate variable.

Enter the labels **INTEREST** Ⓔ at A20, **CONT %=** Ⓔ at A21, and **RATE=** Ⓔ at C21. We have designated the locations B21 and D21 to hold the contribution and the interest rate percentage respectively while row 20 will be used to hold the amount of interest earned each month. Enter **.7** Ⓔ **/FL** in B21 to set the contribution at 70 percent and **.12** Ⓔ**/FL** in D21 to set the interest rate at 12 percent. Whenever we need these values in our calculations we will refer to these locations directly.

Now let us calculate the interest that we will earn on our deposits.

Move the cursor to C20. First, we must find out how much cash will be deposited in the savings account each month. The amount available for deposit is equal to the January earnings times the contribution factor, which we have stored at B21. So the deposit amount is +B19*B21. This corresponds to the "Deposit amount" in our interest rate formula. The complete formula to enter at C20 is **(+B19*B21*D21)/12 Ⓔ**. We multiply the deposit amount times the interest rate and divide this by 12 to find the interest earned in February.

To complete our interest rate calculations we will replicate this formula across the interest row, but watch which options we need to use.

Enter **/R Ⓔ D20.M20 Ⓔ**. The first coordinate of the formula, +B19, is highlighted on the Edit line. We select the **R** option since the accumulated earnings change from month to month. Now the second coordinate, B21, is highlighted. This time we select the **N** option for no change. Since B21 tells us how much to contribute to savings each month, we want this cell used in each calculation. We still want to deposit 70 percent of this cash, or whatever percent value is stored in B21, regardless of the amount of accumulated cash. The last formula coordinate, D21, is now highlighted. Will you select R or N for this coordinate? Since we want the interest rate variable to be equal to the value stored in D12, regardless of which column the formula is in, we select the **N** option.

Move the cursor across this row and watch as the formulas appear in the Entry line. Which coordinates change as you go and which do not? You will see that each reference to the accumulated cash changes as we go from month to month. This amount, however, is always multiplied by the contents of B21 and D21, regardless of the column.

We now have to tack this interest onto our accumulated cash formula. Move the cursor to D19. The formula "+C19+D18" appears on the Entry line. To account for the interest payment we need to add the contents of C20 to this formula. Enter **+C19+C20+D18 Ⓔ** at D19. Now replicate this formula across the row. The accumulated cash will now contain the interest payments. With your cursor at D19 the keystrokes that accomplish this are **/R Ⓔ E19.M19 Ⓔ RRR**.

Now try changing the interest rate and the contribution factor. The sheet shimmers for a moment and the new results are displayed. This is what a flexible model is all about. Ted may decide that he wants to end up with $33,000 at the end of the year. He can juggle the contribution percentage until he achieves his goal. He may also select an investment with a higher yield. Ted is also free to select any middle ground between the two as a path to his goal. He can put more cash into savings each month, or he can seek a more aggressive investment. VisiCalc will quantify the how much and when for him.

Take some time now to enter various values for the rate and contribution. You should appreciate how the model digests any combination

Modifying an Existing Model: Two for the Price of One 59

of these variables and instantly reveals the new cash flow for the year. When you are done, return the contribution and rate back to their original values of .7 and .12 respectively.

A further enhancement that could be added to this model would be to show the annual expenses and income for each separate category. This way we can see how much was spent on rent and other expenses over the entire year as well as what our total earnings have been for each account.

Up to now, column M marked the last column of our cash flow model. We will now use the next column over to keep track of the annual expense totals. First let us use the name ANNUAL for column N. Move your cursor to N4 and enter **ANNUAL** Ⓔ **/FR**.

Now place the cursor at N5. To add the rent for the year you will use the sum function. Try to enter the correct formula in this location before you read on.

You should have entered the following keystrokes at N5: **@SUM (B5.M5)** Ⓔ. Now, to total up all the expense and income categories replicate this formula down the entire column. To do this, enter the following keystrokes: **/R** Ⓔ **N6.N20** Ⓔ **RR**. Watch closely as several unexpected things happen.

Looking down the column the totals appear as they should for the next three rows, but then "0" is displayed followed by the total for more of the expenses followed by another zero. Also one cell is displaying "<<<<<<<<<". Let us start to unravel this mystery one step at a time.

Move the cursor to the first 0 at N9 and look at the formula. The Entry line looks like this: "@SUM(B9...M9)". We have added up a line of dashes and found the answer to be 0. You may ask, since when does a line of dashes equal zero? When we replicated the sum formula down this column, VisiCalc obliged us by summing all the rows in the replicate range, including the border row. VisiCalc has responded to this somewhat eccentric request with characteristic forgivingness. When a label is referenced in a formula the assumed value is zero. The sum function which is acting on the border rows is essentially adding up a line of zeros. So the zeros displayed at N9, N11, and N15 can be replaced by a line of dashes. Continue the border lines into these three locations by entering "---------" Ⓔ in each of these three locations. Row 17 is left blank to separate the summary results from the rest of the model. During the replication a zero appears at N17 because we are summing an empty row. To blank this result out move your cursor to N17, and using the /B(lank) command type **/B** Ⓔ.

The blank command removes any value, formula, or label in the highlighted location. You should note that it will not remove a specific format. If you have a label in a location that you have specified as, for example, /FR, you can blank out the label, but the next label or value entered in that location will still be displayed as right justified. The way to alter an existing format is to specify a new format at that location or use the /FD command to cause the format to default to the Global format.

Now we can turn our attention to a strange looking entry that is inhabiting N19. Move the cursor down to this location and notice that the formula reads: "@SUM(B19...M19)". The row of greater than signs is warning us that an overflow condition has occurred at N19. The value is too large to be displayed by the cell, given its current width. There are too many digits. Regardless of the size of the number, it really doesn't have any meaning for us since it represents the total of the monthly accumulated cash. We only need to know the accumulated cash figure for the year.

In the next section we will learn how to widen each cell on our sheet so that more digits or longer labels can be displayed. For now let us just erase the contents of N19. With your cursor over N19 enter these keystrokes: /B Ⓔ. The contents of this location disappear and you are left with a blank location.

The final addition to this column is to extend the line of equal signs across row 3. Move your cursor to N3 and enter "=========Ⓔ. Now the new total expense column fits neatly into our model.

So far in this section we have added several new features to our cash flow model. It is not that we started out to make these changes as much as the model itself seemed to suggest them to us. We have been illustrating the process of enhancement and the way VisiCalc is used to apply these types of changes. We now not only have a model that does everything we wanted it to in the beginning, but it also suggested new ideas to us as we went along. VisiCalc is great for helping the intuitive problem solving process along, because as you improve the model the forces at play in the specific problem become clearly visible. While you are in this "enhancement mode" you will often find that new ideas surface.

We will now shift our attention to a different type of change and discuss how it affects our VisiCalc models. Earlier, we compared these types of changes to a house that had just received new occupants. These changes leave the structure of the model intact but alter the elements that are stored in the sheet. We end up with a model that performs the same task as it did before, but the input data and labels are different. The model may have to grow or shrink to accommodate the new data, but its function still remains the same.

Many of you will find that the specific categories used in this model do not match your specific expenses and income. There will be differences in the types of income and expenses incurred, their number, and their dollar amount. We will show you how to transform the Applied

Modifying an Existing Model: Two for the Price of One 61

Systems model to a model that suits your specific purposes. This ability will come in handy in several situations. You will find that changing business considerations will cause you to make both major and minor changes to your models. Often you will have models where certain sections can be used by other models. For example, you might be using the same type of complex interest or tax calculations for different parts of your business. You can save these "utility" sections for use in many different models. If you are using VisiCalc in a large company you may create standard models which people can then customize to solve their own specific problems. An example would be a detailed job cost sheet that your individual estimators could use. You may also want to purchase a predesigned VisiCalc sheet that has much of the work already done for you. This can save time and energy. All you will have to do to use the models is enter your own specific information and the calculations will be done for you.

All of these examples require you to alter the VisiCalc model by entering your own data. This way you can customize it for a specific application. We will be spending the rest of this section learning how to make these types of changes.

Take a minute now to store the cash flow model on disk. You will then have a permanent copy of the enhanced version. If you want to keep the original model for comparison, you will need to save the enhanced sheet under a new name. If you save this model under the same name, i.e., CASH, it will overwrite the original model, the same way that a new cell entry replaces the one that was there before. Save the enhanced version under the name "CASHFLOW" using the following keystrokes: **/SSCASHFLOW** ⓔ.

After you have done this, examine the spread sheet with your own business in mind. To make this easier, enter these keystrokes: **>A2** ⓔ **/B ▶/B** ⓔ. You have now erased the APPLIED SYSTEMS title and are free to imagine how your own expenses and income would fit on this sheet.

Start by changing the expenses to match those of your own business. Is the rent too low? If this is the case, enter the appropriate amount. Suppose that you own your premises instead of rent. Change the RENT label to MORTGAGE; you can enter the payment amount in B5 and VisiCalc does the rest. This new amount causes our total expenses to change as well as our net income, accumulated cash, and interest earned. Not bad for changing only a single expense figure.

Suppose that you do not pay for parking. Since this expense was paid quarterly, we did not bother to set up a flexible expense line as we did for rent and telephone. We do not need this line at all and so are faced with the task of removing it.

We have a VisiCalc command that will do this. The /D(elete) command is used to erase a row or column. As with any VisiCalc command that erases data it should be used carefully, lest hours of hard work vanish.

With your cursor at A6 enter **/D**. The Prompt line responds with "DELETE: ROW OR COLUMN". You must respond with either the letter R or C. The R indicates you would like to delete the row your cursor is currently in, while C indicates that the column defined by your present cursor position should go. Enter **R** and watch what happens. After the screen does some shuffling, the line that contained the parking expense is gone. The line containing the telephone expense, that was just below it, has moved up to take its place. We have used the delete command to remove a line from our model. Notice that all the formulas we have previously defined are still doing their jobs as if nothing had happened. The total expense line and the other calculated amounts are displayed correctly. Since the parking expense line is gone our monthly expenses have now decreased.

Move the cursor down one line to the SECRETARIAL line, and assuming this expense is not applicable to you, let us delete this line as well. To do this place your cursor on the label SECRETARIAL and enter **/DR**. What does the screen look like now?

It appears that this deletion did not work as well as the previous one. The word ERROR is displayed at many locations on our sheet. Don't be concerned. We are about to learn another interesting fact about VisiCalc.

Move the cursor to B8. Since we have deleted two lines of our model this is now the total expense line. Look at the formula that is stored in the Entry line. It reads: "@SUM(B5...@ERROR)". The @ERROR is VisiCalc's way of informing you that it is unable to perform a requested calculation. For example, if you tried to divide a number by zero, VisiCalc would respond by placing a @ERROR in the offending cell or cells.

In our current case we deleted a coordinate that defined the ending range of the sum function. We had requested a sum over the range B5...B8. So VisiCalc started adding at location B5 and continued to add the numbers in the column until it tried to reference B8. When we deleted row 8 the B8 that was referenced in the sum range was no longer there. As a result, @ERROR appeared as the terminal point of the sum function, and the same result occurred in each formula stored in the row. The ERROR entry is displayed in each cell of the total expense row as well since VisiCalc cannot calculate the sum of the expenses. Every location that required the results of this calculation displays the ERROR message as well. The ERROR condition actually propagates through the model so that every location that references a cell with an error also has an error. This happens because the values that these other cells need to display

Modifying an Existing Model: Two for the Price of One   63

their own results depend on cells that cannot display their own results. It's like a house of cards.

Why didn't this happen when we deleted the parking expense line? When we deleted this row it was in row number 6 at the time. Because this row fell within the range of the sum function there was no problem. The function simply added up everything from B5 to B7. Since the parking expense at B6 was gone it had no effect on the function being able to perform its task. It still knew where to begin adding and where to stop.

It is time to go back to the drawing board. We could fix up this model, but it is a lot easier to simply read in the latest version of our model that we saved on disk.

Let us reload our latest version of the Cash Flow model and make our modifications over again from the start. Enter **/CY** before you reload the cash flow model. If you do not enter /CY, the two models will appear mixed together. Now load the model, CASHFLOW, using the following keystrokes: **/SLCASHFLOW Ⓔ**. You should now be looking at the enhanced cash flow model as it appeared before we made any changes to it.

Flexibility in the design of your models is the key to getting the most out of VisiCalc. We know that as time goes on we will have to add new expenses and drop old ones. Our model should anticipate these changes and be able to adjust to them quickly and easily.

Our last experience with deleting a row pointed out an area where our model's structure could be improved. We want to be able to add and delete expense rows without causing errors to occur throughout the model.

Remember when we summed up a line of dashes and got an answer of zero? We learned that any time a label is involved in a calculation VisiCalc assumes it has a value of zero. We can actually use the cells containing our label borders as the starting and ending ranges of our sum function. All the contents of a column between the two border lines will be totaled up by the sum function. This will solve the problem that deleting the wrong row can cause, provided, of course, we do not delete the border rows!

The fact that we can delete any rows that lie between two border rows points out another powerful VisiCalc feature. The terminal points of a function, such as the sum function, change to reflect changes in the VisiCalc sheet. This is an important concept that we will use often in the models section of this book. For example, suppose the formula "@SUM (A1...A4)" was stored in A5 of a model. If you moved the cursor into line 3 and deleted the line, the formula would actually change. The formula "@SUM(A1...A3)" would be stored at A4. The range of the SUM function has contracted along with the sheet. The locations of the functions are intelligent. As long as you do not wipe out a starting or ending coordinate they will shrink and grow right along with all of your spread sheets. We use these border rows in the same spirit that utility companies put up signs reading "Danger: Buried Cable." As long as we do not delete a border row the model will perform as designed, and our function ranges will continue to work.

Place your cursor at B10. The formula "@SUM(B5...B8)" appears on the Entry line. Instead of adding the locations between B5 and B8, try using the coordinates B3 and B9 as the starting and ending coordinates for the sum function. Enter **@SUM(B3...B9)** Ⓔ in this location. The answer displayed at B10 does not change even though you have modified the range of the sum function. This is because the new range differs from the old range only because some cells that contain labels have been included. Since these cells are considered to have a value of zero, the calculated total is unchanged. Replicate this formula across the row. You should be able to do this yourself. To double check you should use these keystrokes: **/R** Ⓔ **C10.M10** Ⓔ **RR**.

Now you can delete any expense row that does not apply to you, and you do not have to worry about the error problem.

Do the same for the TOTAL INCOME line. The range over which this sum function should act will be from row 11 through row 15. Enter the new sum function in row 16, and replicate across the necessary rows. To do this place your cursor at B16 and enter **@SUM(B11.B15)** Ⓔ **/R** Ⓔ **C16.M16** Ⓔ **RR**.

This is the final enhancement that we will make to the Applied Systems cash flow model. Before we go any further, save this model using the following keystrokes:**/SSCASHFLOW**Ⓔ. Our old "CASHFLOW" model will be replaced by this newer, more flexible version. Now, let us go back and reapply the changes we made earlier. First, use the Blank command to erase the APPLIED SYSTEMS portion of the model's title. Next, delete the parking and secretarial expense rows as we did before. We are now left with rent and telephone as our only expenses. What do we do if we want to add a new expense?

We have used the /D(elete) command to remove lines. Its counterpart, the /I(nsert) command, inserts either a blank row or a column at the current cursor location. With your cursor at A6 enter these keystrokes: **/I**. The Prompt line shows "INSERT: ROW COL". As with the /D command you need to specify whether you want to insert either a row or a column. In this case we enter **R** to signify that we want to insert a row. As soon as we enter this last response a blank row appears above where the cursor is positioned. The rows below the cursor have all moved down a line to make room for the new arrival.

Suppose that we want to add the cost of leasing a car into our cash flow model. Enter the label **CAR** Ⓔ at A6. Assume that the lease payments are fixed at $325 per month. Enter **325** Ⓔ in location B6 and replicate it across the entire row. There is no need to use the domino technique since each monthly payment will remain the same.

When we include this new expense, the model immediately displays how leasing a car affects our total cash flow picture. The only feature we need to add to this row is to calculate the annual cost of the car. Move your cursor to N6 and enter the correct formula. If you are not sure what to do move the cursor up one line and look at the formula that is stored in N5.

You should enter the formula **@SUM(B6...M6)** Ⓔ at location N6 to get the desired result.

By repeating the process of inserting and deleting sources of income and expenses, you can customize this cash flow model to suit your specific business application.

Take some time now to add expense and income categories that apply to your business situation. By deleting and adding rows you should be able to build an exact model of your business's cash flow.

If you decide that you do not want to see the results of investing some of your excess cash, you can do one of two things. You can enter 0 at B21, the CONTRIBUTION % cell. This allows for no contribution to savings and zeros will appear across the interest earned row. Your other alternative would be to delete the interest earned row and the row below it which contains the interest rate and contribution cell.

Of these two methods it is better to enter 0 for the contribution %. This way you still have the option to model the impact of investing some of your spare funds. After all, you may change your mind later about investing and char.ge is what this section has been all about.

After you have altered the model to suit yourself, you may wish to save a permanent copy of it on disk. The key strokes that accomplish this are **/SSMYFLOW** Ⓔ. This will save a copy of the model under the name MYFLOW.

Below you will find a summary of the section on altering existing models. Look it over and review the new commands that we have learned in this section. A few minutes of review will help firm up your understanding.

SUMMARY

- This section illustrated how to cope with different types of changes that affect the structure and the content of VisiCalc models.
- We began our look at structural enhancements by calculating the cumulative cash flow for Applied Systems. This allowed us to see

how much money the company retained as the months passed by.

-When we noticed the accumulation of excess cash we decided to deposit some of these excess funds into a savings account.

-To make the model as flexible as possible, we decided to make the deposit amount variable. This introduced the idea of designating a special cell to store a value that is used in a later calculation.

-Both the percent of accumulated cash to be deposited monthly as well as the interest rate paid were stored in these designated cells.

-When it was time to replicate our interest formulas, we selected the N option for the interest rate and contribution variables since they always referred to the same location, regardless of the column into which the formula was copied.

-Once we calculated the interest earned each month we had to include this amount in our new cumulative cash flow formulas.

-Ted could use this model to see what combination of interest paid and contribution amount would yield him a specific year-end retained earnings figure.

-Our final enhancement was to add annual totals for the various expense and income categories.

-Upon replicating the sum functions in column N, we noticed several strange results. We summed up our border rows and learned that a label is assumed to have a value of zero. We experienced an overflow problem because a number had too many digits to be displayed in a cell.

-We introduced the /B(lank) command to solve our overflow problem.

-Operating in "enhance mode" helped us gain a more complete understanding of the problem, as well as stimulate our creative process.

-Our second type of change showed us how to turn the Applied Systems model into our own cash flow.

-These internal modifications are useful when creating utility models, altering model assumptions, and using prepackaged models.

-Overwriting labels and entering new expense and income values was the first step in customizing the cash flow.

-We introduced the powerful /D(elete) command to erase the line containing the parking expense.

-Things got a bit out of hand when we deleted the line containing secretarial expenses. Since this line was used to define the range of

Modifying an Existing Model: Two for the Price of One 67

a sum function, VisiCalc was unable to do certain calculations. It displayed ERROR in the problem cells.

- The border lines were used to define the starting and ending points of the sum function. This allowed for the error-free deletion of rows and so made for a more flexible model.
- To complete our set of modification tools, we used the /I(nsert) command to add new expense and income categories.
- We are now able to transform the Applied System cash flow into our own by adding and deleting income and expenses where necessary. We can also turn off our interest calculation should we desire.

Chapter 8

Manipulating the Electronic Sheet

In the last few sections we have been discussing how to build and modify VisiCalc models. In this section we will learn how to use the VisiCalc commands that are concerned with the display and manipulation of the spread sheet as a whole.

Building your model is only one part of the VisiCalc problem-solving process. It may seem that once the model is defined and the data is entered, the job is complete. Actually, the real benefits of using VisiCalc appear once this initial work is done. At this point, the model actually gets *used*. This is when a production manager can see how many widgits he needs to make in order to reach and surpass breakeven points; or an investor can see how various investment strategies will affect his tax exposure; or a sales manager can play "what if?" in assigning quotas to his sales force. This is the time you can really cash in on your model-building effort.

Manipulating the sheet means altering the model's appearance so that we can easily examine and compare the data that is displayed on the electronic sheet. Since we can only see a small portion of the whole screen at any one time, we need to learn how to view different pieces of the sheet at the same time. We will be "juggling" pieces of the sheet around so that the specific information we require is displayed in the most convenient manner possible. For example, we will learn how to compare the first to the last quarter's cash flow without moving the cursor back and forth at a dizzying pace. It is like learning how to fold a newspaper for the first time. It takes a bit of practice before you can get from the comics to the sports page.

We will continue using the Applied Systems cash flow model as our example. Start by loading VisiCalc and then load the model we saved in the last chapter as CASHFLOW.

We have dropped several hints in previous chapters about how the column width could be either expanded or reduced. We will start our discussion of the screen commands by introducing this powerful feature.

Place your cursor at A1 and enter **/G**. The options available appear on the Prompt line as "GLOBAL:C O R F". We will select the C(olumn) option. When this character is entered you will see the Prompt line now displays "Column width:". You can enter any number from two to the maximum number of characters that your screen can display across a row as a response to this prompt.

Enter **15 Ⓔ** and watch what happens. Each cell has gotten wider. The numbers are spaced further apart and only two columns appear if you have a 40-column screen while five columns are displayed on an 80-column display. Since the cells have become wider, VisiCalc cannot display as many columns on a screen at one time.

Notice that all our border rows are filled with gaps where the dashes in one cell fail to meet those of the next. When the cells grew, the nine dashes we entered in each location are no longer enough to fill up the entire cell. We have lost the illusion of a straight line.

To solve the problem of the shrinking label, VisiCalc has a special command that is designed to be used when creating border rows. With your cursor at A9, enter these keystrokes: **/-**. The dash is used to indicate that we want to enter a repeating label in the highlighted location. The Prompt line reads "Label:repeating". Enter **- Ⓔ** and notice that A9 is now filled with a line of dashes. When you use the repeating label command, the character that you enter in response to the "label repeating" prompt will always fill the cell, no matter how much you alter the column width.

Replicate the repeating label across row 9 as you would any other label. Do this now using A9 as the source range and B9 through N9 as the target range. Now change the column width with the command **/GC12 Ⓔ**. The other border rows still have gaps showing while row 9 looks as it should. Try entering **/GC18 Ⓔ**. The line of dashes in row 9 still looks like a solid line of dashes. Change the border rows 3, 11, and 15 so that they use repeating labels. When you have done this, enter **/GC15 Ⓔ,** to return the column width to 15.

Take a close look at the labels in column A. Before you widened the cells you could only see TOTAL EXP displayed at A10; now, TOTAL EXPENSES appear in this location. The screen is like a venetian blind; as you open it wider you can see more of what lies behind. As you increase the width of the columns, you can see more of what lies in the cell. You use wide columns when a model has long labels that are difficult to abbreviate meaningfully, or when you are displaying large numbers with a lot of significant digits. Unfortunately, there is a tradeoff here: the wider you make the columns, the fewer can fit on the screen at once. If your labels are especially long, you can use two or more columns to hold them.

Let us use the /GC command to pack many months of data onto one screen. Enter **/GC6 Ⓔ**. Look at the screen now. Many locations have filled with greater than signs, indicating that an overflow condition has occurred. The numbers are too large to be displayed in the cells given the current column width. There are several ways to solve the problem. We can either increase the cell width or we can somehow make the numbers more narrow. We will use the less obvious solution first and shrink the numbers down a bit.

Recalling the section on formats, we can select either integer, general, left, or right justification, $, or * format. Currently, the /GF$ option is in effect. In order to decrease the number of digits displayed, enter these keystrokes: **/GFI,** and look at how the screen changes. The overflow condition has disappeared. Now you can see more months of data than you could before.

VisiCalc can display five digits in integer format when the columns are six spaces wide. This is because the left-most space in each cell containing a value is padded with a blank. This blank is used to prevent columns of numbers running together and creating an unreadable row of continuous digits. This leading blank is also reserved for displaying a negative sign when necessary. Since we selected the integer format, the decimal point and the following two digits are no longer displayed. We have saved the three spaces that were previously taken up by the ".00" in numbers such as 1100.00.

If you tried setting the column width to five, you would find that you could get even more columns on the screen. All numbers would be displayed without problem except for some in the accumulated cash row. This row would have an overflow condition after the month of February because after this month the amount of accumulated cash is too large to be displayed in a cell that is only five spaces wide.

You may want to spend a few minutes now just growing and shrinking the column width of the cash flow model. Satisfy yourself that the repeating label performs as advertised. Get a feel for how altering the column widths affects the screen's appearance. When you are comfortable with the now elastic electronic sheet, enter the following keystrokes: **/GC9 Ⓔ**. By specifying a column width of nine you are now back to the column dimension that is in effect each time you load the VisiCalc model. We refer to this width as the default width.

Move the cursor to A1. During your previous experience with scrolling across the sheet you may have felt some irritation at the way the titles disappear off the left-hand side of the screen as you scroll to the right. To illustrate this problem start moving the cursor to the right and continue until you have just made column A disappear. Now that you can no longer refer to the appropriate labels, it is difficult to tell which expense belongs to which particular category. In many cases you will want to refer to distant locations of a large model and you will want to know what it is you are looking at. If you cannot see the label and the value at the same time this is hard to do. Often you will have to move the cursor a long way to find the label that identifies the object of your interest. The way to solve this problem is to fix the specific row or column titles so that they are not pushed off the edge of the screen as you scroll across the page.

The /T(itles) command causes the titles of rows, columns, or both to be fixed on the screen so that they no longer fall off the edge as you scroll. With your cursor at A1 type **/T**. The Prompt line responds with the options "H V B N". They stand for Horizontal, Vertical, Both, and None. Select the vertical option by entering the letter **V**. This causes all the columns to the left of the cursor position, including the current position, to become fixed. In our case we have just fixed column A in place. Since this command applies to the entire column, the result would have been the same if the cursor was in any row of column A at the time the command was issued.

To see how this affects your scrolling, move your cursor to the right until you expect column A to fall off the screen. Surprised? The cash flow data for the month of January actually disappears while the column of labels remains in place. It is as if the edge of the screen has been moved over to the right of column A. Now you can look at the data in the last few columns of the model and refer to the labels at the same time. Try experimenting to get the feel of using fixed titles by moving the cursor back and forth.

To "unstick" the row, enter **/TN**. Now if you move the cursor over to the right, column A will disappear off the left-hand edge of the screen as it did before. By specifying the N(one) option of the Titles command the screen reverts to having no rows or columns that are fixed.

Move your cursor to A1 to insure that the top of the screen is in view and then move the cursor to A4 and type **/TH**. You have requested that several horizontal rows be fixed. When you specify the H option all the rows above the cursor, including the row currently defined by the cursor, become fixed. In this case all the rows beginning from the row containing the month names to the top row will become fixed. Move the cursor down until you would expect the top row of titles to move off the screen. Like the column of labels before, the top rows stay in place. The columns of numbers disappear below the fixed row titles as you scroll down the page.

The last option available with the Title command allows you to fix both rows and columns at once. With your cursor at A4 type **/TB** to fix both the rows above and the columns to the left of the cursor position. Both the row and column defined by the current cursor location are also fixed. You have now combined the two column and row fixes we made earlier.

Try moving the cursor around. No matter what you do you cannot dislodge those tenacious row and column headings. Try direct cursor movement to J18. Once the cursor gets there you can easily tell that you are looking at the net cash earned in September. Since the row and column labels remain in place, the contents of any location is quickly identified.

Once again it is suggested that you try your own hand at fixing and unfixing various rows and columns to aquaint yourself with the Title command. When you feel comfortable using /T and its variations, return the sheet to its default by entering **/TN** command.

The next set of commands are a great help when we need to compare different parts of the screen to each other. VisiCalc accomplishes this task by actually splitting the screen into two parts, allowing you to treat each half of the screen as a complete model.

Let us begin by trying to compare our cash flow in January with that of December. If we wanted to do this using our current set of skills, we would be forced to move the cursor back and forth between the two ends of the sheet. This would be tedious to say the least. It would be much better if we could line up the months of January and December side by side so that comparisons could be made easily. The /W(indow) command helps us do this.

The Window command gives you a second window through which you can examine the electronic sheet. In effect, you are gaining a second vantage point on your model. This is another VisiCalc feature that is more easily seen than explained.

Move the cursor to A1 to reset the screen location. Now move to column C. The exact location does not matter as long as the cursor is in column C. For comparison purposes, let us select C1. Enter **/W**. The

74 Learning to Use VisiCalc

Prompt line shows the following options: "H V 1 S U". Like the Title command, the H and V refer to horizontal and vertical, respectively. We will cover the other three options as we go.

Our goal is to compare January's cash flow to that of December. Since we want to compare one column to another, we will want to split the screen into two vertical sections. Enter the letter **V**. Watch as the amazing VisiCalc screen proceeds to clone itself.

Two screens now appear side by side where we had only one before. What better way to compare one part of the screen to another than by having two entire screens at your disposal?

Your cursor is currently on the left-side screen. You should be seeing what is shown in Fig. 8-1:

	JAN		FEB	MAR	APR	MAY	JUN	JUL
APPLIED SYSTEMS		CASH FLOW						
RENT	350		350	350	350	350	350	350
PARKING				90			90	
PHONE	56		56	56	56	56	56	56
SECRETARI	150		100		100			75
TOTAL EXP	556		506	496	506	406	496	481
FREEMAN	1100		1100	1100	1100	1100	1100	1100
TRANSPACI	3000		1000	1000	1000	1000	1000	1000
BROWN & B	1500		1500	1500	1500	1500	1500	
TOTAL INC	5600		3600	3600	3600	3600	3600	2100
NET CASH	5044		3094	3104	3094	3194	3104	1619
ACCUMULAT	5044		8138	11277	14428	17701	20906	22649
INTEREST			35	57	79	101	124	146

Figure 8-1

The column containing January's data bumps up against the highlighted line that divides the screen in two. This line actually lists the row numbers for the sheet on the right. We want to scroll the right-hand screen over until the data for December is next to the January data. To do this we will first have to get the cursor over into the screen on the right. To do this enter **;** while watching the screen. The cursor will jump over into the other screen. Now, move the cursor to the right until you have the data for December bumping up against the left edge of the screen. Voila!

By using two screens you can compare any column to any other column with ease. This is how we fold the electronic spread sheet into sections that allow us to assess and compare whatever information we want.

Try moving the cursor around the different sheets. By entering ; at any time, the cursor will flip-flop back and forth between the two sheets. Once you are satisfied that there are actually two complete sheets available for your use, move the cursor to the sheet on the left side.

One advantage of having two screens to play with is that you can use different Global formats in each screen. When would this ability come in handy?

Suppose that we have a model that contains long labels which act as row or column headings. If we want to display the entire label, we need to increase our column width. Unfortunately, when we do this all the columns get wider. The labels may be easier to read, but you cannot fit much else onto the screen. The few columns of numbers that do appear on the sheet will be quite far apart. There is a way to reconcile these two different needs by combining the split screen with the judicious use of the Global format command.

In terms of our existing model, we would like to see the full text of our labels, but at the same time we want to see as many months of data at one time as possible. We can get the best of both worlds by using a different set of Global formats in each screen. The left screen will contain only one column of labels, formatted to display a wide column. The second screen will use a narrow column combined with the /GFI format so that many columns of data will fit on the screen. In that way we can see the entire label and, at the same time, view months of cash flow data.

In order to do this with our current screen configuration we first need to redefine where we split the screen. The left side of the screen currently contains two columns and we want only one column—the wide column containing the labels—to be displayed on the left screen. If you want to change the current window, you must first return to a regular screen before you enter a different window specification. To "undo" the window we use the 1 option of the Window command. This indicates that we want to view the electronic sheet from a single vantage point. Enter **/W1** and watch as the screen returns to its original form.

Now we need to split the screen so that only the labels in column A remain on the left. Enter **/GC13 Ⓔ** to display all the row labels in their entirety. Move the cursor to column B. With the cursor anywhere in column B enter **/WV**. Now enter ; to move the cursor to the screen on the right. Enter **/GC6 Ⓔ** to display as many rows as possible on this screen. Your screen should look like what you see in Fig. 8-2.

You now have the combination of a wide column that displays labels and a set of narrow columns that displays numbers. The application

76 Learning to Use VisiCalc

		JAN	FEB	MAR	APR	MAY	JUN	JUL	AUG	SEP	OCT
APPLIED SYSTEM CASH FLOW											
RENT		350	350	350	350	350	350	350	350	350	350
PARKING				90			90			90	
PHONE		56	56	56	56	56	56	56	56	56	56
SECRETARIAL		150	100		100			75			100
TOTAL EXPENSE		556	506	496	506	406	496	481	406	496	506
FREEMAN		1100	1100	1100	1100	1100	1100	1100	1100	1100	1100
TRANSPACIFIC		3000	1000	1000	1000	1000	1000	1000	1000		
BROWN & BROWN		1500	1500	1500	1500	1500	1500				
TOTAL INCOME		5600	3600	3600	3600	3600	3600	2100	2100	1100	1100
NET CASH FLOW		5044	3094	3104	3094	3194	3104	1619	1694	604	594
ACCUMULATED C		5044	8138	11277	14428	17701	20906	22649	24489	25252	26017
INTEREST			35	57	79	101	124	146	159	171	177

Figure 8-2

of screen manipulation should be coming clear. Getting the most out of VisiCalc does not stop at building the model; there are many ways to display the sheet so as to increase the information you can receive.

Take some time now to see what different changes you can make to the screens. Notice how changes in one window affect the overall screen appearance. You may like to change the location where the screen is split. Practice altering the screens and see how they can combine to give you a more useful overall spread sheet format. After you have tried your hand at jockeying the two screens around, enter **/W1** to revert back to a single window.

When you revert to a single window, the current location of the cursor controls the format of the remaining window. The formats in effect in the screen that the cursor is in at the time the /W1 command is given will define what the remaining screen looks like. If the cursor is in a /GC6/GFI window, then the single remaining screen will have these formats. It is as if the screen that the cursor is in at the time the /W1 command is issued expands until it engulfs the other window. Before going on, define your current screen to have the default column width of

Manipulating the Electronic Sheet

nine and a Global $ format by entering the following keystrokes: **/GC9/GF$.**

A variation of the Window command that we have not tried yet is the /WH command. This splits the sheet horizontally so that row comparisons can be made more easily. Let us use this command to see how the various monthly expenses compare to the net and accumulated cash flow that are shown near the bottom of the model.

First, we will fix column A so that we will always be able to refer to the row names. With your cursor in any row of column A, enter **/TV.**

It is not too difficult to decide where to split the screen. We want to be able to see all the expenses in the top screen, so we will choose the border line in row 11 as the dividing line between the two screens.

Place your cursor in row 12. Enter the keystrokes **/WH.** This will cause the row that the cursor is in to move down a row and make room for the solid line that divides the screen. Move the cursor into the lower screen by typing **;**. Now move the cursor down the rows until the TOTAL INCOME label is bumping up against the screen divider. You can now see the expense levels contrasted with the total income, and the net and accumulated cash.

It would be helpful if we could scroll both screens at the same time. That way we could examine the month-by-month cash flow to see how changes in the expense levels affected the net income and accumulated cash figures as the year progressed. To do this would require both screens to scroll simultaneously as the cursor was moved across one screen. This synchronized scrolling will ensure that the columns remain lined up. Enter **/WS.** Now move the cursor across the right side of the screen. Notice that when you get to the last column displayed on the screen both the upper and lower screen begin to scroll to the right at the same time. Both of the windows are now in sync. We have folded the sheet in half so that we can easily compare the expenses to the accumulated and net cash figures for each month.

To make our examination of the spread sheet even more convenient, we have fixed the row titles. Note that we did this using the /TV command before we created the extra window. As a result this option is in effect in both the upper and lower screens.

Spend some time moving the cursor across the months to get a feel for how the screen behaves. To reset the windows so that they can be scrolled independently, enter **/WU.** This unsynchronizes the windows.

There are hundreds of ways to combine various window definitions with fixed titles and formats to make the screen look and act exactly as you want it to. You can organize the information contained in the screen to be displayed so that it suits your every purpose. The more you practice with these commands, the more efficient you will become at getting the most from your VisiCalc models.

When you have finished playing with the window and other screen commands, set the screen back to a single window and make sure that the **/GF$/GC9** Ⓔ display options are in effect. Also enter **/TN** to unfreeze the row titles.

As you altered the contents of the VisiCalc sheet, either during the building or modification stages, you probably noticed that a pause occurs after each alteration. This pause grows longer as the model gets larger because each time you enter new data VisiCalc recalculates each formula on the sheet. This insures that the results displayed in each location constantly reflect any changes in the model's data. As the model grows larger, the delay increases to the point that the model building process is seriously slowed down. This is due to the fact that VisiCalc has to perform more and more calculations as the screen grows. To avoid this delay VisiCalc allows us to turn off the automatic screen recalculation feature.

Altering the recalculation feature entails changing an option that affects the entire sheet. Like most of the commands that affect the entire sheet we begin by typing in **/G.** We now select the option **R**(ecalculation). The Prompt line reads : "RECALC: A M". The Prompt line is giving us the choice of selecting either A(utomatic) or M(anual) recalculation. Enter: **M** to set the recalculation feature to manual. As long as the M option is in effect we will have to make a special request each time we want VisiCalc to recalculate the formulas in the electronic sheet.

With the manual option in effect, notice how changes can be made to the model without the accompanying delay. Move the cursor to B8 and enter:**200** Ⓔ. Once you enter this value VisiCalc is instantly ready for your next command. To really see the difference, enter **/GRA** to return to automatic recalculation. Now enter **150** Ⓔ at B8 and note the delay that occurs as VisiCalc recalculates the sheet contents. Each time information is added or altered in the sheet, VisiCalc recalculates all the screen contents.

Set the recalculation back to manual. Enter **400** Ⓔ at B5. Normally this rent increase would immediately begin to roll across the rent row. Since we have turned off the recalculation feature, however, the new rental amount we entered in B5 just sits there. To cause VisiCalc to recalculate the entire sheet, enter **!** and see what happens. The new rent amount moves across the rent row and the entire cash flow is recalculated to reflect the new rent. Return the rent to its original value by moving your cursor to B5 and entering **350** Ⓔ. Save a permanent copy of the final version of this cash flow model by entering the following keystrokes: **/SSCASHFLOW** Ⓔ.

We have now covered practically every VisiCalc command that you will need to build and maintain your models. Our intention in these initial sections was not to replace your reference manual and existing VisiCalc documentation package, but rather to offer an alternate approach to learning VisiCalc. This hands-on instruction was based on the belief that people learn information best when the skills being taught are applied to a specific problem. Thus, we have tried to introduce each VisiCalc command as the development of our checkbook and cash flow models required them. As a result we have been able to introduce most, but not every, VisiCalc command in these instructional chapters. There are several commands that you should examine in your reference manual to complete your knowledge of the VisiCalc commands available.

The commands that were not covered in detail are the /S(torage), /P(rint), /M(ove) commands and the built-in functions. If you read about these commands in your reference manual, you will have examined all the VisiCalc commands available.

The next chapter is crucial to your getting the most out of this book. We will show you how to use the models that are developed in the applications section of this book. If you take the necessary time to work through the example presented in the next section, you will be assured of getting the most out of the various business models presented in the following chapters.

There are quite a few models developed in the separate applications chapters contained in this book. Many of these models will require you to spend a certain amount of time and energy entering the appropriate keystrokes into the VisiCalc sheet to set up the models. For those of you who are interested in having instant access to all the different models presented in this book, there is a way you can avoid this time-consuming data entry. Copies of all the models developed in this book are available on disk for your specific microcomputer by sending the order form that can be found immediately preceding the Appendix.

Before moving on to the last of the VisiCalc introduction chapters, we will summarize the major points discussed in this chapter.

SUMMARY

-We learned to shape and manipulate the electronic sheet so that it revealed the information we needed in a form that was easy to use.

- We introduced the /GC command that shrinks and expands our model's column width on demand.
- Using our existing cash flow model, we saw that after expanding the column widths our border line no longer looked like a solid line. To create a border that always works regardless of the column width, we introduced the repeating label command: /-.
- Reducing the column widths can cause the cells to be too narrow to display large numbers. We observed this in our example and used the /GFI command to reduce the space that the numbers required.
- Every value is padded with a blank space in its left-most position. As a result only five digits can be displayed in a column that is six spaces wide.
- Since titles that disappear off the edge of the screen are not much help in identifying the contents of a distant cell, we introduced the /T(itle) command.
- The /T command has the H, V, B, and N options. The H and the V allow you to fix horizontal or vertical titles. The B lets you fix titles in both directions, and the N removes the "glue" from all the titles that have been previously fixed.
- In order to compare different locations of the sheet to each other we learned how to use the /W(indow) command.
- The /W command has the H, V, 1, U, and S options. The H and V cause the screen to be divided horizontally or vertically. Once the new window has been introduced you can specify that the two windows scroll together, using the S(yncronize) option, or you can cause two screens that are in sync to revert to independent motion using the U(nsyncronize) option.
- We combined the /W and the /GF commands to create a custom screen. It had wide columns on the left side to display labels and narrow columns on the right so that we could see lots of values. The values on the left-hand screen were packed closely together using integer format.
- By using the /WH command we were able to compare monthly expenses to net and accumulated cash flow.
- To reduce the delay caused by automatic recalculation, we introduced the /GR command to set the recalculation feature to either A(utomatic) or M(anual). You can have VisiCalc recalculate the sheet at any time by entering the "!" character.

-Finally, we discussed our "learn-as-you-need-them" philosophy behind introducing the VisiCalc commands. We listed the commands that were not covered in detail in the VisiCalc introduction chapters.

Chapter 9

Learning How to Use the Models in this Book

This is the final chapter in our introduction to VisiCalc. We will illustrate how you can take the models that are developed at the end of each applications chapter and customize them to suit your own special needs.

Each applications chapter is structured the same way. After the initial application introduction, the specific models are defined and built. It is this "models" section that we are concerned with now. Each models section begins with a brief description of the spread sheets contained in the chapter. One at a time each model will be examined in detail. First, the layout of the spread sheet will be shown so you can get an overview of the model. Then you are directed to the appendix where the keystrokes that compose the model are listed so that you can type them into the VisiCalc program. Alternatively, if you have the disk you can load the model directly. Finally, we get to the most important part of the chapter. We use an example to show you how to enter information into each model. You learn how to make the model fit your own circumstances by watching how someone else would do it.

All the models have been designed so that they are easy to alter. This lets you change the spread sheet to represent your specific business situation. To facilitate this ease of alteration, all the models in this book are stored in "packed format." Each sheet is a skeleton of a model that you customize with your own data.

84 Learning to Use VisiCalc

We originated the idea of the packed model after many hours of experience in instructing VisiCalc. These models are filled with the formulas and formats needed to solve your specific business problems. It is our "just add water and stir" approach to getting VisiCalc to work for you. You do not need to be a VisiCalc expert to use these models. By using a small subset of VisiCalc commands you can quickly create complex models that grow as you enter information about your own business. Some of the models are in a "fill-in-the-blank" format, while others allow you to insert and delete sections, gradually shaping the model to match your own business.

This chapter will show you how to unpack a model. The example we will develop is in the same format as all the other model sections, so it is like a warm-up exercise. You will have a chance to practice on this model before you go on to the applications chapters. To get the most out of this exercise you should be reading this chapter in front of your computer so that you can actually modify the model as we go.

Our sample model is used to analyze cash flow. For those of you who have read all the previous chapters you will be familiar with this example. We are using it again, with some variations, so that you can concentrate on the unpacking technique. For those readers who, because

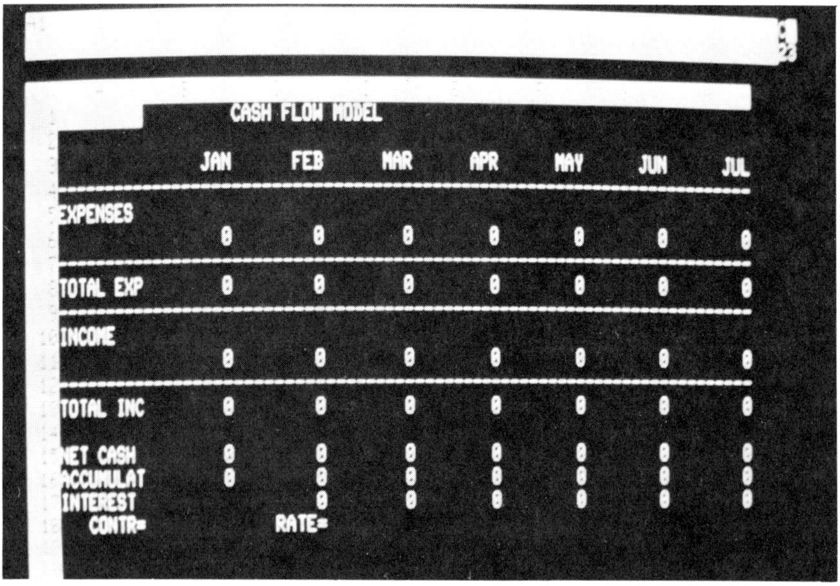

Figure 9-1

they were already familiar with VisiCalc, have skipped forward to this section, it is important that you go through this example step-by-step. This is your opportunity to learn how to get the most out of the models that are developed in this book.

Below you will see how our packed cash flow model appears. This illustration is followed by the keystrokes necessary to create the model. There are several calculations embedded in the model that you cannot see by simply examining the picture. If you try to type in the model based on what it looks like you will be missing many of its important functions. Once you have loaded the VisiCalc program you can either type in the keystrokes listed below the model, or if you have purchased the model disk, simply type **/SLCASHF** ⓔ and the model will be loaded directly from disk.

CASH FLOW MODEL INSTRUCTIONS

>C1 ⓔ CASH FLOW ⓔ /FR►" MODEL ⓔ /FL
>B3 ⓔ /FR /R ⓔ C3.N3 ⓔ
JAN►FEB►MAR►APR►MAY►JUN►JUL►AUG►SEP►OCT►NOV►DEC►ANNUAL ⓔ
>A4 ⓔ /-- ⓔ /R ⓔ B4.N4
▼EXPENSES
▼►0►+B6 ⓔ /R ⓔ D6.M6 ⓔ R
>A7 ⓔ /-- ⓔ /R ⓔ B7.N7 ⓔ
>A8 TOTAL EXPENSES►@SUM(B4.B7) ⓔ /R ⓔ C8.M8 ⓔ RR
>A9 ⓔ /-- ⓔ /R ⓔ B9.N9 ⓔ
>A10 ⓔ INCOME ⓔ
>B11 ⓔ 0►+B11 ⓔ /R ⓔ D11.M11 ⓔ R
>A12 ⓔ /-- ⓔ /R ⓔ B12.N12 ⓔ
>A13 ⓔ TOTAL INCOME►@SUM(B9.B12) ⓔ /R ⓔ C13.M13 ⓔ RR
>A15 ⓔ NET CASH►+B13-B8 ⓔ /R ⓔ C15.M15 ⓔ RR
>A16 ⓔ ACCUMULATED CASH►+B15►+B16+B17+C15 ⓔ /R ⓔ D16.M16 ⓔ RRR
>A17 ⓔ INTEREST►►(B16*B18*D18)/12 ⓔ /F$/R ⓔ D17.M17 ⓔ RNN
>A18 ⓔ CONTR= ⓔ /FR►/F$►RATE= ⓔ /FR►/F$
>N6 ⓔ @SUM(B6.M6)▼▼@SUM(B8.M8)▼▼▼@SUM(B11.M11)▼▼@SUM(B13.M13)▼▼▼▼@SUM(B17.M17) ⓔ
>A1 ⓔ /GFI

86 Learning to Use VisiCalc

If you type in the model be sure to save a copy of it before you proceed any further. This way you will always have an untouched cash flow model to use. You may want to use the name CASHF.

After either loading the model or typing it in, refer back to the illustration on the cash flow model. Check the picture to be sure that your screen looks the way it should.

We will illustrate how to unpack the cash flow model by seeing how a small furniture manufacturer would enter his specific information into the model. Keep in mind that the goal of this exercise is to use the model to project cash flow for the coming year. You will find it useful as you go through this exercise to pause once in a while and think about what your own business's cash flow would look like on this spread sheet.

First, take a look at how the sheet has been designed. It is divided into three sections. The first section is used to record expenses, the second records sources of income, and the third section contains a summary of retained earnings.

Here is the list of expense categories and their projected costs as supplied by the A&A Furniture Company, Ltd.

Owners draw	: $1,500/month
Payroll	: $2,500/month January to April, then $3,000/month until December
Materials	: $8,000/month until June, then $9,500/month until December
Rent	: $600/month
Utilities	: $110/month
Accounting	: $100 on last month of each quarter
Taxes and licenses	: $60/month
Interest	: $55/month

This summarizes the projected expenses for the coming year. Now we have to insert this information into our cash flow spread sheet so that it represents A&A's financial condition.

To start, let us add a title to the model. The title will help us identify the model in the future. Enter the following keystrokes: >B1 (E) ►A&A LTD. (E) /FR.

Now we need to expand the expenses section of our model so that we can fit in the various expense categories. Let us start by inserting a few rows. With your cursor at A6, type the following keystrokes: **/IR/IR/IR/IR.** Watch the space in the expense section grow as you insert the four rows. We are prying apart the border lines that define the expense section. This is one of the methods used to unpack a model.

Learning How to Use the Models in this Book 87

The line of zeros has been pushed down and now appears in row 10. This line of zeros has been set up to behave like a line of dominoes. If you enter a number at any cell along this line it will be copied into all the cells to its right. We will refer to this type of line as a repeating line throughout the book.

The first expense we want to insert will be the owner's draw. This expense is well suited to a repeating line since it is projected to remain the same all year. By entering the draw just once in the first month it will be carried forward to all the subsequent months. We will first enter the label for this row and then replicate the "dummy" repeating row into row 6.

To set the label at A6 enter **OWNERS DRAW** Ⓔ. To replicate the repeating line, proceed as follows: >**B10** Ⓔ /**R.M10:B6** Ⓔ **RRRRRRRRRRR**; that is eleven Rs in a row. You have now produced a repeating line at row 6. Enter the owner's draw by using the following keystrokes: >**B6** Ⓔ **1500** Ⓔ. Once you enter the owner's draw for January it automatically spreads across the entire year. In order to reduce the delay caused by the spread sheet recalculating each time we enter any data, set the recalculation feature to manual with the following keystrokes: /**GRM.**

The next expense category to enter is the payroll. Notice that payroll is expected to increase from $2,500 to $3,000 during the year. A repeating line will suit this type of changing expense extremely well. Enter the label at A7 as follows: >**A7** Ⓔ **PAYROLL** Ⓔ. Now replicate our repeating row into row 7 as we did before: /**R BS B10.M10:B7** Ⓔ **RRRRRRRRRRR.** Notice that this time we used the *BS* key so that we could enter the source and target ranges directly. When we do this it makes no difference where our cursor is located when the Replicate command is issued. To enter the appropriate payroll amounts, type the following: >**B7** Ⓔ **2500** Ⓔ ▶▶▶▶ **3000** Ⓔ. Now type **!** to cause the screen to recalculate. The correct amounts for payroll appear across row 7.

Notice that calculations appear in other spots on the sheet. In particular, notice that the total expense line is filled with the total monthly expenses. The expense area that lies between the border rows acts as an automatic expense accumulator. The top border line is used to define the starting point of the @SUM function, while the lower border line is used as the ending point of the range. This means that all the numbers that you add between the dotted lines will be summed and displayed on the total expense line. So when you are using the packed models you can add or delete rows between the dotted lines as much as you like. If you clobber a border line, however, you will probably cause an error condition to occur. In all the models in this book add and delete lines between the borders, but leave the borders alone. They are the bones of our skeletal models.

Next, we can add the raw material expense. It is handled the same way as the payroll. Enter the label at A8 as follows: **MATERIALS▸**. Now replicate the repeating row into row 8 with the following keystrokes: **/R BS B10.M10:B8 Ⓔ RRRRRRRRRRR.** To enter the actual expenses the following keystrokes will suffice: **>B8 Ⓔ 8000 Ⓔ ▸▸▸▸▸▸9500 Ⓔ**. Remember that since you turned off the automatic recalculation, the raw material costs will not flow across the page. We have to request a manual recalculation to get the screen to respond. But we will put this off for the time being.

The rent and utilities expenses are easily handled if we use the repeating line. We need to make more room, however, because we are running out of expense rows.

Since we have three other expenses to add, as well as the rent and utilities, we will add the four extra rows that we need. With the cursor at A9, enter these keystrokes: **/IR/IR/IR/IR**. Now we have room to add the remaining expenses.

Both the rent and utilities can use the repeating row. Now let us replicate the dummy row into both these expense rows at the same time. We do this by specifying a multiple target range. Type in these keystrokes: **/R BS B14.M14:B9.B10 Ⓔ RRRRRRRRRRR.** That is eleven Rs in all. Notice how both the rows are filled at once. First, enter the labels with the following keystrokes: **>A9 Ⓔ RENT ▾ UTILITIES Ⓔ**. Now we can enter the amounts required with these keystrokes: **>B9 Ⓔ 600 ▾ 110 Ⓔ**.

The cost for accounting services does not lend itself to the repeating line format, because the expenses occur only once a quarter. We will enter the label first and then add each quarterly payment directly by typing **>A11 Ⓔ ACCOUNTING▸▸▸100▸▸▸100▸▸▸100▸▸▸100 Ⓔ**.

The last two expenses are taxes and licenses, and interest charges. We enter these expenses in the same way we entered the rent and utilities. First, we input the labels, then replicate the repeating line into both rows, and finally we will enter the appropriate amounts. Use the following keystrokes: **>A12 Ⓔ TAX & LICENSES ▾ INTEREST Ⓔ /R BS B14.M14: B12.B13 Ⓔ RRRRRRRRRRR >B12 Ⓔ 60▾55 Ⓔ**.

This completes the expense categories for our sample manufacturer. Enter ! to cause the screen to recalculate. You will notice that the screen fills with numbers in the expense section. The bottom section of the sheet shows a negative accumulated cash flow. This is to be expected since we have recorded only expenses and no income.

The procedure for using the packed sheets should be getting clearer. The first step is to insert rows between the borders as you need them. Should you need a repeating row, all you need to do is replicate the "dummy" row into the appropriate row or rows. The next step is to enter the values and labels in the specific locations. All the totals, accumulated earnings, and interest calculations will be done for you. This will be easier to see after we have filled in the income section of the model.

Before we move on to the income section we need to calculate the annual totals for the various expenses. This means totaling the expenses across the rows. To do this, position your cursor at N14. This location holds the formula to sum across the rows and is an extension of the dummy row. To replicate this formula for all the expense categories, type the following: **/R Ⓔ N6.N13 Ⓔ RR.** Watch as the annual totals are displayed as the formula is replicated.

Now let us move on to the income. The A&A Furniture Company receives income from two sources: cash sales and collections of accounts receivable. The table below describes the income projections for the coming year. The figures for cash sales and collections are averages. We will assume that they represent income received for each month of the quarter.

Quarter	Cash Sales	Collections
1ST	$10,000	$7,000
2ND	10,500	7,100
3RD	11,500	7,200
4TH	12,500	7,500

We will need to expand our income section to hold the two income categories. First, insert two rows with the following keystrokes: **>A19 Ⓔ /IR/IR.** Now enter the two income labels: **CASH▾COLLECTIONS Ⓔ.** Both of these income categories are entered on a quarterly basis so the dummy repeat line will not help us out. We will enter the income forecasts directly. Use the following keystrokes: **>B19 Ⓔ 10000 ▸10000 ▸ 10000▸10500▸10500▸10500▸ 11500▸11500▸11500▸12500▸12500▸12500>B20 Ⓔ 7000▸7000▸7000▸7100▸7100▸7100▸ 7200▸7200▸7200▸7500▸7500▸7500 Ⓔ >B20 Ⓔ.**

Force the screen to recalculate by entering **!**. You can now see the cash picture for the coming year for A&A Furniture. Take a minute to scroll along the net and accumulated cash rows. You can see how the retained income grows each month.

We need to add the annual totals for the income categories. We can use the dummy formula stored in N21. Enter the following keystrokes: **/R BS N21 Ⓔ N19.N20 Ⓔ RR.** Again, we see the annual totals appear as the formula is replicated into the cells.

The final step is to add the interest that the excess funds could be earning. Move the cursor to A28. You will notice that cell B28 has been designated to hold the contribution (CONTR=), while D28 is reserved for the rate (RATE=). The contribution refers to the percentage of the retained earnings that will be deposited in an interest-yielding investment. The rate refers to the interest rate that the invested money will earn. Suppose that A&A decides to invest 25 percent of their retained earnings at 12 percent. To see how this would affect cash flow, enter ▶.25 ▶▶.12 Ⓔ. Now enter ! to recalculate the screen. Notice how the interest earned is compounded each month. You can see how various contribution percentages contrast with differing investment yields by simply altering amounts in B28 and D28 and recalculating the sheet. It is easy to see how these factors affect the annual retained earnings.

Scroll around the screen and look at the total cash flow picture. Take some time to imagine how your own cash flow would look if entered into this spread sheet. Would you need more or less expense categories? How many of your expenses could use the dummy repeating line? Do you have enough retained income to warrant investing some of the cash in short-term notes? If not, you can set RATE= 0, and no interest will be added to your cash flow.

The principle of unpacking the models in order to make them suit your specific business needs is present in each of the applications models. After completing this example you should be able to load the original packed cash flow that you saved under "CASHF" and fill in the blanks with your own financial information. If you are not sure that you can do this, you may want to review this final chapter. If you would like more of a review you could reread the chapter on modifying an existing model.

As has been the case throughout this introduction to Visi-Calc, we will review the major points covered in this chapter. This concludes the introduction section. Happy modeling!

SUMMARY

- Each applications chapter is divided into an introduction and a models section.
- Each models section begins by describing the models that will be developed. Then, one at a time, each spread sheet is discussed in detail.
- A picture of each packed model is shown, and the instructions necessary to create it are provided.
- The most important part of the models section follows. Specific examples are used to show you how to modify the models to suit your special application needs.

- Once the model was either typed in or loaded from disk, we began to unpack the sheet. We first added a descriptive title.
- To enter A&A's expense information, we need to expand the expenses section of the model. We did this using the "/IR" command.
- Once the rows have been inserted we added the expense data.
- The dummy repeating line was replicated when necessary into the appropriate row or rows.
- As we filled in the expense section we noticed that the monthly expense totals were being calculated. The border rows were used to define the range of a sum function.
- In general, when using the models in this book, we can add or delete as many rows as we like, as long as we stay between the border rows. If you delete a border row, you will usually create error conditions in many locations.
- When we completed entering the expense data we replicated the last formula in the dummy row to sum the annual expense totals.
- We then repeated this process for the income categories—first expanding the income section by inserting rows between the border lines, and then entering the actual income information.
- Once all the income and expense information was entered, we assigned specific values for the contribution and rate variables. This allowed us to see how various combinations of cash invested and investment yield affected the retained earnings.

PART 2

Applications and Models

Chapter 10

Credit Control

Credit policies can affect a business in several key, but not necessarily obvious, ways. Complaints from your sales department about customer reluctance to buy might be related to your credit policy being too tight, not to problems with your product. On the other hand, being too loose with credit can result in increased losses due to bad debt. Credit is an important part of your total business operation. When used efficiently it can help sell goods and increase operating profit. Poor credit management can tie your cash flow in knots, decreasing profitability.

In this chapter we will try to gain a better understanding of credit and examine ways to improve credit management.

The VisiCalc models we will develop in this chapter will provide you with an overview of your receivables. One model will let you analyze your outstanding accounts by age and see your cost of offering credit, both in interest payments and bad debts. The second model will let you track the payment history of each credit customer. You will see the year-to-date sales, as well as the average collection period for each customer.

When you offer credit you increase the amount of cash required to run your business. Extending credit to a customer is like lending him money. Instead of receiving cash at the time of the sale, you receive the promise that cash will be paid later. You have exchanged the opportunity to collect a dollar now for the hope of receiving it later. Meanwhile, your own cash needs have not changed. Your creditors still expect to be paid on time. In order to stay in business you need to replace the inventory that was sold on credit. The credit sale has created a vacuum in your cash flow.

You have to fill this hole in your cash flow by borrowing or investing more cash. The longer it takes for you to collect on your customers' promise to pay, the more expensive it becomes for you to plug the hole.

You offer credit to increase your sales. By minimizing the cost of offering credit, you increase the profits that extending customer credit can provide.

How can you measure how efficiently you are managing credit? There are several financial ratios that reveal the results your credit policies have on your short-term financial picture. The first two ratios show how your credit policies are affecting short-term cash flow. The Working Capital Ratio and the Quick Asset Ratio are often used by lenders to determine the credit worthiness of a company. These ratios tell the vital story of how well you can meet your short-term financial commitments. We will explain how these ratios are used shortly.

The second group of ratios we will discuss examine how efficiently you manage your credit collections. The three ratios in this group are the Average Collection Period, the Aged Account Analysis, and the Bad Debt Ratio. Each reports on how healthy your credit department is. Individual managers use these ratios to monitor their own performance as well as the company's performance as a whole. Financial officers use these ratios to insure that the credit department is operating as efficiently as possible. An important group that uses these ratios are potential lenders and investors. By combining the information contained in these ratios with some experience and common sense, much can be learned about the stability and future prospects of a company.

The first two ratios we will discuss are the Working Capital and Quick Asset Ratios. Your accounts receivable are corporate assets, while the money you owe your creditors—your accounts payable—appear as liabilities. The difference between your short-term assets and short-term liabilities is called your working capital. Both of these ratios use short-term assets divided by short-term liabilities as the key to measuring how well you can pay your debts. This shows how much money you have left over for running your business after you pay your bills. Large assets divided by small liabilities make for a healthy appearing company. What happens when you collect your bills slowly? These ratios are hit with a double blow. Assets, which appear as the numerator in these ratios, are decreased, while at the same time liabilities, used in the denominator, are increased. This causes the ratio to decrease quickly.

One of the most popular ratios commonly used for credit analysis is the Working Capital Ratio, also called the Current Ratio. To calculate this ratio use the formula below.

Working Capital Ratio = Current Assets/Current Liabilities

Current assets are assets that can readily be turned into cash, usually within one year. Current liabilities represent the amount of money owed by the company and payable within one year.

Let us suppose you have divided a company's current assets by current liabilities and the answer is $2.90. This indicates that for every dollar that the company has to repay in the next year, it has $2.90 of assets. Is this a good ratio? The answer depends on several different factors, including the industry, the rate of inventory turnover, and the composition of the current assets. They all play a major role in interpreting this statistic. For example, suppose company A and company B have the same Working Capital Ratios. Company A has 50 percent of its current assets in cash while company B has 75 percent of its current assets in inventory. Based on this information, company A looks better. From the lender's viewpoint, should there be a desperate need for cash, A is a better credit risk since its assets are more liquid. Company B may have trouble turning its inventory into cash. Many lenders are justifiably concerned about what a company's inventories are actually worth. They do not want to face a crisis situation and discover that an inventory is overvalued or that it cannot be turned into cash at all. While company B has the same ratio as company A, it is not as desirable a credit risk.

As a general rule of thumb, a Working Capital Ratio of 2:1 is thought to indicate good liquidity. Some companies, however, may have a ratio considerably below this and still be considered a good credit risk. For example, a dry cleaning company usually gets paid cash on all its accounts, yet it will get 30 days credit to pay its suppliers for cleaning fluid and other supplies, and it has virtually nothing in the way of inventory carrying costs. This business will have a small Working Capital Ratio since it is paid in cash and it buys its supplies on credit. It is always ahead of the cash flow cycle.

If a Working Capital Ratio of $2 is good, is $20 better? Definitely not. If a company's current ratio exceeds roughly 6:1, there is an unnecessary accumulation of cash and/or inventory. If there is an excess of cash on hand, the company is losing money since it could invest the excess for more interest then it receives lying idle in its checking account. An accumulation of inventory can indicate poor sales forecasting or production control, or both. Since inventories cost money to carry, too much inventory can quickly reduce profit margins. Either way, a high Working Capital Ratio calls for further investigation.

Another popular ratio used to indicate debt capacity is a variation of the Working Capital Ratio called the Quick Asset Ratio, also affectionately known as the Acid Test. This ratio is calculated as follows:

Quick Asset Ratio = (Current Assets-Inventory)/Current Liabilities

The Quick Asset Ratio subtracts the inventory value from current assets. This "solves" the problem of valuing inventory by ignoring it altogether. The lender assumes that none of the inventory could be turned into cash on short notice. The Acid Test, therefore, is a more conservative measure of a company's ability to meet its current obligations. If this ratio is 1:1 or better, a company is considered to be in a good liquid position. A Quick Asset Ratio of less than 1:1 may be just as acceptable, depending on how quickly a particular company turns its inventory. The faster a company moves its inventory, the faster cash becomes available to pay the bills. In the case of rapid inventory turnover, the ratio of short-term assets to liabilities can be less than 1:1 since the inventory is turned into cash at a faster rate. For example, a dairy farmer who has a rapid inventory turnover ratio could function satisfactorily with a Quick Asset Ratio of $.70 to a dollar, while a manufacturer of heavy equipment would have to obey this 1:1 or better rule since his inventory takes longer to turn into cash.

When credit is managed poorly, both the Working Capital and the Quick Asset Ratios sound an alarm. Receivables that are collected slowly or that are not collected at all have a doubly devastating impact on liquidity. Your assets decrease while at the same time your liabilities increase. A potential lender, trade creditor, or investor will view this situation with concern. Inability to collect receivables hurts cash flow. This in turn affects a business's ability to expand, cope with unexpected problems, and take advantage of potential opportunities.

The Working Capital and Quick Asset Ratios depend solely on the levels of the current assets and current liabilities. They do not give you any information about how well your receivables are being managed. A low Working Capital or Current Ratio could be caused by inventory build-up, slow sales, or other problems not necessarily related to credit. The next three ratios we will discuss directly measure how efficiently you are managing your credit. This will let you see whether your receivables are creating a cash flow bind.

The Average Collection Period tells you how long it takes to collect your outstanding accounts. Once you know your average collection period you can judge how far your customers are stretching your credit terms.

Average Collection Period = (Average Accounts Receivable/ Annual Credit Sales) * 365

In the above formula your annual credit sales are projected for the coming year as are your average accounts receivable outstanding. As far as this ratio is concerned, the shorter the average collection period the better.

The Aged Account Analysis shows you the percentage of your accounts receivable that are of a specific age. For example, the percentage of your accounts receivable that are current can be calculated using the formula below.

% Current A.R. = (Current Balance/Total A.R. Outstanding) * 100

Similarly, the percentage of accounts receivable that have been outstanding for over one month can be calculated as follows:

% A.R. Over 30 Days = (A.R. Over 30-Day Balance/Total A.R. Outstanding)*100

You can calculate these ratios for each age category. This gives you a complete picture of the age of your receivables. By monitoring the distribution of account balances, you can be alerted to any change in your collections. The object is to keep as high a percentage of accounts as possible in the current column.

The final ratio we will discuss is the Bad Debt Ratio. This is the ratio of bad debts to total accounts receivable.

Bad Debt Ratio = Bad Debts/Total Accounts Receivable

All of the ratios we have been discussing become more meaningful if you compare your results to those of other companies within your industry. Both Dun and Bradstreet and Robert Morris Associates publish hundreds of operating ratios for almost all industries. By examining your operating ratios in comparison to other companies in the same industry you can see where your operations can stand improvement.

The five ratios we have discussed are particularly helpful in assessing businesses that offer credit directly to their customers. In many cases, particularly in the manufacturing sector, offering 30-day credit is standard practice. Retail institutions, however, are making more use of credit cards to satisfy their customers' demand to purchase goods on credit. We can understand why if we take a moment to examine the credit card phenomenon.

The first national credit card was the Diners Club card. It was offered as a form of payment for the very first time in 1950. Several years later American Express and Carte Blanche climbed on the credit card bandwagon. The two major bank cards, MasterCharge and BankAmericard did not really become established until the early 1960's. What the banks lacked in pioneering spirit, they more than made up for in growth. In 1980 the banks had over 80 million of their credit cards in circulation. The travel and entertainment card companies claimed over 15 million card holders.

It is no wonder, then, considering the growth in the use and acceptance of credit cards and the acknowledged fact that credit card customers spend more money than cash customers, that many retailers will honor at least some of the major credit cards. For a large percentage of businesses it will be their only experience with credit. For a percentage of sales, usually related to the level of gross sales and the average dollar amount of each sale, the credit card company will maintain and assume all the administrative costs, overhead, and risk associated with consumer credit. This fee is usually between 2 and 5 percent of sales. This cost is acknowledged by most businesses to be less than the cost of offering credit themselves. In some cases the savings can be quite significant.

For many, the decision to accept credit cards for payment will seem like a necessity. It is a decision that should not be taken lightly. Offering credit will alter the way you do business. You will most likely find that your typical credit card customers will spend two to three more than your cash customers. As a result, you may also find that more and more of your sales are credit card sales. You will have to factor in the result of giving up between 2 and 5 percent of your sales margin to the credit card company. If your margin is slim, an increasing portion of credit sales may completely wipe out an already thin profit margin. If you can afford to pay for credit, and you feel that the added sales volume will more than compensate for this cost, you must add the credit cost to your cost of goods sold for all your future sales projections.

You may find that the proportion of credit card sales increasing with respect to cash sales can have some negative effects on your business. You may come to depend more and more on the credit card customers and hence the credit card system. This "golden" or, more appropriately, "plastic handcuffs syndrome" can be dangerous. Your dependence may not become apparent until the card company, which you depend on for a vast majority of sales, decides to pass on its increasing operating expenses to you in the form of increased premiums. If you become locked in, several other problem areas may arise. What can you do if you want to raise your assigned floor limit and the major credit card company says no? What happens if you experience difficulty dialing up the credit department to get an authorization because the line is often busy? What if the credit card company is slow delivering required charge slips or other supplies? Be sure that you make decisions involving credit policy with the long- and short-term ramifications in mind.

On the one hand, the growth in consumer credit is pressuring you to accept credit cards, but on the other hand, you do not want to be left at the mercy of the credit companies. One solution to this credit dilemma is to offer your own credit in conjunction with standard credit cards. There are several advantages to this approach. First, you avoid the problem of depending too heavily on the major credit card companies. Second, a private credit system is an excellent means to promote your products. Third, since credit customers spend more than cash customers, it may be an opportunity to get some of your cash customers to increase their purchases. Fourth, it is a way of telling your better customers that you value their business.

The added responsibility of record-keeping is in part offset by the increased knowledge you will receive from your customer base. You will be able to keep track of your customers' purchasing patterns, and you will know which accounts are becoming less active and perhaps be able to take corrective action. Even if an inactive account can not be revived, you may learn how to improve your business. Let us say you decided to examine all of your charge customers that have not purchased anything from you in the last 120 days. You could make up a list and phone four or five of these people every day. If you are lucky, or if your interviewing skills are particularly good, you may be able to find out what has been keeping them away. Is there a salesman on the floor you should be watching more closely? Is there something lacking in your inventory? Is there something about the service in general or the appearance of the store that put them off? Is there a new competitor in the area? Feedback from inactive accounts is a good way to keep your business healthy.

A general rule of thumb regarding credit cards is that the cost for the vendor is between 40 and 80 percent less than if the vendor set up and administrated his own credit department. For many businesses this is true, but things may be changing. If you already own a computer and are using it for some other purpose, adding an accounts receivable system increases the value of your computer. By letting your computer help you manage receivables, you may find that offering your own credit is not as expensive as you once thought.

SUMMARY

Consumer credit can have a profound effect on your business. Properly used, it can attract customers and increase sales. Mismanage credit, however, and you run the risk of drying up your company's cash flow.

Various ratios are used to monitor the health of your collections department both directly and indirectly. The indirect ratios compare current assets to current liabilities to see if there is any sign of a cash flow problem. If there is, further investigation is needed to determine if the problem originates in your credit department or not. The direct ratios report on how well the credit department is being run. These ratios help you find out if it is your collections department that is causing the problem or not.

We discussed the role of the credit card in retail sales. While these cards may seem to solve all your credit problems, one should "beware of banks bearing gifts." Know the long- and short-term effects that credit cards can have on your business.

THE MODELS

Two credit models will be developed in this section. The first model is a credit analysis spread sheet. This spread sheet is designed to keep you on top of your receivables. You will be able to see your accounts receivable by age, and within each age group you will see the largest amount outstanding. In addition, you can project your allowance for bad debt, calculate your average collection period, and given current interest rates, you can see exactly how much it is costing you to carry your customers' receivables.

The second credit model tracks the credit history of each of your customers. You will find out how long on the average a customer takes to pay, as well as how much he/she has spent with you in the past.

This information, when taken together, will give you a complete report on the health of your credit department. Danger signals, such as a growing percentage of receivables 60-days old or older, are quickly spotted and prompt corrective action can be taken. With the high cost of borrowing, collecting your receivables faster can pay for your computer software and hardware investment by reducing the amount of borrowing required to cover your outstanding accounts. In addition to allowing better control of credit, these models will help you get to know your customer better. They will let you observe spending patterns and alert you to inactive accounts, which may signal possible customer dissatisfaction or increasing levels of local competition.

Before we proceed, a warning is in order. These models are especially suited to companies that have no more than 200 accounts to manage. Each of these accounts should have no more than three transactions per billing period. This is because the work involved in keeping the accounts current is too time consuming. The number of accounts and transaction rates are meant as a rough guideline. For those companies that are too large, there are two alternative solutions. You can buy an accounts receivable package, or you can put only the largest of your accounts on these spread sheets. If your company is large, the purchase of a set of accounting programs is well worth the investment.

Model I: Credit Analysis

Load the model CREDIT from the model disk by typing **/SLCREDIT** (E), or enter the keystrokes under this name in the appendix. Your screen should look like Figure 10-1.

The principles you use to unpack this model are the same as those used with the Cash Flow example. You will expand the model and enter the information. In some cases you will be replicating dummy lines that contain necessary formulas and formats.

Most of the column headings in this model are self-explanatory, but some require discussion. As we describe the specific columns, you can follow along by scrolling the cursor to the right across the top of the sheet.

The account number shown in column E is optional. You can use your own numbering system, or depending on the size of your client base, you might find a name is simply good enough.

The credit limit is shown in column F. It provides a way to control your level of credit risk, especially where a new customer is concerned. At the foot of this column you will find the total amount of your credit exposure.

The billing date in column G is used to spread the work of sending out your customers' invoices over the entire month. Instead of having one hectic day each month where you and your staff have to get all the invoices out, the billing date lets you split up accounts into smaller and more manageable groups. There are several ways to divide up your customer base for invoicing purposes. One way is to select account numbers that fall within a specific range. Another way is to divide customers into groups whose last names fall within a range of letters. One such group could be composed of all customers whose last names begin with the

CREDIT   ANALYSIS   CURRENT TO:

NAME	ADDRESS	HOME#	BUS.#	ACCT#	LIMIT	BILLING DAT	INVOICE#	DATE	BALANCE	CREDIT
									0.00	0.00
				====TOTALS:	0.00				0.00	0.00

	ANNUAL	PROJECTED AVERAGE COLLECTION	CREDIT INTEREST CARRYING	ALLOWANCE	SALES: PERIOD: RATE: COST:	LARGEST FOR BAD ALLOWANCE	% AGED ANALYSIS: OUTSTANDING: DEBT % ESTIMATE: FOR BAD DEBT:
					NA NA ERROR		

CURRENT	>30 DAYS	>60 DAYS	>90 DAYS	BAD DEBT	COMMENTS
0.00	0.00	0.00	0.00	0.00	
0.00	0.00	0.00	0.00	0.00	

CURRENT	>30 DAYS	>60 DAYS	>90 DAYS	BAD DEBT
ERROR	ERROR	ERROR	ERROR	ERROR
0.00	0.00	0.00	0.00	0.00
.01	.02	.08	.2	TOTAL
0.00	0.00	0.00	0.00	0.00

Figure 10-1 This illustration is wrapped around to fit on one page. The top half shows columns A through K and the bottom half shows columns L through R.

letters "A" through "G." These separate groups are then assigned different billing dates. Not only will the billing date help you spread the workload through the month, but it also helps establish a well-defined pattern of billing and repayment for each customer.

Columns H and I show the invoice number and the invoice issue date.

Column J contains the balance owing on the invoice, while column K shows any payments that have been applied to the invoice. Since no

Columns L through O show the age of the invoice. Each month that the invoice goes unpaid you move the amount owing one column to the right. We will illustrate how this invoice aging is done shortly.

Column P is used to record bad debt. We will find this information helpful when we gather statistics about our overall collection efficiency.

The last column, column Q, is reserved for any comments you might have regarding a particular account. For example, suppose a customer has had an account outstanding for a long period of time but has agreed to make partial payments on the account. You can write a brief note in column Q (and beyond, if necessary) indicating your last contact with the customer and the terms of repayment that have been agreed on.

The total amounts outstanding for the receivables age groups are shown at the foot of the respective columns. The total balance outstanding and the total of all your credit limits are also displayed in this line. This TOTALS row is in row 8 when you first load the model.

Let us illustrate how you can use this model from the initial data entry step to ongoing day-to-day account maintenance.

We will assume that it is June 30 and you are entering customer information into the model for the first time. It is a good idea to start using the model immediately after you have sent out your invoices as this will give you the most time to get used to the sheet.

Move the cursor to J1 and enter **JUNEb30 Ⓔ**, to show that the credit sheet will be current to this date. To make room for customer data move the cursor into row 6 and enter **/IR/IR/IR**; this will insert three rows that we can use to hold customer data. The first customer we will enter is Joe Adams of 10 1st St. His business telephone number is 783-8244, his home telephone number is 442-1010, and his account number is 123. He has been assigned a credit limit of $2,000 and he is billed on the 15th of each month.

The model is used in two steps. First, the general customer information is entered in columns A through G. Then, on the next line, we begin listing the active invoices.

106 Applications and Models

We will begin by entering the customer information. Move your cursor to A5 and enter **JOE ADAMS▶"10▶1ST▶ST▶"783-8244▶"442-1010 ▶123▶2000▶15▶**. You need to enter the quotes in front of the address and telephone numbers so that VisiCalc does not expect values. This is all we need to do to enter the customer background information.

The table below shows this customer's outstanding invoice information.

Invoice #	Date	Amount
1121	April 15	$50
1145	May 10	350
1165	June 2	400

Since we know that we will be entering three invoices, we will replicate the dummy line into all three lines at once. This dummy line contains the formulas and formats that make the model work. To replicate the invoice line, type **/R BS H9.P9:H6.H8 Ⓔ RRR**. By specifying a target range we have duplicated the line three times and used only one Replicate command. Now we can start entering Adam's outstanding invoices. To enter the first invoice, move the cursor to H6 and enter **1121▶APR▶15▶▶0 ▶▶▶50 Ⓔ**. The invoice amount of $50 is entered in the column labeled >60 DAYS to let us know the age of the receivable. When this data has been entered, the balance of 50 appears in column J.

Now move your cursor to H7, and we can enter the other two invoices as follows: **1145▶MAY▶10▶▶▶350 ▼ 400◀◀◀JUN▶2◀1165 Ⓔ**.

To give you an idea of how the sheet looks with more than one customer we will add another. The customer is Atom Stores, located at 10 Main St. The proprietor's home telephone number is 788-1954 and the business telephone number is 440-2424. The account number is 120, the credit limit is $3,500, and the billing date is the 15th of the month. To enter this information we need to make some more room by inserting four new rows. With your cursor in row 9, enter **/IR/IR/IR/IR**. Now replicate the customer information that is in row 5 between columns A and G as follows: **/R BS A5.G5:A10 Ⓔ**. This is the same principle as replicating the dummy line, except that this time there is some data in the row we are copying. Also, this row contains only formats and no formulas. As we enter new data we will overwrite this duplicate customer information. Now move the cursor to A10 and enter the customer information as follows: **ATOM▶STORES▶"10▶MAIN▶ST▶"788-1954▶"440-2424▶120▶3500 ▶15 Ⓔ**. This customer has the following invoices outstanding:

Invoice #	Date	Amount
1180	June 10	$750
1195	June 12	1200

We want to enter two invoices, so as before we will make two copies of the dummy row. One copy will go in row 11 and the other in row 12. Enter these keystrokes: **/R BS H13.P13:H11.H12 Ⓔ RRR**. Now that the rows are in place we can put the invoice information into the sheet by moving the cursor to H11 and entering **1180▶JUN♭10▶▶▶750 ▼ 1200◀◀◀ JUN♭12◀1195 Ⓔ**. Since all the other columns contain zeroes, we are finished entering these two invoices.

You can add more customers by inserting lines, adding the customer information line, and then entering the customer invoices. To improve readability you should leave a blank line between the customers.

To be sure you are entering the information correctly, check your sheet against Figure 10-2.

Notice the analysis section at the bottom of the screen. This area contains important information about your credit department. It shows you the percentage of your receivables that are of a specific age. It displays the largest single outstanding invoice in each age group. The line labeled "ALLOWANCE FOR BAD DEBT ESTIMATE:" holds the percentage of receivables in each age category that you can expect to lose due to nonpayment. In our example it is estimated that 8 percent of the receivables outstanding for over 60 days will be lost due to nonpayment. You can change these estimates to suit your business experience by entering a new percentage value in any of the locations. The line below contains the actual dollar amount that your bad debt percentage estimates say you stand to lose for each age category. The total amount you expect to lose from all age categories is shown in the last column below the label TOTAL.

Below and to the left of the aged account analysis there are two ratios that carry valuable information about your receivables as a whole. The first line asks you to enter your projected annual credit sales. Once you have entered this estimate in the cell indicated, the line below will tell you how many days it takes you to collect the average account. The formula used for this calculation is

Projected Average Collection Period = (Average Accounts Receivable Balance / Annual Projected Credit Sales) * 365

Below this you can calculate what your credit customers are costing you to carry each month. Just enter your short-term borrowing rate across from the label INTEREST RATE: and your monthly carrying cost will appear on the line below. The formula used to calculate this cost is

Cost = (Accounts Receivable Outstanding * Interest Rate)/12

The analysis section will start to give you useful information once you have all your accounts in place. Since our example has so few invoices outstanding it is difficult to use the cost of credit and projected average collection period statistics meaningfully. Once you have a number of your outstanding accounts in this spread sheet you will find these two sources of information useful.

Let us illustrate how to use this model to record receivables collection.

Suppose it is now July 15 and you want to update the credit analysis sheet. You have finally caught up with the elusive Mr. Adams, who apologized profusely for being out of town for so long, but his great aunt has been very ill. He has hand delivered a check for $400 to cover two of his outstanding invoices and vowed it will never happen again.

You have also received two checks from Atom Stores to cover their June invoices.

First, change the date on the credit analysis sheet by moving your cursor to J1 and typing **JULY 15** ⓔ. Now, to apply these payments move the cursor to K6 and enter **50 ▼ 350 ▼▼▼ 750 ▼ 1200** ⓔ. You have recorded credits that offset the amount of these invoices. Notice that the balance of the paid invoices is now 0. Once you have your receivables information in the sheet you can go through and follow a similar routine for each account. When funds have been received you apply them to the invoices by entering the appropriate amount in the credit column; if you have received no payment, you move the invoice amount one column to the right to show the new age of the invoice amount. You can also take this opportunity to add any interest penalty onto the outstanding amount. In this way, VisiCalc paints an up-to-date portrait of your receivables.

For example, it seems that Mr. Adams is on the road again. We have not received the check for invoice #1165. Since it is now over 30 days we move the amount of this invoice one column to the right. To do this, move your cursor to M8 and enter **400◄0** ⓔ. You have aged the account receivable.

After you have gone through the spread sheet and applied payments and aged the receivables, the next step is to print out a copy of the updated credit analysis spread sheet. Once you have a "hard copy" of the latest payments, you can delete the rows that contain the paid invoices.

CREDIT   ANALYSIS   CURRENT TO: JUNE 30

NAME	ADDRESS	HOME #	BUS. #	ACCT#	LIMIT	BILLING DAT	INVOICE#	DATE	BALANCE	CREDIT
JOE ADAMS	10 1ST ST	783-8244	442-1010	123	2000.00	15	1121	APR 15	50.00	0.00
							1145	MAY 10	350.00	0.00
							1165	JUN 2	400.00	0.00
ATOM STORES	1C MAIN ST	788-1954	440-2424	120	3500.00	15	1180	JUN 10	750.00	0.00
							1195	JUN 12	1200.00	0.00
									0.00	0.00
			=TOTALS=		5500.00				2750.00	0.00

```
                                          ALLOWANCE     LARGEST        % AGED ANALYSIS:
                                                        FOR BAD           OUTSTANDING:
                                                        ALLOWANCE      DEBT % ESTIMATE:
                                                                          FOR BAD  DEBT:
                              ANNUAL    PROJECTED    CREDIT
                                        AVERAGE   COLLECTION   SALES:         NA
                                                  INTEREST   PERIOD:         NA
                                                  CARRYING    RATE:
                                                              COST:        ERROR
```

Figure 10-2 Note: Figure 10-2 is continued on the following page.

CURRENT	>30 DAYS	>60 DAYS	>90 DAYS	BAD DEBT	COMMENTS
0.00	0.00	50.00	0.00	0.00	
350.00	0.00	0.00	0.00	0.00	
400.00	0.00	0.00	0.00	0.00	
750.00	0.00	0.00	0.00	0.00	
1200.00	0.00	0.00	0.00	0.00	
0.00	0.00	0.00	0.00	0.00	
2700.00	0.00	50.00	0.00	0.00	

CURRENT	>30 DAYS	>60 DAYS	>90 DAYS	BAD DEBT
98.18	0.00	1.82	0.00	0.00
1200.00	0.00	50.00	0.00	0.00
.01	.02	.08	.2	TOTAL
27.00	0.00	4.00	0.00	31.00

Figure 10-2 (cont'd.)

To do this, move your cursor into a row that shows a balance of 0, indicating that the invoice has been paid. Enter **/DR** to erase the row. When you do this be sure that you are not in a row containing customer information or you will wipe it out. As a safeguard we suggest you move the cursor down column J, as this holds the balance owing on the invoice. If your cursor highlights a 0, you are safe to delete the line. Once you have updated the sheet be sure to resave it or you will lose all your hard work.

After you have applied the payments, printed the sheet, and deleted the rows containing the paid invoices your sheet should look like Figure 10-3.

The memory capacity limits the number of accounts you can store on one sheet. Storing 100 accounts takes up approximately ten units on your memory indicator. If you cannot fit all your accounts on one sheet, you can split them into two models. For example, a hardware store has a total of 135 credit customers. The A/R files are on two saved models called CREDIT1 and CREDIT2. CREDIT1 has a total of 70 customers with names beginning with the letters "A" through "L," while CREDIT2 has the records of the remaining customers. To get the analysis on your total accounts receivable you will have to transfer the total shown at the bottom of one spread sheet into a customer line of the second sheet. You are simply carrying a balance forward from one sheet to the other. One way to do this is to designate a special customer name, say BAL FORWARD in CREDIT2, to hold the total line carried forward from CREDIT1. This way the analysis section will reflect realistic totals. Note that the statistics on the largest outstanding debts in each category will only apply for the receivables in CREDIT2.

As you enter and delete customers you should decide on an order that you will use to display the receivables information. This will allow you to locate specific accounts for examination and will make updating the sheet much easier. You can either select to keep the receivables in alphabetical order by customer name or in numerical order based on your account number. They both accomplish the same thing so you can choose the one you prefer.

Model II: Credit Record

This spread sheet is used to keep track of your customers' payment histories. It tells you which customers are your friends and which ones are not. You store all the customer invoices that have been paid during the year and also record the time it took to receive each payment. As time goes on you will have a complete portrait of the customers' payment characteristics. This can be a very effective tool in helping an habitually slow paying customer to improve his payment style.

CREDIT ANALYSIS   CURRENT TO: JULY 15

NAME	ADDRESS	HOME #	BUS. #	ACCT#	LIMIT	BILLING DAT	INVOICE#	DATE	BALANCE	CREDIT
JOE ADAMS	10 1ST ST	783-8244	442-1010	123	2000.00	15	1165	JUN 2	400.00	0.00
ATOM STORES	10 MAIN ST	788-1954	440-2424	120	3500.00	15			0.00	0.00
			TOTALS:		5500.00				400.00	0.00

		% AGED ANALYSIS:
		OUTSTANDING:
	LARGEST	
ALLOWANCE	FOR BAD	DEBT % ESTIMATE:
	ALLOWANCE	FOR BAD DEBT:
SALES:	NA	
PERIOD:	NA	
RATE:		
COST:	0.00	

ANNUAL PROJECTED CREDIT
AVERAGE COLLECTION INTEREST
CARRYING

CURRENT	>30 DAYS	>60 DAYS	>90 DAYS	BAD DEBT	COMMENTS
0.00	400.00	0.00	0.00	0.00	
0.00	0.00	0.00	0.00	0.00	
0.00	400.00	0.00	0.00	0.00	

CURRENT	>30 DAYS	>60 DAYS	>90 DAYS	BAD DEBT
0.00	100.00	0.00	0.00	0.00
0.00	400.00	0.00	0.00	0.00
.01	.02	.08	.2	TOTAL
0.00	8.00	0.00	0.00	8.00

Figure 10-3

Credit Control 113

The keystrokes necessary to create this model are found in the appendix under CREDREC. If you type in the keystrokes or load the model CREDREC from your disk, it should look like Figure 10-4. Make sure you have a copy saved in its packed form.

If you have loaded a copy of the model from disk, enter ! to remove the ERROR message from directly below the Y-T-D (Year-to-Date) column title. We will explain why it appeared there later.

Each sheet carries the complete invoice history of one customer. Let us continue with our previous example and enter the credit history of Joe Adams. The information we need is shown below.

Invoice #	Days	Amount
192	30	$ 340
231	28	650
301	42	530
449	30	1034
1010	46	425
1121	91	50
1145	65	350

We start by moving the cursor to C1 and entering **JOE ADAMS** Ⓔ to identify the credit record.

Next, we make room in the model to enter invoices and customer information. We know that we need room for seven customer invoices, so we will insert all the lines we need at once. Move your cursor to row 7 and enter **/IR/IR/IR/IR/IR/IR/IR**.

Now we will add the customer background information. We use an abbreviated set of customer information since we have a complete record stored in the credit analysis model. All we will enter is the customer name, account number, and credit limit. Move your cursor to A6 and enter **JOE ADAMS▶123▶2000** Ⓔ.

The rest of the information that we will add to this spread sheet will be historic invoice information. We will replicate seven copies of the dummy row displayed in row 14 as follows: **/R BS E14.J14:E7. E13** Ⓔ. We do not need to replicate the entire line, because the invoice information only takes up part of the sheet.

Now we can enter the invoice information a line at a time. Move your cursor to E7 and enter **30▶192▶340◀◀ ▼ 28▶231▶650◀◀ ▼ 42▶301▶▶ 530◀◀◀ ▼ 30▶449▶1034◀◀ ▼ 46▶1010▶▶425◀◀◀ ▼ 91▶1121▶▶▶▶50▶▶ CLAIMS⌿AU▶NT⌿ILL** Ⓔ **>E13** Ⓔ **65▶1145▶▶▶350** Ⓔ. Remember that you enter the invoice amount in the column that represents its age at the time it was paid.

The Y-T-D formula depends on numbers that are stored to its right on the sheet; this is why it shows as an error when the model is first

CREDIT TO:

NAME	ACCT#	LIMIT	Y-T-D	DAYS	INVOICE#	CURRENT	>30 DAYS	>60 DAYS	>90 DAYS	BAD DEBT	COMMENTS
			0.00			0.00	0.00	0.00	0.00		
					TOTALS:	0.00	0.00	0.00	0.00	0.00	

AVERAGE COLLECTION PERIOD: ERROR

Figure 10-4

loaded. It is referencing a cell that does not yet hold a value. You must enter the "!" symbol to force another recalculation of the sheet after you enter the last invoice. This lets the Y-T-D formula catch up to your latest entry. You will not cause an incorrect result if you enter "!" too many times. If you are not sure if you have entered it, you can enter it again and not worry. Check your model against the one shown in Figure 10-5.

At the bottom of each customer history spread sheet you will find the average collection period. This displays the average length of time it has taken this customer to pay your invoices in the past.

After you actually enter your customer information onto the sheet, be sure to save each sheet under a separate name. In our example you might like to save the sheet under the name JADAMS or CUST123. The first way would suit you if you were maintaining your accounts receivable by customer; the second is a better choice if you organize your receivables by customer account number. Selecting a logical naming convention for your customer spread sheet is important. If you do not remember how to find a specific spread sheet, you cannot update it or examine it. Either way, you will have a separate saved sheet for each customer. If you keep these spread sheets up to date, you will see which customers abuse your credit policies and which do not.

Since the turn of the century the use of dunning letters has been touted as the way to increase collection rates. The only time credit collections are discussed seems to be in reference to collection problems. We wonder if the old-school "nag" approach to bill collecting works as well with the generation that experienced the depression, the birth of television, and saw man walk on the moon, as it did with the turn of the century Oliver Twist crowd. There are plenty of times when a heavy hand is necessary, but there is another side to the credit picture—i.e., those customers that pay consistently and on time.

We have two suggestions on how to use these VisiCalc sheets to improve your receivables. Look at the customer credit records monthly. When you find a customer abusing your credit, let him know. Tell him you are prepared to stop doing business with him unless his payment habits improve. Let him know how long he usually takes to pay your bills (he probably does not know). If this fails, discontinue offering him credit. You probably cannot afford to have this customer. The other suggestion we have, and it is the one that pays dividends, is that when you notice a customer has a consistently good payment history, call him up and thank him. Tell him that you are aware of his good payment habits and that you appreciate it. These two steps, when taken together, reduce the credit freeloaders who use your working capital as a low-cost loan and let your better customers know you appreciate their patronage.

CREDIT TO: JOE ADAMS

NAME	ACCT#	LIMIT	Y-T-D
JOE ADAMS	123	2000.00	3379.00

DAYS	INVOICE#	CURRENT	>30 DAYS	>60 DAYS	>90 DAYS	BAD DEBT	COMMENTS
30	192	340.00	0.00	0.00	0.00	0.00	
28	231	650.00	0.00	0.00	0.00	0.00	
42	301	0.00	530.00	0.00	0.00	0.00	
30	449	1034.00	0.00	0.00	0.00	0.00	
46	1010	0.00	425.00	0.00	0.00	0.00	
91	1121	0.00	0.00	0.00	50.00	50.00	CLAIMS AUNT ILL
65	1145	0.00	0.00	350.00	0.00	0.00	
==TOTALS:		2024.00	955.00	350.00	50.00	0.00	

AVERAGE COLLECTION PERIOD: 47

Figure 10-5

FURTHER READINGS

Hendrickson, Robert. *The Cashless Society.* New York: Dodd, Mead and Co., 1972.

Sanzo, Richard. *Dynamics of the Credit Decision.* New York: Dun & Bradstreet, 1972.

Schultz, William J., and Reinhardt, Hedwig. *Credit and Collection Management,* 3rd ed. Englewood Cliffs, N.J.: Prentice-Hall, 1962.

Chapter 11

Financial Statement Analysis

Financial statements reveal the inner workings of a company. Hidden within these numbers lie clues to the effectiveness of a company's management, the desirability of their product or service, and their general financial health and future prospects. All this and more can be divined by careful investigation of financial statements. In this chapter we will create a VisiCalc spread sheet that will calculate key corporate financial ratios. The model can be used to examine trends in these ratios as well as to compare similar companies within a specific industry. Each ratio will be discussed in detail, and we will suggest possible messages that each of the ratios convey.

Financial ratios can be used to analyze the entire spectrum of a company's operations. There is a wide range of information to choose from, and different people look for different things when they analyze a financial statement. You will save a lot of time and avoid mistakes if you decide what you need to know before you begin looking.

If you are a potential trade creditor, then you will be concerned with short-term debt and how well a company can handle that debt. A bank manager is different. He will usually be interested in the ability of the company to generate the necessary profits to repay a loan and whether there are enough assets available to guarantee the loan. It is no wonder that many businesses say that by the time a bank will lend you money you probably do not need it anymore.

In many cases, the owner or the manager uses ratios to examine his own company's financial statements. He wants to insure the continued profitability of his company. He wants answers to such questions as: "How well are the corporate assets being used?" "Where can operating efficiency be improved?" "Are receivables being collected quickly?" or "Does inventory stay on the shelf too long?" In the finance area he can find out if there is a comfortable working capital cushion, or if he has enough cash to consider expansion plans. The manager wants to increase operating efficiency and have enough information about the company's financial position to form intelligent plans.

Perhaps the largest single group of people who make use of financial ratios are stock market investors. The use of ratios has reached its most exotic form in this area. A potential investor wants answers to questions such as: "Can the company afford to pay dividends now and in the future?" "How large a price must be paid for the earnings of a company?" "How many times over do the corporate earnings cover the interest payment on long-term debt?" These and many other questions are asked by hundreds of investors daily.

Each of these pursuers of corporate truth has a lot in common, even though the specific information they seek is different. Each wants to better understand the financial position and profitability of a business and better gauge its future prospects. In this chapter we will break out our crystal ball and learn what secrets financial ratios can tell us about a company's chances for success.

We will proceed with our examination of financial ratios by examining the financial statements of a simple manufacturing company. We will use a hypothetical income statement and balance sheet of The Widget Manufacturing Company to practice calculating common financial ratios. The purpose of this exercise is to practice using the ratios and to try to understand what they are telling us. Widget is used for illustrative purposes, and any resemblance to any company living or dead is purely coincidental. The exact nature of Widget's product is not important, because in this section we will be discussing the ratios in general terms. Below we show the balance sheet and income statement of the Widget Manufacturing Company.

Financial ratios can be classified into four broad categories. Each of these categories reveals information about a different aspect of a business's operations. The first type, liquidity ratios, is used to show how well a company can handle short-term debt. On the other end of the scale, we have the long-term solvency ratios. These are used by potential long-term lenders to see how well a company can absorb a large loan that is to be repaid over a long period of time. The third group of ratios we will discuss are the efficiency ratios. They tell us how well management

WIDGET MANUFACTURING COMPANY
(in thousands)
Balance Sheet
December 31, 1981

ASSETS		
1. Cash	20,500	
2. Receivables	46,500	
3. Inventory	37,000	
4. Deferred Taxes (current)	6,000	
5. Total Current Assets		110,000
6. Investments	1,000	
7. Property Plant and Equipment	298,000	
8. Accumulated Depreciation	201,000	
9. Net Property Plant and Equipment	98,000	
10. Goodwill	5,000	
11. Total Assets		213,000
LIABILITIES		
12. Accounts Payable	38,500	
13. Income Tax	11,000	
14. Long-term Debt (due within one year)	3,500	
15. Total Current Liabilities		53,000
16. Long-term Debt	49,000	
17. Deferred Income Tax	11,000	
18. Total Liabilities		113,000
SHAREHOLDERS' EQUITY		
19. Preferred	12,500	
20. Common	54,000	
21. Retained Income	33,500	
22. Total Shareholders' Equity		100,000
23. Total Liabilities and Shareholders' Equity		213,000

is controlling such key areas as inventory and accounts receivable. The final group of ratios we will discuss are the profitability ratios. These ratios show how well a company is using its capital, resources, and other assets. Each group of ratios will be discussed in turn, and within the group, each sample ratio will be calculated using appropriate numbers from the Widget financial statements. Their possible interpretations will also be examined.

The first type of ratios we will discuss are the liquidity ratios. Liquidity refers to the amount of cash a company can raise, in relation to its total assets, on relatively short notice. This is a good measure of how secure a company is over the short-term and also shows whether cash and other short-term assets are being managed efficiently. Keep in mind that these liquidity ratios are focused specifically on the short-term.

A key measure of liquidity is working capital. Working capital is the difference between current assets and current obligations. Each

WIDGET MANUFACTURING COMPANY
(in thousands)
Income Statement
For year ended December 31, 1981

24. Net Sales		249,000
25. Cost of Goods Sold	215,500	
26. General and Administrative	18,000	
27. Depreciation	3,500	
28. Total Operating Costs		237,000
29. Operating Income	12,000	
30. Interest and Debt Expense	(3,500)	
31. Investment and Other Income	2,500	
32. Income Before Taxes		11,000
33. Provision for Income Tax	3,100	
34. Net Income		7,900

Consolidated Statement of Retained Income
For the years ended December 31, 1981

35. Retained Income (beginning)	31,700
36. Net Income	7,900
Dividends	
37. Preferred	800
38. Common (2,500,000 outstanding)	5,300
39. Retained Income	33,500

of us examines our own working capital at least every month. We have a certain amount of money coming in and a certain amount going out. The object of the game is to try to pay the bills that need to be paid and still have some money left over for fun.

A company goes through the same type of balancing act, except that their idea of fun is making profits for the shareholders. Cash comes in and goes out each month, and the excess of corporate current assets over current liabilities is referred to as working capital. Current liabilities refer to the money that a company owes and must pay in the near future. These liabilities are usually short-term bank loans, payroll, accounts owing for raw materials or other supplies that are necessary for the daily operation of the business, and any other debt that must be paid within a year. The other side of the working capital picture—current assets—refers to the assets a company could turn into cash within one year should the need arise. Securities, accounts receivable, and many types of inventory are typical examples of current assets.

Working capital is important, because a company that runs out is usually on the verge of going out of business. To get a better understanding of what working capital is all about, imagine a water pump. The pump will function as long as water remains in its reservoir. If the reservoir goes dry, the pump must be primed before it will work again. A company needs a certain reservoir of excess cash on hand to keep the cycle of production and sales in motion. This reservoir lets a company meet its obligations, expand its volume of business, and take advantage of opportunities as they arise, without having to wait to collect on sales to do so. Lack of sufficient working capital is frequently blamed for poor business performance and often leads directly to business failure.

The first ratio that we will discuss is called the Working Capital Ratio, sometimes called the Current Ratio. Throughout this chapter we will introduce a ratio by first giving its formula, and then we will plug in actual data from the Widget statements to see what the ratios reveal.

Working Capital Ratio = Current Assets/Current Liabilities

You will notice that the Widget financial statements contain numbers for each entry. These numbers provide a convenient way to refer to the numbers we will use for our ratio calculations.

Working Capital Ratio = Current Assets / Current Liabilities
= Item 5 / Item 15
= 110,000 / 53,000
= 2.1

The Working Capital Ratio comes out to be 2:1 for Widget. Is this result good, bad, or so-so? Generally speaking, for a manufacturer a Working Capital Ratio of 2:1 is good, but not exceptional. It says simply that Widget has about two dollars of current assets available to cover each dollar of current debt. If 2:1 good, is 20:1 ten times better? Definitely not. If a company's Current Ratio exceeds 6:1, it probably has an unnecessary accumulation of cash and other current assets and this indicates several possible problems. Slow sales can result in a large inventory. This increases assets which in turn increases the Working Capital Ratio. Poor credit management can cause accounts receivable levels to increase and this increases the Working Capital Ratio as well. Any of these problems can contribute to an unreasonably high Working Capital Ratio and should be examined in detail if the ratio seems too large. On the other hand, a ratio of less than 2:1 points to a possible cash bind forcing creditors to wait a long time for payment. A low ratio is a warning to potential trade creditors and investors that all is not well with the company.

When examining the Working Capital Ratio, keep in mind that not all current assets are created equal. Suppose two manufacturing companies have similar ratios. One company may have a large percentage of its current assets in inventory while another company may have the majority of its current assets in cash and accounts receivable. The company with the larger percentage of current assets in inventory is not as liquid as the company having a greater portion of its current assets in cash and accounts receivable. This is because inventories are sometimes very hard to turn into cash, and they are difficult to value, especially in times of high inflation. As a result, inventory values can be overstated, giving a false impression of the company's liquidity. The next ratio we will examine, called the Quick Asset Ratio, will help us deal with the problem of inventory valuation.

First, there are a few important points to mention about interpreting ratios. Many of us have developed a belief in the reliability of numbers. We pay bills, read reports, and draw conclusions based on the mountains of figures we are force-fed each day. In many cases these infallible-looking numbers are anything but infallible. They represent trends, approximations, or just plain educated guess work. When it comes to interpreting financial ratios, it should be understood that these numbers are representative of the general condition of corporate operations. This is especially true considering that a corporate balance sheet is a reflection of just one day out of the company's operating year. As a result, ratios are best used when they are examined over several years. The VisiCalc model that we will develop in this chapter will allow us to make more meaningful use of ratios by examining their trends over several years.

When comparing one company's financial ratios to another, you should compare companies that are within the same industry group. A ratio considered acceptable for one industry could be a sign of impending doom in another. We will see some examples of this when we examine the next ratio. Throughout this chapter, when we make a statement such as "For a manufacturer, the Working Capital Ratio of 2:1 is good," the ratio 2:1 is meant only as a rough guideline. Like most rules, there are exceptions. The best way to apply these ratios is to understand their underlying meaning; in that way, you will know what they can and cannot tell you about a company.

The Current Ratio that we calculated for Widget Manufacturing was 2:1. Based on this ratio it looks like there is no problem with Widget's working capital reservoir.

We observed that the Working Capital Ratio could be misleading because the value of inventories, often the largest of all the current assets, can be difficult to accurately ascertain. The Quick Asset Ratio, also referred to as the "Acid Test," analyzes the ability of a company to service its short-term debt without figuring in the value of its inventories.

Quick Asset Ratio = (Current Assets-Inventory)/Current Liabilities

If you refer to the Widget financial statements, we can perform the calculation as follows:

= (Item 5 - Item 3) / Item 15
= (110,000 - 37,000) / 53,000
= 73,000/53,000
= 1.4

This gives us a ratio of approximately 1.4:1. The Quick Asset Ratio is a more conservative test of a company's ability to meet its current obligations; as a result, we would not expect the ratio to be around 2:1 as was the case of the Working Capital Ratio. Generally speaking, if this ratio is 1:1 or better, it is indicative of a good liquid position. However, companies with a Quick Asset Ratio of less than 1:1 may be just as liquid if they have a high inventory turnover rate. For example, a meat packer can turn his inventory over once every seven days. A Quick Asset Ratio of 0.6:1 would be acceptable in this business, because we know the inventory can be readily turned into cash. In the case of a manufacturer who produces a relatively small number of high-cost products, we would require a larger Quick Asset Ratio. It is much more difficult for this manufacturer to turn his inventory into cash.

This illustrates the point we discussed earlier about the problems of comparing different industries to each other. To make valid conclusions based on the ratios you calculate, you need to compare them to the industry average. In order to see what the average ratios are for any type of industry, Dun and Bradstreet and Robert Morris and Associates publish complete lists of financial ratios by industry type. By comparing the ratios from the companies that interest you with the industry averages, you will know whether or not a ratio is acceptable.

In the case of Widget Manufacturing, the Quick Asset Ratio of 1.4:1 is within generally acceptable limits.

Based on both the liquidity tests, Widget seems to be in good, but not exceptional, shape.

The next ratios we will discuss are concerned with long-term solvency. Investors and lenders are interested in these ratios because they help decide whether a long-term investment or loan in a company is advisable. Using these ratios you can tell how easily a company can pay its long-term debts and examine the company's present mix of financing. The specific ratios that fit into this category are the Debt-Equity, Times Interest Earned, and the Asset Coverage Ratios.

The first ratio we will examine is the Debt-Equity Ratio. Aside from the money a company generates through product sales, there are two other ways it can raise funds. A company can borrow money or issue stock. Borrowing creates more debt, while issuing stock creates more equity.

A company needing to borrow a large sum of money for a period usually longer than a year may issue a bond or debenture to raise the required capital. This creates a commitment on the part of the company to repay the debt holder both principal and interest over a prescribed period of time and at a prescribed rate of interest. A bond pledges specific assets to cover its promise to pay, while a debenture is a loan unsecured by any specific assets. Since most corporate borrowing of this kind is in the form of debentures, the ratios we are going to discuss will help measure the relative "sincerity" of a company's promise to pay.

Equity financing refers to capital that has been raised through the issue of corporate stock. Like borrowing, it is a way that a company can raise funds to use for further long-term growth and development. The two major types of stocks, common and preferred, come in many different varieties, each with its own set of investor-inducing features. Shareholders are actually part owners in the company and participate in the growth of the company. They forgo the guarantee of periodic dividend payments to participate in the company's future growth.

A key difference between debt and equity financing is that the interest payments of debt must be paid regularly, regardless of how well the company does. If a company has several bad years, the interest on its debentures still must be paid or it can be forced into liquidation. This is not the case with equity financing. It is up to the board of directors to decide whether they will pay the common or preferred shareholders any dividends or not. As a result, in years of poor performance where there are slim or no profits at all, the directors of a company may decide not to pay dividends, retaining earnings for more urgent requirements. In some cases, companies may not pay dividends even if performance has been good. This can happen when there is an expected need for cash on hand for a new business expansion or for building a larger cash reservoir to face anticipated lean times. Thus, equity capitalization does not necessarily cost the company money year-in and year-out regardless of what kind of year they have, and so adds flexibility to financial planning. But you pay for what you get. Equity capital is more expensive to raise than debt.

This brings us to the examination of the Debt-Equity Ratio. This ratio tells us how well balanced a company's financing is. The larger the ratio of debt to equity, the greater the risk to the common and preferred shareholders. This is because the debt holders must be paid their interest before the stockholders get any dividends. Should the company go under, the debt holders also have prior claim on the company's assets. The larger the debt, the smaller the level of protection given the shareholder should the worst happen. The ratio of debt to equity tells the shareholders how far back they stand in the line for company earnings. For Widget Manufacturing we can make the following calculation:

Debt-Equity Ratio = Total Long-term Debt/Total Shareholders' Equity (Book Value)
= Item 16/Item 22
= 49,000/100,000
= 0.5

For a manufacturing company, a Debt-Equity Ratio of 1:1 is considered to be an upper limit. Widget Manufacturing is comfortably below this suggested maximum.

A company with a high Debt-Equity Ratio has a greater commitment to pay interest charges. In times of economic difficulty, such a company may have its hands full just servicing its interest payments, let alone paying salaries, suppliers, or shareholders' dividends.

The next of the long-term solvency ratios is the Times Interest Earned Ratio. This ratio indicates how well a company can afford to pay the interest costs on its debt, based on what it earns.

Times Interest Earned = Earnings Before Interest & Tax/Interest Charges
= Item (29 + 31)/Item 30
= 14,500/3,500
= 4.1

This gives us a ratio of about 4:1. In other words, Widget Manufacturing earns four times the interest it needs to service its long-term debt. For manufacturing companies, interest payments should be earned at least three times over. Widget's Times Interest Earned Ratio tends to the lower limit of safety. When examining this ratio, the larger the earning's cushion, the safer the lenders' and the shareholders' investment.

Next, we examine the Asset Coverage Ratio. This ratio helps to fill in the long-term solvency picture for the debenture holders and other lenders. It indicates the amount of assets that backs a company's long-term debt. Since a debenture is an unsecured loan, it is only backed by the general assets and earning power of a company. The potential lender needs to know if his loan is covered by a high level of assets.

Asset Coverage = Net Tangible Assets/Long-term Debt
= Item 11-Item 10-Item 15-Item 17/Item 16
= 213,000-5,000-53,000-11,000/49,000
= 144,000/49,000
= 2.939

From this calculation we see that for each $1,000 of long-term debt, Widget has $2,939 of assets.

Notice that to calculate net tangible assets we subtract goodwill, deferred tax, and current liabilities. This gives a better picture of the true value of the company's available assets. The guideline for manufacturing companies is that there should be at least $2,000 of assets for each $1,000 of long-term debt. Widget again passes inspection but not by a large margin. Comparing Widget to another manufacturer in its own specific industry will yield better information.

In reviewing Widget's long-term solvency ratios we noted that both the Times Interest Earned and Asset Coverage Ratios are close to the suggested limits. We might want to examine Widget's competitors to see if this is typical for the industry. If not, then the low ratios would provide a focus for more research. A potential bond holder might well find an investment candidate that appears more solid. However, it may be that if Widget were to offer a new debenture, its interest rate might be attractive enough to compensate for its slightly higher risk level.

The next set of ratios we will examine measure management efficiency in certain key areas. The Inventory and Accounts Receivable Turnover Ratios are important here. The ratio of Sales to Working Capital will also be examined.

The Inventory Turnover Ratio measures how many times a year a company turns its inventory. A company with an above average inventory turnover rate shows a balance between inventory levels and sales volume. There is less risk that this company will be caught with a backlog of inventory in difficult economic times. If a company shows a higher Inventory Turnover Ratio than its competition, you can credit management with a superior product mix or an excellent sales and marketing department. These are the attributes of an above average corporation. When a company has a lower than average inventory turnover, it may be due to inventory that contains a large portion of slow moving or unsalable goods or to poor sales forecasting, resulting in overproduction of goods. A company in this position incurs heavy interest and other carrying charges associated with inventories which eat into profit margins. We discussed earlier the importance of working capital. When a large part of a company's working capital is tied up with inventory, it means that funds are not free for other uses such as reducing debt, expanding plant, or paying dividends. A comparatively low inventory ratio is cause for concern.

We can calculate the Inventory Turnover Ratio for Widget using the following calculation:

$$\begin{aligned}
\text{Inventory Turnover} &= \text{Cost of Goods Sold/Inventory} \\
&= \text{Item 25/Item 3} \\
&= 215{,}500/37{,}000 \\
&= 5.8
\end{aligned}$$

Widget turns its inventory 5.8 times a year. We can express the inventory turnover in days as well: 365/5.8 = 63 days. Widget turns over one cycle of its inventory once each 63 days.

There is no standard yardstick that can be used to evaluate this ratio since it differs so much from one industry to another. Useful insights can only be gained by comparing a company's performance to that of its competitors.

The next management efficiency ratio measures the Accounts Receivable Turnover Ratio. This ratio shows how quickly the company is able to collect its receivables. With high interest rates making the financing of receivables so expensive, improving the rate of collections should be a management priority. A long collection period is indicative of a poorly run credit department. The size of the accounts receivable and the speed with which they are collected also have an important impact on working capital. A longer collection period means more funds are tied up financing customers' purchases, and the percentage of bad debts tends to increase.

To calculate the Accounts Receivable Ratio for Widget Manufacturing, we proceed as follows:

Accounts Receivable Turnover = (Accounts Receivable*365)/Sales
= (Item 2*365)/Item 24
= (46,500*365)/249,000
= 68 days

This ratio will also vary from one industry to another since credit terms differ. Many industrial companies take up to 60 days to collect their accounts receivable. The Widget Manufacturing Company is over even this long collection period, indicating that there is room for improvement. The shorter the average collection period, the better.

The final efficiency ratio we will examine shows us how well management is using working capital.

For Widget this ratio is:

Sales/Working Capital = Item 24/(Item 5-Item 15)
= 249,000/(110,000-53,000)
= 249,000/57,000
= 4.4

Each dollar or working capital is able to generate $4.40 of sales. When used to compare companies in the same industry, this ratio can help you spot management that makes the best use of its working capital. The more sales dollars generated from each dollar of working capital, the better.

Some efficiency ratios can only be applied to specific industries. For example, if you are a restaurateur you may like to know how many times you turn over a table in an evening. If you were a manager for an airline company, you might like to know the average revenue per passenger mile flown; this could help you set more competitive ticket prices. These special efficiency ratios can be very revealing when comparing companies. Several of the books listed in the suggested reading section at the end of this chapter outline some of these special efficiency ratios.

The last set of ratios we will examine is designed to measure corporate profitability and will probably attract the most attention. These are the most commonly used ratios. These ratios are the Gross and Net Profit Margins, Return on Common Equity, Earnings per Share, and the Price Earnings Ratio. Each ratio examines a different corporate area to see how profitably it is being run.

Potential investors make frequent use of these ratios when evaluating a company. A manager or owner can use these ratios to keep track of his own operating efficiency.

We will begin by looking at the Gross Profit Margin. This ratio tells us how much gross profit a company earns displayed as a percentage of sales. It shows whether the product pricing is sufficient for the company to operate at a profit. This ratio is also useful when comparing competitive companies in the same industry, the ones with the highest ratios being more attractive.

Gross Profit Margin = (Net Sales − (Cost of Goods Sold + Depreciation)/Net Sales)*100
= (Item 24 − (Item 25 + Item 27)/Item 24)*100
= (249,000 − (215,500 + 3,500)/249,000)*100
= (30,000/249,000)*100
= 12.0%

Notice that in the numerator of this ratio we include depreciation as a cost of goods sold. This helps represent the true cost of manufacturing a company's product.

For a manufacturer, Widget shows a relatively low profit margin and this would affect the company's overall profitability. A potential investor or motivated manager might want to investigate the reason for this low margin. It may be caused by inappropriate product pricing.

The Net Profit Margin is calculated in a similar way. This ratio reflects a company's performance after all operating costs have been deducted. While the Gross Margin shows how well management can turn over its product at a profit, the Net Margin measures how well management runs the entire business operation. This includes the cost of running areas like sales and administration as well as distribution and marketing. To make a meaningful comparison between different companies, the earnings figure must be taken before minority interests and extraordinary items. This is because many companies do not have subsidiaries and extraordinary items are not truly indicative of a business's regular operations.

Net Profit Margin = (Net Profit (Before Minority Interests and
               Extraordinary Items)/Net Sales)*100
            = (Item 34/Item 24)*100
            = (7,900/249,000)*100
            = 3.2%

The difference between the Gross and Net Profit Margin is that Gross Profit Margin evaluates the manager solely on operating performance. By the time you get down to the net profit line, nonoperating factors such as debt expense have been deducted. Gross Operating Margin may show that the management may be doing a good job handling production operations, but the Net Profit Margin may be poor. This could be caused by heavy financing expense or some other nonoperating factor.

Our Gross and Net Margin calculations for Widget were 12.0 percent and 3.2 percent, respectively. By examining these two ratios we can see if specific areas of the company's operation are below par.

The Net Return on Common Equity is another way to see how hard a company makes its cash work. It shows the earnings created by each dollar of equity that the common shareholders have invested in the company. This ratio is very useful when compared to other companies both in and out of the same industry.

Net Return on Common Equity = (Net Profit Before Extraordinary
                         Items Less Preferred Dividends/
                         Common Equity)*100
                    = (Item 34 − Item 37/Item 20
                         + Item 21)*100
                    = (7,900 − 800/54,000 + 33,500)
                         *100
                    = (7,100/87,500)*100
                    = 8.1%

The better the return on common equity, the better the job management is doing using the equity that the common shareholders own.

Another measure of business profitability is the Earning Per Share. This helps shareholders predict whether or not the board of directors is likely to pay dividends. This ratio first finds the annual earnings that are left over for the common shareholders, then divides this by the number of common shares outstanding to reveal the earnings per common share. If earnings are high, the directors are more likely to pay dividends. They realize that most shareholders like to feel that some of the profits are flowing back into their pockets, and as a result, they try to pay dividends when possible. Since the numerator in this calculation is the income net of all prior claims, each individual shareholder can see on how much of the year's earnings they actually have a claim.

To calculate this ratio, we proceed as follows:

Earnings Per Share = Net Profit Before Extraordinary Items Less Preferred Dividends/Number of Common Shares Outstanding
= Item 34 − Item 37/2,500
= 7,900 − 800/2,500
= 7,100/2,500
= $2.84

Widget was able to earn $2.84 for each share of common stoc.. outstanding. If the annual dividend was $1.00 per share, then the earnings of $2.84 per share will cover this expense quite well. This ratio also lets you know whether or not a company is paying dividends out of earnings. Companies with a long tradition of paying dividends will often continue paying through good and bad times. But a company has to earn the dividends at some point. If not, it will eventually have to stop paying the dividends or go broke. If a company has not earned its dividends but has continued to pay them over several years, this can be a signal that investors requiring income should stay away.

The Price Earnings (P.E.) Ratio is the final ratio we will discuss in this chapter. It is used by potential investors to add more meaning to the earnings per share figure. Comparison of a straight earnings per share between different companies can be confusing because common share prices vary from company to company. For instance, company "A" may earn $2 per share with its stock priced at $20 per share, while company "B" earns $1 per share with stock selling for $10 per share. Though the earnings of company "A" are twice those of company "B," the shares of each company represent equivalent value. You have to pay twice the price for "A" stock. In the end you have paid the same price for a dollar of earnings. Suppose that Widget common stock is currently trading at $12. To eliminate the price factor, the Price Earnings Ratio for Widget is calculated as follows:

Price Earnings Ratio = Current Price of Stock/Earnings Per Share
= 12.00/2.84
= 4.22

Going back to companies "A" and "B," if you calculate each of these companies' P.E. Ratio, you will find them to be the same even though one company's earnings are twice the other.

By examining the Price Earnings Ratio for Widget we are able to learn that the market is willing to pay $4.22 for $1.00 of Widget earnings. When comparing the P.E. ratios of companies, a higher ratio is indicative of the market being more positive about the future earnings potential of a company. The average investor is willing to pay a high P.E. Ratio for a company's earnings today, because future prospects look even better.

SUMMARY

Sifting through financial statements searching for useful facts is hard but rewarding work. Ratios are used to help us get to the bottom, or at least closer to the bottom, of how well a company is being managed and what its prospects are for the future.

We divided ratios into four main groups, examining a company for liquidity, long-term solvency, efficiency, and profitability. The financial statements of our sample company, Widget Manufacturing, were used to show how to calculate the various ratios and we also discussed ways to interpret results both above and below industry averages.

The limitations to the use of ratios were discussed, and because of their importance, we will list them again.

- Since the balance sheet represents a snapshot of a company on only one day of the year, and the income statement represents the results of only one year of corporate operation, conclusions based on ratios are more reliable if several years of financial data are used and trends in ratios are examined.
- Acceptable ranges for ratios are only guidelines and, like the ratios themselves, indicate only general information.
- Compare the ratios of companies in similar industries.
- Always stop to think what the ratio really says about the company in question. Look before you leap to any conclusions.
- If investing is your key aim in employing these ratios, ask an investment professional for his opinion before you act. You may be missing something.

THE MODEL

We will now create a VisiCalc model that will paint a detailed financial portrait of any company you care to examine. Thirteen financial ratios will be calculated that describe a company's health in the areas of liquidity, long-term solvency, efficiency, and profitability.

Users of this model should have some familiarity with financial statements.

If you are a potential investor, a manager with financial responsibility, or a potential creditor, you will find this model very useful. For the investor, the model will judge the investment desirability of a specific company or select an investment candidate from a group of competitive companies. If you are a manager, you will be able to measure your performance, and those of your peers, in the areas of contribution to net income, overall operating efficiency, and other key areas. This will provide excellent insight into how your company performs and enable you to make suggestions to your management about areas of possible improvement. The potential trade or capital creditor will see at a glance a company's financial structure and relative solvency. This will greatly aid the decision of whether or not to offer credit.

To use the model you first need to enter the company's financial data into the spread sheet. This data is entered from the company's balance sheet and income statement. Once these numbers are in place, you will see the key financial ratios displayed at the bottom of the model.

The keystrokes that make up this model appear under RATIOS in the appendix. To be sure you have entered the model correctly, compare it to the one shown below.

Take a minute now to examine the layout of the spread sheet. It is divided into four main sections. The first section will hold the income statement information and starts at the top of the model. The second section will hold the statement of retained earnings and begins in row 41. The third section is used to record the balance sheet data and begins in row 54. The final section is the analysis section which begins in row 135. All the ratios are displayed in this section and appear ordered by ratio type. Familiarize yourself with the spread sheet. If you know where to look for the various types of financial data, you will find it much easier to get the information from a corporate financial statement into the spread sheet.

Each sheet can hold up to ten financial statements, one per column. You can choose to analyze one company per sheet displaying past data in the columns or use a sheet to analyze several businesses within the same industry for comparative purposes.

There are several ways to use this model. If you are an investor, you could keep a separate model for each company. You could update the sheet annually or quarterly as the financial information becomes available. This would allow you to monitor important trends in a company's performance. If the financial press is projecting a 15 percent growth in

```
                    FINANCIAL STATEMENT ANALYSIS
INCOME STATEMENT

I N C O M E
******************-----------------------------------------------------------------
NET SALES
OTHER INCOME
-----------------------------------------------------------------------------------
TOTAL INCOME            0    0    0    0    0    0    0    0    0    0
-----------------------------------------------------------------------------------

E X P E N S E S
*****************

COST OF GOODS SOLD
* GROSS PROFIT          0    0    0    0    0    0    0    0    0    0
-----------------------------------------------------------------------------------
GEN. SALES & ADMIN
DEPRECIATION
RESEARCH & DEVEL.
-----------------------------------------------------------------------------------
TOTAL OPERATING EX      0    0    0    0    0    0    0    0    0    0
-----------------------------------------------------------------------------------
* NET OPER. INCOME      0    0    0    0    0    0    0    0    0    0
INTEREST EXPENSE
* INCOME BEF. TAX       0    0    0    0    0    0    0    0    0    0
TAXES
* NET BEF MIN & EX      0    0    0    0    0    0    0    0    0    0
MINORITY INTEREST
EXTRAORDINARY ITEM
DISCONTINUED ITEM

* NET INCOME            0    0    0    0    0    0    0    0    0    0

# PREF SH. (000'S)
# COM. SH. (000'S)
COM. MARKET PRICE
***********************************************************************************
STATEMENT OF RETAINED EARNINGS

RETAINED INCOME
*ANNUAL NET INCOME      0    0    0    0    0    0    0    0    0    0
*TOT RET. INCOME        0    0    0    0    0    0    0    0    0    0

DIVIDENDS PAID:
PREFERRED
COMMON
* TOTAL DIVIDENDS       0    0    0    0    0    0    0    0    0    0

* BALANCE YEAR END      0    0    0    0    0    0    0    0    0    0
***********************************************************************************
```

Figure 11-1

earnings, you can enter the projected earnings and see how this will impact other areas of the company. You can also have several competitive companies on one sheet so that industry-wide patterns can be seen.

If you work in a credit department, you can have a sheet devoted to each customer with whom you do a volume of business. As new financial information becomes available, you can update the sheet in the next column and see if there is a negative change in any of the key ratios.

If you are a manager, you can enter the annual or quarterly results for your company. This will give you a unique opportunity to spot problems well in advance and to suggest ways to improve operations.

While it takes time to enter the financial data of a company, we believe you will find the insights you gain from this model well worth the effort.

```
BALANCE SHEET

CURRENT ASSETS:
-----------------------------------------------------------------------------------------------------------------
CASH
SECURITIES
RECEIVABLES
INVENTORY
DEFERRED TAXES
OTHER CUR. ASSETS
-----------------------------------------------------------------------------------------------------------------
TOTAL CURRENT          0       0       0       0       0       0       0       0       0       0
-----------------------------------------------------------------------------------------------------------------

FIXED ASSETS:
-----------------------------------------------------------------------------------------------------------------
PROPERTY PLANT,EQU
LESS ACC. DEPRECIA
OTHER FIXED ASSETS
-----------------------------------------------------------------------------------------------------------------
TOTAL FIXED ASSETS     0       0       0       0       0       0       0       0       0       0
-----------------------------------------------------------------------------------------------------------------

INTANGIBLE ASSETS:
-----------------------------------------------------------------------------------------------------------------
GOODWILL
OTHER
-----------------------------------------------------------------------------------------------------------------
TOTAL INT. ASSETS      0       0       0       0       0       0       0       0       0       0
-----------------------------------------------------------------------------------------------------------------
* TOTAL ASSETS         0       0       0       0       0       0       0       0       0       0

CURR. LIABILITIES:
-----------------------------------------------------------------------------------------------------------------
ACCOUNTS PAYABLE
NOTES PAYABLE
LOANS PAYABLE
INCOME TAX PAYABLE
-----------------------------------------------------------------------------------------------------------------
TOTAL CURRENT L.       0       0       0       0       0       0       0       0       0       0
-----------------------------------------------------------------------------------------------------------------

DEBT:
-----------------------------------------------------------------------------------------------------------------
LONG-TERM DEBT
OTHER L.T. DEBT
OTHER L.T. DEBT
-----------------------------------------------------------------------------------------------------------------
TOTAL L.T. DEBT        0       0       0       0       0       0       0       0       0       0
-----------------------------------------------------------------------------------------------------------------
```

Figure 11-1 (Continued)

As you look down the rows of this model, you will notice two features. Border rows composed of dashes appear from time to time, and some labels in column A begin with an asterisk (*). The dashed border lines are used to enclose areas where lines can be either added or deleted. For example, the lines in rows 7 and 10 enclose the area used to list income information. Lines can be added between these border rows as necessary to show different types of income, such as the income contributed by separate areas of a company. Lines can also be deleted between the dashed borders if they are not necessary. These areas are designed to give you the flexibility you need to enter different types of financial statements. The total line shown in row 11 and the others that will appear below these "variable zones" should not be deleted or changed. Each contains a formula which calculates the total of the numbers contained between the lines. If you are not sure how this works, you

```
OTHER LIABILITIES
-----------------
DEFERRED TAXES
OTHER LIABILITIES
OTHER LIABILITIES
-----------------
TOTAL OTHER          0    0    0    0    0    0    0    0    0    0
-----------------
*TOTAL L.T. LIABIL   0    0    0    0    0    0    0    0    0    0

*TOTAL LIABILITIES   0    0    0    0    0    0    0    0    0    0

OWNERS EQUITY:
--------------
PREFERRED
PREFERRED
COMMON
COMMON
CAPITAL SURPLUS
RETAINED EARNINGS
LESS TREAS. STOCK
-----------------
TOT. OWNERS EQUITY   0    0    0    0    0    0    0    0    0    0
-----------------
*TOT LIA. OWN EQU    0    0    0    0    0    0    0    0    0    0
###############################################################################
            ANALYSIS SECTION

LIQUIDITY:
WORKING CAPITAL    ERROR  ERROR  ERROR  ERROR  ERROR  ERROR  ERROR  ERROR  ERROR  ERROR
QUICK ASSET        ERROR  ERROR  ERROR  ERROR  ERROR  ERROR  ERROR  ERROR  ERROR  ERROR

L.T. SOLVENCY:
DEBT-EQUITY        ERROR  ERROR  ERROR  ERROR  ERROR  ERROR  ERROR  ERROR  ERROR  ERROR
TIMES INT. EARNED  ERROR  ERROR  ERROR  ERROR  ERROR  ERROR  ERROR  ERROR  ERROR  ERROR
ASSET COVERAGE     ERROR  ERROR  ERROR  ERROR  ERROR  ERROR  ERROR  ERROR  ERROR  ERROR

EFFICIENCY:
INVENTORY TURNOVER ERROR  ERROR  ERROR  ERROR  ERROR  ERROR  ERROR  ERROR  ERROR  ERROR
ACCTS. REC. TURNOV ERROR  ERROR  ERROR  ERROR  ERROR  ERROR  ERROR  ERROR  ERROR  ERROR
SALES/WORKING CAP. ERROR  ERROR  ERROR  ERROR  ERROR  ERROR  ERROR  ERROR  ERROR  ERROR
SPECIFIC

PROFITABILITY
GROSS PROF. MARGIN ERROR  ERROR  ERROR  ERROR  ERROR  ERROR  ERROR  ERROR  ERROR  ERROR
NET PROF. MARGIN   ERROR  ERROR  ERROR  ERROR  ERROR  ERROR  ERROR  ERROR  ERROR  ERROR
RETURN ON COMMON   ERROR  ERROR  ERROR  ERROR  ERROR  ERROR  ERROR  ERROR  ERROR  ERROR
EARNINGS PER SHARE ERROR  ERROR  ERROR  ERROR  ERROR  ERROR  ERROR  ERROR  ERROR  ERROR
PRICE/EARNINGS     ERROR  ERROR  ERROR  ERROR  ERROR  ERROR  ERROR  ERROR  ERROR  ERROR
###############################################################################
```

Figure 11-1 (Continued)

might find it helpful to reread the section entitled "How to Use the Models in this Book."

The second feature we noted was that some labels begin with an asterisk. These lines are special lines that contain formulas. You should not enter data into any of these special rows or you will lose the formulas. These rows will automatically display the correct amounts as you proceed with entering a company's financial information.

To use this spread sheet you have to enter the financial data of the company or companies you want to examine. Unfortunately, this is often easier said than done. The problem is not the typing in of all the numbers (which really does not take long and provides a good way to become familiar with a company) but in the way financial statements differ. There is no standard format that all companies follow. Even different names are used to describe the same statements. The statement of profit and loss, earnings statement, or income statement are all different names for the same report. There is no easy way around this financial Tower of Babel.

To help you practice using this spread sheet, we will enter the financial information for the Tandy Corporation for the years 1980 and 1981. This example is fairly complex and it is designed to give the model a good workout. If you are using it to examine a small private company, you will not find the model as complex to use as it appears in this example. The financial statements for Tandy are shown below.

Refer to these statements as we go along and enter the data into your own spread sheet. We will begin with the income statement and enter Tandy's numbers for 1980 and 1981. Enter the company name by moving your cursor to A1 and typing **TANDY ▶ CORP Ⓔ**. Next, move your cursor to C6 and enter **1981 ▶ 1980 Ⓔ** to indicate the years of the data. The Tandy income statement begins by listing "Net sales." We can enter the net sales for 1980 and 1981 directly into the model by moving the cursor to C8 and entering **1691373 ▶ 1384637 Ⓔ**. The next category we come to on the Tandy income statement shows "Other income." To enter this data into our sheet, move the cursor to C9 and enter **15697 ▶ 11360 Ⓔ**. Notice that the total income automatically appears on line 11 for both 1980 and 1981. A good way to make sure that you are entering the correct numbers is to periodically compare the subtotals shown on the spread sheet to the subtotals shown on the financial statements. In this case the subtotals for total income should be the same: 1707070 for 1981 and 1395997 for 1980.

Next, the "Cost of Products Sold" appears on the Tandy income statement. This information is placed across from the label COST OF GOODS SOLD in row 17. Do this by moving your cursor to C17 and entering **701777 ▶ 594841 Ⓔ**. You will often find that there are differences between the labels on our model and the ones on a corporate statement. You will have to take a close look at each category to figure out where the matches occur.

Once you have entered the cost of goods (products) sold, the line below automatically displays the gross profit. Notice that the label in line 18 appears as * GROSS PROFIT. This is our first encounter with an asterisk line. Remember that the asterisk acts as a warning symbol. Do not enter any numbers in this row. If you do, you will wipe out the formula it contains.

Next, you can enter the "Selling, general and administrative" costs from the statement into row 20 of the model. Then you can enter the depreciation charges into row 21 of the model. Your model should now display the total operating expenses in row 24. For 1980, the result should be 565435 and for 1981, 669222.

We left line 22, Research and Development, blank because Tandy shows no such expenses. If we wanted to we could delete the line because it is between two dashed border rows. It is better to leave it in place. If you later decide to compare Tandy to another company, the other company may have this expense. If you delete the line, it will be more difficult to compare the two companies.

Next, enter the values shown across from "Interest expense" into the appropriate positions in the row labeled INTEREST EXPENSE. The net income before taxes is shown in line 28. Check it against the totals shown in the income statement. It appears across from the boldfaced label "Income from continuing operations before income taxes."

Since there is no amount shown for minority interest, extraordinary items, or discontinued operations on the Tandy income statement, we can move the cursor down to row 38. This is where we enter the number of common shares outstanding. This is shown in the bottom line of the statement. In 1981 there were 102578 common shares outstanding and in 1980 there were 103644 (as with all the numbers used so far, the outstanding shares are shown in thousands).

In the next line we need to enter the market price of Tandy's common stock. Move your cursor to C39 and enter **30 ▶8.50 Ⓔ**. These amounts represent average share prices for the years 1980 and 1981. They are found in the annual report but are not shown in the section we have reproduced.

This completes the entering of the Tandy income statement information for 1980 and 1981. We can now turn our attention to the Statement of Retained Earnings. In our model this section begins on line 41. We will be referring to the Tandy Corporation's Consolidated Statements of Stockholders' Equity. They are the same statement, but as we said at the start of this model, different companies use different names.

This is one of the more complicated statements of shareholders' equity that you will see. To start with, we need to find the balance of retained earnings at the start of 1980 and enter this amount in location D43. Look for the boldfaced line on the left of the Tandy report labeled "Balance at June 30, 1979." Look across to the column labeled retained earnings and you will see the amount 185183 also shown in boldface. Enter this amount in D43. Now we need to find the balance at the start of 1981. Look down the same column to find the balance at June 30, 1980. This is also shown in boldface and is 297418. Enter this amount in C43. Since no dividends were paid during these years we are finished with the retained earnings section of our model.

Now we can move on to the balance sheet. Refer to the balance sheet shown for Tandy as we go along. The balance sheet section of our model begins on line 54. The left side of the Tandy report lists the

Review of Operations and Financial Information

Consolidated Statements of Income

Tandy Corporation and Subsidiaries
(In thousands, except per share amounts)
(Per share amounts restated for two-for-one stock splits in May 1981, December 1980, June 1978 and December 1975)

	1981	1980
Net sales	**$1,691,373**	$1,384,637
Other income	15,697	11,360
	1,707,070	1,395,997
Costs and expenses:		
Cost of products sold	701,777	594,841
Selling, general and administrative, net of amounts allocated to spun-off operations in fiscal 1976 and prior	645,934	546,325
Depreciation and amortization	23,288	19,110
Interest expense, net of interest income and interest allocated to spun-off operations in fiscal 1976 and prior	15,454	25,063
	1,386,453	1,185,339
Income from continuing operations before income taxes	**320,617**	210,658
Provision for income taxes	151,015	98,423
Income from continuing operations	169,602	112,235
Loss from discontinued operations, net of income taxes	—	—
Net income of Tandy Corporation before income from operations spun off	**169,602**	112,235
Income from operations spun off, net of income taxes	—	—
Net income	**$ 169,602**	$ 112,235
Income (loss) per average common share and common share equivalent:		
Continuing operations	$1.65	$1.12
Discontinued operations	—	—
Spun-off operations	—	—
Net income	**$1.65**	$1.12
Average common shares and common share equivalents outstanding	102,578	103,644

Figure 11-2 Financial Statements reprinted with the permission of the Tandy Corporation.

			Year Ended June 30,			
1979	1978	1977	1976	1975	1974	1973
$1,215,483	$1,059,324	$949,267	$741,722	$528,286	$411,241	$313,758
11,403	5,629	3,763	2,649	3,963	2,153	1,864
1,226,886	1,064,953	953,030	744,371	532,249	413,394	315,622
535,549	491,509	434,031	331,400	249,006	198,067	158,050
484,249	403,173	350,878	270,308	204,107	158,792	119,240
17,121	13,879	11,140	8,034	7,392	5,461	4,161
28,466	30,260	15,192	7,282	14,044	8,544	4,274
1,065,385	938,821	811,241	617,024	474,549	370,864	285,725
161,501	126,132	141,789	127,347	57,700	42,530	29,897
78,272	59,986	69,970	63,066	29,078	20,669	14,232
83,229	66,146	71,819	64,281	28,622	21,861	15,665
—	—	(2,777)	—	(1,820)	(7,072)	(1,944)
83,229	66,146	69,042	64,281	26,802	14,789	13,721
—	—	—	3,243	7,794	5,657	5,632
$ 83,229	$ 66,146	$ 69,042	$ 67,524	$ 34,596	$ 20,446	$ 19,353
$ .81	$ .69	$ .54	$ .44	$ .20	$ .13	$ .09
—	—	(.02)	—	(.01)	(.04)	(.01)
—	—	—	.02	.05	.03	.03
$ .81	$ .69	$ .52	$ .46	$ .24	$ .12	$ .11
106,004	96,136	132,336	144,824	145,408	169,992	176,304

Figure 11-2 (cont'd.)

Consolidated Statements of Stockholders' Equity

Tandy Corporation and Subsidiaries
Three Years Ended June 30, 1981

(In thousands)

Balance at July 1, 1978
Purchase of treasury stock
Settlement of lawsuit
Stock issued to officer
Sale of treasury stock to Tandy Corporation Employee Stock Purchase Program
Net income

Balance at June 30, 1979
Purchase of treasury stock
Conversion of 6½% Convertible Subordinated Debentures
Sale of treasury stock to Tandy Corporation Employee Stock Purchase Program
Net income

Balance at June 30, 1980
Conversion of 6½% Convertible Subordinated Debentures
Two-for-one split of common stock in December 1980
Two-for-one split of common stock in May 1981
Sale of treasury stock to Tandy Corporation Employee Stock Purchase Program
Other
Net income

Balance at June 30, 1981

Figure 11-2 (cont'd.)

Consolidated Balance Sheets

Tandy Corporation and Subsidiaries
(In thousands)

	June 30, 1981	June 30, 1980
Assets		
Current assets:		
Cash and short-term investments	$141,994	$ 56,365
Accounts and notes receivable, less allowance for doubtful accounts	42,088	25,725
Inventories	513,709	435,160
Other current assets	11,416	13,809
Total current assets	709,207	531,059
Property and equipment, at cost:		
Consumer electronics operations, net of accumulated depreciation	122,208	95,640
Tandy Center, net of accumulated depreciation	68,221	69,500
	190,429	165,140
Other assets	36,909	14,099
	$936,545	$710,298

Figure 11-2 (cont'd.)

	Shares			Amount			
Issued	Treasury Stock	Outstanding	Common Stock	Additional Paid-in Capital	Retained Earnings	Treasury Stock	Total
25,026	(951)	24,075	$25,026	$24,666	$102,359	$(13,055)	$138,996
—	(1,246)	(1,246)	—	—	—	(27,396)	(27,396)
124	(47)	77	124	783	(405)	(420)	82
—	20	20	—	151	—	337	488
—	526	526	—	4,841	—	8,113	12,954
—	—	—	—	—	83,229	—	83,229
25,150	(1,698)	23,452	25,150	30,441	185,183	(32,421)	208,353
—	(1,975)	(1,975)	—	—	—	(53,342)	(53,342)
2	—	2	2	44	—	—	46
—	578	578	—	3,507	—	12,326	15,833
—	—	—	—	—	112,235	—	112,235
25,152	(3,095)	22,057	25,152	33,992	297,418	(73,437)	283,125
3,443	—	3,443	3,443	95,109	—	—	98,552
25,638	—	25,638	25,638	(61,051)	—	35,413	—
51,412	—	51,412	51,412	(69,369)	—	17,957	—
—	421	421	—	14,846	—	6,231	21,077
—	(49)	(49)	—	2,996	—	(3,489)	(493)
—	—	—	—	—	169,602	—	169,602
105,645	(2,723)	102,922	$105,645	$16,523	$467,020	$(17,325)	$571,863

Figure 11-2 (cont'd.)

	June 30,	
	1981	1980
Liabilities and Stockholders' Equity		
Current liabilities:		
Notes payable	$ 34,862	$ 25,918
Accounts payable	54,560	58,926
Accrued expenses	67,206	59,170
Income taxes payable	47,152	24,703
Total current liabilities	203,780	168,717
Notes payable, due after one year	3,903	6,523
Subordinated debentures, net of unamortized bond discount	122,428	122,221
6½% convertible subordinated debentures due 2003	—	99,954
Store managers' deposits	11,972	14,045
Deferred income taxes	12,069	8,902
Other non-current liabilities	10,530	6,811
	160,902	258,456
Stockholders' equity:		
Preferred stock, no par value, 1,000,000 shares authorized, none issued or outstanding	—	—
Common stock, $1 par value, 110,000,000 shares authorized with 105,645,000 and 25,152,000 shares issued, respectively	105,645	25,152
Additional paid-in capital	16,523	33,992
Retained earnings	467,020	297,418
Common stock in treasury, at cost, 2,723,000 and 3,095,000 shares, respectively	(17,325)	(73,437)
Total stockholders' equity	571,863	283,125
Commitments and contingent liabilities		
	$936,545	$710,298

Figure 11-2 (cont'd.)

corporate assets. The amount of cash and short-term investments are combined and appear as the first entry of the current assets. Move your cursor to C58 and enter the amounts shown for 1981 and 1980; they are 141994 and 56365, respectively. Enter the amounts shown for receivables, inventories, and other current assets. Be sure to leave the rows labeled SECURITIES and DEFERRED TAXES blank. Once you have entered this data the total current assets shown on line 65 of your model should match those shown on the Tandy balance sheet labeled as "Total current assets."

Let us move on to the fixed assets section of our model. Property plant and equipment is divided into two parts on the Tandy balance sheet—Consumer Electronics and Tandy Center. We will record the Consumer Electronics operations in the row labeled PROPERTY PLANT, EQU since this accounts for the majority of their fixed assets. Next, enter the value shown for Tandy Center in row 72 as OTHER FIXED ASSETS. Since both amounts are shown net of depreciation there is no need to enter a value for depreciation in row 71.

It is important to note that depreciation is deducted from the value of the fixed assets. It appears as a separate number on many financial statements. When entering depreciation into this model it must be entered as a negative number. If you enter it as a positive amount, it will be added to the value of the fixed assets, producing an extremely misleading value. Be sure to remember this point when you examine other companies.

Line 80 is used to hold the last of Tandy's assets. These amounts are listed on the bottom of the balance sheet as "Other assets" and are entered in the row labeled OTHER ASSETS in the INTANGIBLE ASSETS section of the model. Once you have entered all the assets, check your total shown in line 84 against the total assets shown on the balance sheet.

Now we move on to the Liabilities section of our model. Information for this section comes from the right-hand side of the balance sheet labeled "Liabilities and Stockholders' Equity." Enter the amounts shown for accounts payable, shown on the second line of the Tandy statement, into line 89 of our model in the section labeled CURR. LIABILITIES. Next, enter the values shown for notes payable. We now have to change a label in our model to match one on the Tandy balance sheet. Change the label LOANS PAYABLE to ACCRUED EX PAYABLE by moving your cursor to A91 and entering **ACCRUED∅E ➤ X∅PAYABLE Ⓔ**; then, enter the values for accrued expenses in this row. The final current liability is listed as "Income taxes payable." Once you have entered this amount, check to see if your total current liabilities match those shown on the Tandy balance sheet.

We can now enter the data on Tandy's long-term debt. The "Notes payable, due after one year," are entered in line 99 of our model. Next, the values shown as subordinated debentures are entered in line 100. The value of the convertible debentures is entered in D101. Note that these debentures only appear in 1980.

So far we have entered three types of long-term debt and we still need to add "Store manager's deposits." To do this we insert a new row. We can do this because the new line will be between two dashed border rows. To do this, move your cursor to row 102 and enter **/IR**. With your cursor in A102, enter **STORE♭DEP ➤ OSIT Ⓔ**. You can now enter the values for the two years in this row.

Move your cursor down to the other liabilities section in row 107. Enter the values for "deferred income taxes" and, below that, "Other noncurrent liabilities."

This brings us to the final section in our model, the Owners' Equity in line 120. On the Tandy balance sheet it appears as "Stockholders' equity" at the bottom of the right-hand side of the balance sheet.

Beginning on line 122 our model leaves us room to record two types of preferred stocks and two types of common stocks. Tandy only has common stock outstanding. We can enter the values in line 124 as 105645 and 25152 for 1981 and 1980, respectively.

We still need to enter the amounts for "Additional paid-in capital" and "Retained earnings." Change the label at A126 from CAPITAL SURPLUS to ADDITIONAL CAPITAL to better represent the Tandy statement. Do this by placing your cursor at A126 and entering **ADDITIONA ➤ L♭CAPITAL Ⓔ**. Now enter the values for this category. The final entries are for the retained earnings and treasury stock. The retained earnings are entered just as you would any other value, but the treasury stock is treated like depreciation. Since treasury stock reduces the owners' equity, you must enter this number as a negative amount. To record the treasury stock move your cursor to C128 and enter **–17325 ➤ –73437 Ⓔ**.

This completes the information we need to enter from the Tandy statements. Now that we have entered all this information, let us see what we can learn from the analysis section that begins in line 136.

The analysis section is divided into four sections: liquidity, long-term solvency, efficiency, and profitability. The exact way each ratio is calculated is described in the first part of this chapter. The category SPECIFIC, shown as the last of the efficiency ratios, has been left blank intentionally. You can use this empty row for any special ratio you would like.

The Tandy Corporation represents a challenge. It is not simply a retailer of electronics equipment but a manufacturer as well. If you look for a company to compare with Tandy for analysis purposes, you will have a hard time finding one. If you look in the Standard and Poor's industry guide, you will find that Tandy appears with no less than six SIC (Standard Industry Code) numbers, indicating it is active in many different business sectors. No one said that corporate analysis was easy! Good analysis calls for ingenuity and imagination. Normally, we could compare the ratios for a company with the industry averages, and for many companies, this works very well.

We could try to compare Tandy with retailers of radios, televisions, and stereos. This is one industry classification that matches part of Tandy's business. But this is far from an exact match.

If you cannot find industry averages, you could get the financial information for Tandy going back five to ten years to see the trends in Tandy's ratios. If you do this, certain trends will be spotted immediately. For example, Tandy has experienced a consistent growth in gross margin. Currently, the gross margin is an impressive 57 percent. If you compare this margin to other industries, you will be impressed. This margin is related to Tandy's dual nature of manufacturer/retailer. Favorable trends will also be seen in the Working Capital Ratio, the Quick Asset ratio, and all the long-term solvency ratios. There is no reason to be concerned about Tandy's debt structure.

Contrasting the trends of Tandy's ratios with general business statistics such as inflation, GNP, or disposable income may also help evaluate the future prospects of the company.

We will not go into a detailed analysis of Tandy Corporation here. This example was intended to show you how one company's ratios could be calculated using this model and to suggest some ways to get the most information you can from this spread sheet. The actual model, with the Tandy figures included, appears in Figure 11-3.

FURTHER READINGS

Foster, Louis O. *Understanding Financial Statements and Corporate Annual Reports*. Philadelphia: Chilton Book Co., 1968.

Spohn, Robert F., and Allen, Robert Y. *Retailing*. Reston, Va.: Prentice-Hall, 1977.

Wortman, Leon A. *Successful Small Business Management*. New York: Amacom, 1976.

```
TANDY    CORP
                  FINANCIAL STATEMENT ANALYSIS
INCOME STATEMENT

I N C O M E
******************    1981      1980
------------------------------------------------------------------------------------------
NET SALES            1691373   1384637
OTHER INCOME           15697     11360
------------------------------------------------------------------------------------------
TOTAL INCOME         1707070   1395997     0     0     0     0     0     0     0     0
------------------------------------------------------------------------------------------

E X P E N S E S
******************

COST OF GOODS SOLD    701777    594841
* GROSS PROFIT       1005293    801156     0     0     0     0     0     0     0     0
------------------------------------------------------------------------------------------
GEN. SALES & ADMIN    645934    546325
DEPRECIATION           23288     19110
RESEARCH & DEVEL.
------------------------------------------------------------------------------------------
TOTAL OPERATING EX    669222    565435     0     0     0     0     0     0     0     0
------------------------------------------------------------------------------------------
* NET OPER. INCOME    336071    235721     0     0     0     0     0     0     0     0
INTEREST EXPENSE       15454     25063
* INCOME BEF. TAX     320617    210658     0     0     0     0     0     0     0     0
TAXES
* NET BEF MIN & EX    320617    210658     0     0     0     0     0     0     0     0
MINORITY INTEREST
EXTRAORDINARY ITEM
DISCONTINUED ITEM

* NET INCOME          320617    210658     0     0     0     0     0     0     0     0

# PREF SH. (000'S)
# COM. SH. (000'S)    102578    103644
COM. MARKET PRICE      30.00      8.50
*****************************************************************************************
STATEMENT OF RETAINED EARNINGS

RETAINED INCOME       297418    185183
*ANNUAL NET INCOME    320617    210658     0     0     0     0     0     0     0     0
*TOT RET. INCOME      618035    395841     0     0     0     0     0     0     0     0

DIVIDENDS PAID:
PREFERRED
COMMON
* TOTAL DIVIDENDS          0         0     0     0     0     0     0     0     0     0

* BALANCE YEAR END    618035    395841     0     0     0     0     0     0     0     0
*****************************************************************************************
```

Figure 11-3

```
BALANCE SHEET

CURRENT ASSETS:
CASH                      141994        56365
SECURITIES                 42088        25725
RECEIVABLES               513709       435160
INVENTORY
DEFERRED TAXES             11416        13809
OTHER CUR. ASSETS
TOTAL CURRENT             709207       531059        0        0        0        0        0        0

FIXED ASSETS:
PROPERTY PLANT,EQU        122208        95640
LESS ACC. DEPRECIA         68221        69500
OTHER FIXED ASSETS
TOTAL FIXED ASSETS        190429       165140        0        0        0        0        0        0

INTANGIBLE ASSETS:
GOODWILL
OTHER                      36909        14099
TOTAL INT. ASSETS          36909        14099        0        0        0        0        0        0
* TOTAL ASSETS            936545       710298        0        0        0        0        0        0

CURR. LIABILITIES:
ACCOUNTS PAYABLE           54560        58926
NOTES PAYABLE              34862        25918
ACCRUED EX PAYABLE         67206        59170
INCOME TAX PAYABLE         47152        24703
TOTAL CURRENT L.          203780       168717        0        0        0        0        0        0

DEBT:
LONG-TERM DEBT              3903         6523
OTHER L.T. DEBT           122428       122221
OTHER L.T. DEBT                          99954
STORE DEPOSIT              11972        14045
TOTAL L.T. DEBT           138303       242743        0        0        0        0        0        0
```

Figure 11-3 (Continued)

DEFERRED TAXES	12069	8902							
OTHER LIABILITIES	10530	6811							
OTHER LIABILITIES									
TOTAL OTHER	22599	15713	0	0	0	0	0	0	0
*TOTAL L.T. LIABIL	160902	258456	0	0	0	0	0	0	0
*TOTAL LIABILITIES	364682	427173	0	0	0	0	0	0	0
OWNERS EQUITY:									
PREFERRED									
PREFERRED									
COMMON	105645	25152							
COMMON									
ADDITIONAL CAPITAL	16523	33992							
RETAINED EARNINGS	467020	297418							
LESS TREAS. STOCK	-17325	-73437							
TOT. OWNERS EQUITY	571863	283125	0	0	0	0	0	0	0
*TOT LIA. OWN EQU	936545	710298	0	0	0	0	0	0	0

###

ANALYSIS SECTION

LIQUIDITY:									
WORKING CAPITAL	3.48	3.15	ERROR	ERROR	ERROR	ERROR	ERROR	ERROR	ERROR
QUICK ASSET	0.96	0.57	ERROR	ERROR	ERROR	ERROR	ERROR	ERROR	ERROR
L.T. SOLVENCY:									
DEBT-EQUITY	0.24	0.86	ERROR	ERROR	ERROR	ERROR	ERROR	ERROR	ERROR
TIMES INT. EARNED	20.75	8.41	ERROR	ERROR	ERROR	ERROR	ERROR	ERROR	ERROR
ASSET COVERAGE	4.94	2.14	ERROR	ERROR	ERROR	ERROR	ERROR	ERROR	ERROR
EFFICIENCY:									
INVENTORY TURNOVER	1.37	1.37	ERROR	ERROR	ERROR	ERROR	ERROR	ERROR	ERROR
ACCTS. REC. TURNOV	9.08	6.78	ERROR	ERROR	ERROR	ERROR	ERROR	ERROR	ERROR
SALES/WORKING CAP.	3.35	3.82	ERROR	ERROR	ERROR	ERROR	ERROR	ERROR	ERROR
SPECIFIC									
PROFITABILITY									
GROSS PROF. MARGIN	57.13	55.66	ERROR	ERROR	ERROR	ERROR	ERROR	ERROR	ERROR
NET PROF. MARGIN	18.96	15.21	ERROR	ERROR	ERROR	ERROR	ERROR	ERROR	ERROR
RETURN ON COMMON	56.07	74.40	ERROR	ERROR	ERROR	ERROR	ERROR	ERROR	ERROR
EARNINGS PER SHARE	3.13	2.03	ERROR	ERROR	ERROR	ERROR	ERROR	ERROR	ERROR
PRICE/EARNINGS	9.60	4.18	ERROR	ERROR	ERROR	ERROR	ERROR	ERROR	ERROR

###

Figure 11-3 (Continued)

Chapter 12

Forecasting

"Our plans miscarry because we have no aim. When a man does not know what harbor he is making for, no wind is the right wind."

Seneca (4 B.C-65 A.D.)

The words of this great Roman orator conjure up a grim scene. We can imagine a ship lost at sea, blown aimlessly from place to place. Even if by luck the wind should change and blow in a favorable direction, the captain would be unable to take advantage of his good fortune. He does not know where he is going.

A surprising number of businessmen resemble this confused sailor. Do you recognize good fortune when it appears? Do you know if an increase in the prime rate, a competitor going out of business, or a new piece of government legislation presents a new opportunity?

In this chapter we will develop two VisiCalc models designed to help you forecast your business plans. By plans we mean projecting sales volumes and using these projections to plan for cash, raw materials, labor, and other business requirements. The first model we will develop will help increase the accuracy of your sales projections. The second model will allow you to translate these sales projections into your own projected income statement.

Few tasks are as subject to procrastination as business forecasting. There is something about the effort required to pierce the future's shady veil that sends us scurrying for our favorite coffee cup or searching out pencils that need sharpening. This "future fear" may be one reason why many small and medium-sized businesses do not go through any formal planning process. Despite the evidence pointing out the many benefits gained from forecasting, some key business decisions are made based on scenarios hastily scratched on the back of a cocktail napkin.

Two separate sets of forces contribute to success in business. One is the ability to get the most out of the specific resources at hand such as personnel, equipment, and capital. This is the realm of the management sciences. In many cases optimal solutions to these types of resource problems are available through applied mathematics. The second key contributor to success lies in the ability of management to plot the future direction of the business. Issues such as new product development, plant expansion, or acquisition of other companies come into the picture at this point. These decisions are usually based on incomplete data and made by managers facing uncertain economic conditions, changing consumer tastes, and the unknown actions of competitors. It is this uncertain, unknown aspect of forecasting that makes business planning part art and part science.

To understand the effects of forecasting we will trace the path of a business forecast through a typical company. This will let us see how different areas are affected and how each contributes to the overall forecast.

Businesses work because their products and services are in demand. Since all activity is directed to making and selling products it makes sense that forecasting begins with a sales forecast. There are many different ways to project future sales. Some companies depend solely on their marketing departments, while others involve their entire sales staff. Various methods of sales forecasting will be discussed in detail later in this chapter. For the time being, however, let us assume future sales volumes have already been decided upon and we can proceed to the next leg of the forecasting voyage.

The new sales forecast is sent on to the production department. They plan how they will supply the projected demand. This usually entails dividing up each product into its component parts and projecting the total manufacturing cost based on the amount of each product required. This divide and conquer approach works for a supplier of services as well as a manufacturer. For example, an engineering firm can project the time commitments of each engineer and arrive at a projected billing level for the year.

When the production department uses accurate sales forecasts it can contribute many important benefits to the company. Supplying the right amount of product avoids inventory build-up due to overproducing or the supply shortages caused by underproducing. Planned production allows materials to be purchased at favorable times of the year and in the most economical quantities. Labor is used more efficiently because production can be scheduled to minimize overtime during peak production periods and reduce layoffs during slack times. Also, by avoiding panic production crunches, your own quality standards remain high.

The next operating area to see the sales forecast is the sales department. Here the forecast is used as a basis to assign quotas to the sales force. In many companies the sales projections are passed down the corporate hierarchy like a hot potato from head office to section to region to branch until each salesman is holding his own specific sales targets.

The marketing department uses the forecast as a guide to where its efforts should be concentrated. Development of new products can be directed to areas of growing customer demand. Advertising can be concentrated in areas where sales are slow due to competition, customer taste, or other factors. Historic sales patterns can be combined with forecast patterns to measure the effectiveness of marketing strategies.

Forecast sales go hand-in-hand with sales revenue. The finance department will use the forecast to project collections based on forecast sales volumes for the coming year. This helps in planning short- and long-term financing, retirement of long-term debt, and setting dividend policies. All these factors are heavily affected by sales projections.

We can see that the sales forecast affects practically every major area in a business. The production, sales, marketing, and finance departments all stand to gain from an accurate sales forecast.

With all this money riding on the forecast, how can you stack the odds in your favor? There is no way to guarantee success. We can, however, look at how other companies cope with the sales forecasting challenge.

One of the most commonly used methods for forecasting sales is the Jury of Executive Opinion (JEO). This term refers to a group of top management executives who get together and reach a consensus of opinion about future sales volumes. JEOs are composed of top level management executives, usually drawn from the areas of sales, marketing, and finance. In a small company a JEO may simply be composed of an owner and his two salespeople.

The JEO can be organized in two different ways. The first method has each member produce an individual sales forecast. Then, all the members get together and through a process of compromise arrive at a joint forecast. The second method uses a JEO to critically analyze a forecast that is submitted by another department, usually the planning department. The forecast is presented to the JEO with the personnel responsible for the forecast being rigorously cross-examined on all assumptions contained in the forecast. Many planners come to dread this annual ordeal by fire.

The only published study that surveyed existing forecasting methods was conducted by the National Industrial Conference Board.* According to this survey the JEO system, while the most common and the oldest method of forecasting sales, was found to result in the least accurate predictions of any system that was examined. This is surprising since the image of a sagacious group of gray-headed managers seated at a long conference table has an aura of reliability. Fortunately, most companies that use JEOs use them in concert with other forecasting systems.

Another extremely popular way to forecast sales is the Sales Force Inquiry Method (SFI). The sales force is polled to get its estimates for sales in the coming period. These estimates are broken down on a product-by-product basis. This method has several attractions. It uses the salesman's knowledge of his specific product and market. It allows the sales force to feel it is included in the corporate decision-making process. Finally, the results from the SFI method can be used directly to assign quotas to the sales force.

The way SFI works is that the individual salesperson is asked to project sales for a specified period of time. Each of these estimates is collected by the local sales manager or marketing manager who looks over the total branch estimates and prepares his own estimates for the entire branch. These estimates are consolidated by the region manager and then sent on to the head office. This makes for a grass-roots approach to sales forecasting.

The Conference Board found the SFI model to be considerably more successful in predicting actual sales levels than the JEO system. The SFI technique was found to be accurate for periods of up to one year. One would expect this to be true since most salesmen consider sales on a short-term basis, and are not necessarily concerned with factors that will affect sales over a longer period of time, such as changing customer preferences, economic conditions, or the effects of competition.

---

*Small, Lawrence R., *Sales Forecasting in Canada: A Survey of Practices* (Ottawa: The Conference Board in Canada, 1980), Chapter 3.

In this chapter one of the models we will develop will use VisiCalc to help us collect and interpret SFI data. We will show how estimates can be consolidated up the organizational ladder, from the specific salesman to branch, region, and head office level. The model will also allow the managers to compare on a period-to-period basis how well the particular salespeople and managers below them have done in predicting sales levels. If a particular salesperson is consistently high or low in his projections, the local manager can then adjust these estimates before passing them up to the next level.

The Customer Inquiry System is another way companies try to predict future sales levels. The customers are asked about their future buying plans. This method can be used very successfully by companies who have a small number of customers that account for a large percentage of their total sales. Companies with a larger customer base find that there are problems involved in applying this system. Talking to a lot of customers takes time, which can make forecasting expensive. Also, customers tend to tell you what they think you want to hear, especially when no commitment from them is necessary. While using customers to help in sales forecasting is a good second source of forecast information, it is not a reliable tool in itself.

The use of econometric indicators, such as the Consumer Price Index, Gross National Product, and Disposable Income, are widely used as an aid to forecasting. Other industry-specific statistics such as Housing Starts or Cattle on Feed reports are also used during the forecasting process. This data can provide valuable background information on which you can base some of your forecast assumptions. These economic indicators act as an additional check on your sales estimates. For example, a very bullish report showing large increases in new car sales would look strange placed before a backdrop of high interest rates, high unemployment, and low disposable income.

Finally, there are more advanced forecasting techniques which are based on statistical theory and general mathematics. These methods are usually used by large companies and require highly trained personnel. These forecasting methods are referred to as time series analysis. This is the analysis of past data, searching for patterns in the hope that they will predict future trends. The specific types of techniques used are moving averages, regression analysis, and various types of correlation analysis. For certain types of industries, for example those that have a large seasonal component to sales or those that have been experiencing a steady growth trend, these forecasting methods can be extremely useful and very accurate.

It seems like VisiCalc has been designed especially to help make forecasting easier. For example, no matter how much hard work you do you usually never arrive at a "final" projection. Your forecast will be changing and evolving all the time to fit the latest available information. If you build a flexible VisiCalc spread sheet, you only need to alter a few numbers and your new projections will be instantly displayed throughout your model. The ease of altering the assumptions of your forecasts makes VisiCalc a natural for these kinds of applications.

Many planners make up three sets of forecasts; they display the best, worst, and most likely possibilities. This allows for an entire spectrum of possible results to be seen at a glance. Normally, this analysis would require a lot of time consuming and error prone calculation. With VisiCalc you can quickly generate new business scenarios by entering new forecast data. This lets you see how sensitive your business is to factors like material and labor costs and varying sales volume.

Once you have decided on your sales forecast you can then enter this data into your company's operating model. The sales volume acts as the catalyst that drives the other estimates which compose your total business forecast. We will create a pro forma income statement that you can use to instantly reflect the results of your latest sales forecast. By using this model you will see the results of your expected sales volume translated into actual business profits or losses.

The two models developed at the end of this chapter can be combined to form a complete forecasting system. You begin by using the SFI model to generate your sales forecasts. These forecasts can then be entered into your own pro forma income statement so you can see how the sales volume will affect your business. By using these models you can generate an entire spectrum of financial reports based on different future possibilities.

When you have completed your latest sales forecast, you should try to verify your results by using other methods. See if your predictions are in the same ball park as general industry projections, and see if your numbers look out of place when contrasted with general business trends.

In considering your sales estimates you will need a check list of factors that you should take into account before reaching your "final" conclusions. This type of list will vary from one business to another, but the factors can generally be divided into two types: internal factors and external factors. A short list of factors to think about appears below. There is no implied order to the list and the list itself is by no means exhaustive. It is meant to suggest the type of check list that you could develop for your own specific business. Using a list like this can be invaluable, because it makes you stop and rethink your forecast. It insures that you have not missed any important facts when reaching your final conclusions.

External Factors	Internal Factors
General economic conditions	Changing supply conditions
Population characteristics	Changing distribution costs
Labor factors	Labor
Direct competition	Overhead costs
Indirect competition	Fixed asset replacement
Changing fashions and styles	Credit policy
Government	Advertising campaigns

SUMMARY

We began this chapter with Seneca's warning about why some of our plans are destined to fail. The flip side of this warning is that when we do know where we are going things often seem to fall into place, probably because we learn to recognize good fortune.

A business plan is an important component of success, but many of us still go to great lengths to avoid making a business forecast. Our microcomputer and VisiCalc can help take the pain out of this important task and can even make it enjoyable. The ease of forecasting with VisiCalc can lead to the creation of entire groups of forecasts based on different assumptions about the future. This can help you plan for unexpected events.

The cornerstone of a business forecast is the sales forecast. We examined several ways that companies forecast sales and saw how each department in a company can use the sales forecast to improve its own individual performance.

Since a business plan is only as good as the sales forecast that it is based on, you should be sure that you have not missed any crucial factors before completing the forecast. Using economic indicators and general industry trends is a good way to double check your forecasts. In addition, a list of internal and external factors that specifically affect your business can help you insure that your forecast is the best you can produce.

THE MODELS

In this section we will develop two models that can be used to help create useful business forecasts. The first model uses the Sales Force Inquiry Method to gather forecast data from your sales force. This data can supply the basis for your sales forecast. The second model translates your sales forecast into a projected income statement for your specific business. Both of these models can be used independently or together.

Model I: Sales Force Inquiry

The Sales Force Inquiry Model (SFI) appears in the appendix under the name SFI. If you have the model disk, you can load the packed model directly; otherwise, you can type in the keystrokes listed below the model name. Either way, your packed SFI model should look like the one in Figure 12-1.

This model is designed to help you formulate meaningful sales forecasts. It will be especially helpful if you have several salespeople who are responsible for different types of products. The idea is to use their input to help you decide on future sales volume.

Across the top of the model you will notice a place to enter the period that the forecast applies to, as well as the date that you entered the forecast into the sheet. You can forecast over any time period that suits your particular business; in our sample application, we will be using an annual projection. Let us assume that it is March 1 and we want to forecast our sales over the coming year. To add this information to the model, move your cursor to E1 and type **/FRANNUAL∅F ➤ ROM∅MAR ∅ ➤/FL1 Ⓔ**.

Our sample company is Fastsel Distributors, Inc., who market a line of photocopiers and supplies. The company employs six salespeople and each salesperson sells each of the three different copier models. In addition to the copiers, they sell supplies of ink and paper. So each of the six employees can sell any combination of five different products.

Our first step is to customize our packed SFI model to reflect the size and product mix of Fastsel.

Across the top of our model you will see that there is space for up to ten different products and each one is numbered from 1 to 10 beginning from column D. Since we only have five different types of products in our example, we need to shrink our model so it contains space for only five columns. Move your cursor into column I, which contains the data for product 6. To delete the extra columns, enter **/DC/DC/DC/DC/DC**—that is five delete commands altogether. Now your model should display only five product types across the top with an empty column separating product number 5 from the label TOTAL.

So far so good; the model is beginning to conform to our needs. To further customize it we need to change the product descriptions across the top of the model from uninformative model numbers to product names. To do this move your cursor to D3 and enter the following keystrokes: **MODELI ➤MODELII ➤MODELIII ➤PAPER ➤INK Ⓔ**.

The next step is to make room for our sales staff. The names are GREEN, ADAMS, SALTER, MORRIS, SMITH, and LEWIS. We need to make room for the six salespeople between the border rows that stretch across rows 4 and 6. To insert the five rows (we do not need six because

S F I FORECAST PERIOD:

PRODUCT:	1	2	3	4	5	6	7	8	9	10	TOTAL
SALESMAN	0	0	0	0	0	0	0	0	0	0	0

SUMMARY	1	2	3	4	5	6	7	8	9	10	
TOTAL	1	2	3	4	5	6	7	8	9	10	
AVERAGE	0	0	0	0	0	0	0	0	0	0	
LARGEST	0	0	0	0	0	0	0	0	0	0	

RECOMMENDATION

Figure 12-1

we have one already), move your cursor into row 6 and enter /IR/IR/IR/IR/IR. Now that there is room we need to enter the names of our salespeople in column C. To do this move your cursor to C5 and enter **GREEN ▼ ADAMS ▼ SALTER ▼ MORRIS ▼ SMITH ▼ LEWIS Ⓔ**.

Suppose that you have requested an estimate of expected annual sales by product type from each salesperson. Usually, you will receive lower than expected sales figures, especially if the salespeople think it will lower their sales targets. It is up to you to encourage your staff to take its best shot at designing an honest sales forecast. The grid below summarizes the results of your survey. All estimates are shown as dollar amounts in thousands.

	MODEL I	MODEL II	MODEL III	PAPER	INK
GREEN	50	30	25	10	6
ADAMS	35	40	25	12	6
SALTER	55	40	30	8	4
MORRIS	20	25	15	6	3
SMITH	60	25	0	7	3
LEWIS	55	15	35	11	5

Now we can record the results of the survey on the sheet. You should be able to enter the information for each salesperson into the SFI model yourself, but to be sure we will illustrate how to enter the information for the first salesperson. To enter the information for GREEN, move your cursor to D5 and enter **50 ▶30 ▶25 ▶10 ▶6 Ⓔ**. Take some time now and enter the information for the other five salespeople to get a feel for the model.

Once you have entered the salesforce's estimates, you need to replicate the formula in column J. With your cursor at J5, enter the following keystrokes: **/R Ⓔ J6.J10 Ⓔ RR**.

To enter information for your own company you follow the same procedure. First, adjust the width of the model to fit the number of products you sell and label the columns as desired; then, widen the salesforce section to fit the number of salespeople you have. Once the model is unpacked to fit the correct shape, you can enter the forecast data.

Once the data has been entered you can examine the summary section at the bottom of the model. This area gives you an overview of the forecast information. By examining this summary you can then decide on the overall forecast for your sales group. The line below the summary labeled RECOMMENDATION is reserved for your best guess at total sales of the group.

To complete the unpacking of this model, you should change the product numbers in the summary section to product names as you did on line 3. You can enter the five column headings directly into line 13 or you can use the replicate command as follows: **/R BS D3.H3:D13 Ⓔ**.

To insure that you are using the model correctly, check it against the picture shown below.

```
          S F I FORECAST   PERIOD: ANNUAL FROM MAR 1

                PRODUCT:   MODELI  MODELII  MODELIII  PAPER   INK      TOTAL
                =========================================================
SALESMAN:       GREEN        50      30        25      10      6        121
                ADAMS        35      40        25      12      6        118
                SALTER       55      40        30       8      4        137
                MORRIS       20      25        15       6      3         69
                SMITH        60      25         0       7      3         95
                LEWIS        55      15        35      11      5        121
                =========================================================

SUMMARY                    MODELI  MODELII  MODELIII  PAPER   INK
                TOTAL       275     175       130      54     27
                AVERAGE      46      29        22       9      5
                LARGEST      60      40        35      12      6

RECOMMENDATION
```

Figure 12-2

A large company could use the SFI spread sheet as a useful aid to sales forecasting. At the branch level each manager would be responsible for collecting the individual branch data and forwarding a copy of this sheet, along with the manager's recommendation, to the next level up the corporate ladder. The region manager would receive several sheets containing the forecasts of the various branches in his region. He in turn could design his own sheet, but instead of using employee names he could use branch names instead. That way he would have a complete picture of his forecast region sales. This process would continue until the entire corporate SFI forecast "rolls up" from the individual salesperson to its final destination in the head office.

The danger in using the SFI model is that salespeople often tend to forecast on the low side. This is especially true if they think a lower forecast will result in lower sales targets for themselves. It is up to you to get the most honest estimates from your salesmen as possible. One suggestion is to reward the most accurate predictors on a quarterly or annual basis. An extra benefit in using the SFI model is that as time goes on you will have an ongoing record of how well each salesperson has forecasted sales in the past. This lets you adjust the forecast of an individual salesperson if he or she is habitually over or under in the estimates. You also will be able to spot the salespeople who have the best understanding of the markets they serve—an understanding that could come in handy. An added benefit is that your better salespeople appreciate the chance to affect corporate planning and will try harder to achieve goals that they have helped define.

The SFI method has been used successfully by many companies as an aid to forecasting sales, but a forecast should never be based on only one forecasting method. You should apply one or more of the other forecasting methods discussed in this chapter. Different methods work together and allow you to double check your assumptions.

Model II: Forecasting the Income Statement

Once you have decided on your sales forecast you need to see how these sales will affect the future operation of your business. This VisiCalc spread sheet will let you see the impact of your projected sales on the profitability of your business.

Our model uses historic information on sales and expense levels combined with your sales forecast to project your company's future earnings performance. The keystrokes used to create this model are found in the appendix under INCOME. After you have loaded or typed in the model, your screen should look like Figure 12-3.

The income statement is divided into two major sections—sales and expenses. There is room on the sheet for two historic income statements and a third forecast statement. The idea is to use your past financial information as an aid to forecasting future expense levels.

The first column contains the names of the various income statement categories. The next two columns show the actual amounts paid or received and the percentage of total sales each category represents; they are labeled YEAR and % SALES, respectively. The percentage of sales figure supplies a meaningful way to examine the change in sales and expenses from one year to the next. The next two columns do the same thing but use data from the latest income statement. The effect is that you can fit two previous income statements on the sheet at once. This lets you refer to historic performance while you project your income statement for the coming period.

The next column shows the percentage change in a given category from one year to the next. The percentage change between the two statements appears in column F and is labeled % CHANGE.

It may not be clear at first exactly how this model works, but as we illustrate its use you will see how powerful this spread sheet is as an aid to forecasting. We will continue with our example using the information from Fastsel Distributors, Inc. This company distributes photocopiers and we created an SFI sales forecast for them in the previous section. The chart below shows the sales and expense information taken from the previous two income statements of Fastsel Distributors, Inc.

INCOME STATEMENTS   FORECAST

	YEAR	% SALES	YEAR	% SALES	% CHANGE	YEAR	% SALES	FORECAST %
S A L E S								
A	0	ERROR	0	ERROR	ERROR	0	ERROR	0.00
B	0	ERROR	0	ERROR	ERROR	0	ERROR	0.00
C	0	ERROR	0	ERROR	ERROR	0	ERROR	0.00
D	0	ERROR	0	ERROR	ERROR	0	ERROR	0.00
E	0	ERROR	0	ERROR	ERROR	0	ERROR	0.00
F	0	ERROR	0	ERROR	ERROR	0	ERROR	0.00
TOTAL SALES	0	ERROR	0	ERROR	ERROR	0	ERROR	ERROR
COST OF GOOD	0	ERROR	0	ERROR	ERROR	0	ERROR	0.00
GROSS MARGIN	0	ERROR	0	ERROR	ERROR	0	ERROR	ERROR
E X P E N S								
WAGES	0	ERROR	0	ERROR	ERROR	0	ERROR	0.00
RENT	0	ERROR	0	ERROR	ERROR	0	ERROR	0.00
UTILITIES	0	ERROR	0	ERROR	ERROR	0	ERROR	0.00
PROFESSIONAL	0	ERROR	0	ERROR	ERROR	0	ERROR	0.00
TAXES	0	ERROR	0	ERROR	ERROR	0	ERROR	0.00
DEPRECIATION	0	ERROR	0	ERROR	ERROR	0	ERROR	0.00
INTEREST	0	ERROR	0	ERROR	ERROR	0	ERROR	0.00
TELEPHONE	0	ERROR	0	ERROR	ERROR	0	ERROR	0.00
BAD DEBTS	0	ERROR	0	ERROR	ERROR	0	ERROR	0.00
THEFT	0	ERROR	0	ERROR	ERROR	0	ERROR	0.00
MISC	0	ERROR	0	ERROR	ERROR	0	ERROR	0.00
TOTAL EXPENS	0	ERROR	0	ERROR	ERROR	0	ERROR	ERROR
NET PROFIT	0	ERROR	0	ERROR	ERROR	0	ERROR	ERROR

Figure 12-3

164 Applications and Models

	1981	1982
SALES		
MODEL I	210	260
MODEL II	100	130
MODEL III	71	100
PAPER	45	50
INK	15	18
COST OF GOODS	240	290
EXPENSES		
WAGES	120	160
RENT	15	18
PROF. SERV.	4	5
TELEPHONE	3	4

(in thousands)

We will start by entering in the income statement information into the spread sheet. First, we will replace the general YEAR labels by the correct year. The historic data is from 1981 and 1982 and the forecast period is 1983. Move your cursor to B3 and enter **1981 ▶ ▶1982 ▶ ▶ ▶ 1983 Ⓔ**.

Now we can start to add the historic sales information into our model. Below the title S A L E S in column A you will see the letters A through F. Each of these letters can be replaced by a source of sales. Fastsel has five areas that contribute revenue and we will enter these areas now. Move your cursor to A6 and enter **MODEL␣I ▼ MODEL␣II ▼ MODEL␣III ▼ PAPER ▼ INK ▼**. Your cursor will now be in row 11. This is an extra expense row that we do not need because we only have five areas that contribute to sales. We will delete this extra row by entering **/DR** while our cursor is in row 11.

To enter the historic sales data for 1981 and 1982, go to B6 and enter the following keystrokes: **210 ▼ 100 ▼ 71 ▼ 45 ▼ 15 ▶ ▶ 18 ▲ 50 ▲ 100 ▲ 130 ▲ 260 Ⓔ**.

If you need to use more than six rows to record your specific sources of income, you can insert new rows using the /IR command and replicate an adjacent line into the blank row. When you replicate the line into the newly created row, use the source range of column A through I. The row number you use will be the row number of the adjacent row. The sequence of replicate options to use with these rows is RN RN RRR RR RN. The blanks have been added to make the letters easier to read, but do not include them in your response to the "Relative or No Change" replicate prompt. For example, if you created a new blank row in row 7, you could replicate the row above it into place as follows: /R BS A6.I6:A7 Ⓔ RNRNRRRRRN.

So far we have managed to add the sales information to our model. We can see by looking down the column labeled % CHANGE how the sales have grown during the last two years. For example, location F6 tells us that Model I sales have grown by over 23 percent from 1981 to 1982. By looking down this column we can see growth trends for the different products. Model II sales have grown 30 percent and Model III sales have grown at just over 40 percent.

In order to calculate our gross margin, we need to deduct our cost of goods sold from the total sales figure. Move your cursor to B14 and enter **240 ▶ ▶290 Ⓔ**. We now see the gross margin figure displayed in the line below.

Now we need to record the operating expenses. Various categories are listed in the Expenses section. Among them are wages, rent, professional services, and telephone. Take a minute now and enter the historic expense information in the correct rows. For example, to enter wages move your cursor to B20 and enter **120 ▶ ▶160 Ⓔ**. Remember to skip the % SALES column because this column contains formulas that the model requires. If you enter data in that column, you will wipe out the stored formulas. Repeat this process for the other three expense areas we have listed for Fastsel Distributors. You can get the information from the capsule expense statements listed above. When you are done you will see that there are several rows in the expense section that you do not need; one at a time, move your cursor into these rows and type **/DR** to remove the empty row. When you are done, your model should look like Figure 12-4.

Now that the historic data has been entered into the spread sheet, we can begin to use the model for its intended purpose—as a forecasting tool. Let us see what we can tell about Fastsel's product line and expense patterns by examining our spread sheet. Imagine that we are familiar with Fastsel; since we are involved in forecasting sales this is not too hard to believe. By combining knowledge of the company and its products with the information on the screen we can draw some interesting conclusions about future sales.

The Model I is the oldest model copier currently sold by Fastsel, and it shows the lowest increase in sales, just over 23 percent. Column F shows how sales have changed. The Model II is a newer machine and sales are increasing at a 30 percent clip, indicating growing market acceptance for this copier. The Model III is the newest product in Fastsel's copier line. Its rapid growth indicates a product well suited to current market needs.

Based on this knowledge, we might forecast the increase in Model I sales to slow in the coming year since it may be entering the twilight of its product lifespan. Model II sales could be expected to continue to increase in the coming year. Model III sales could be expected to grow at a somewhat greater rate than last year's impressive rate. Examining

INCOME STATEMENTS

	1981	% SALES	1982	%SALES	% CHANGE	1983	% SALES	FORECAST %
S A L E S								
MODEL I	210	47.62	260	46.59	23.81	260	46.59	0.00
MODEL II	100	22.68	130	23.30	30.00	130	23.30	0.00
MODEL III	71	16.10	100	17.92	40.85	100	17.92	0.00
PAPER	45	10.20	50	8.96	11.11	50	8.96	0.00
INK	15	3.40	18	3.23	20.00	18	3.23	0.00
TOTAL SALES	441	100.00	558	100.00	26.53	558	100.00	0.00
COST OF GOOD	240	54.42	290	51.97	20.83	290	51.97	0.00
GROSS MARGIN	201	45.58	268	48.03	33.33	268	48.03	0.00
WAGES	120	27.21	160	28.67	33.33	160	28.67	0.00
RENT	15	3.40	18	3.23	20.00	18	3.23	0.00
PROFESSIONAL	4	0.91	5	0.90	25.00	5	0.90	0.00
TELEPHONE	3	0.68	4	0.72	33.33	4	0.72	0.00
TOTAL EXPENS	142	32.20	187	33.51	31.69	187	33.51	0.00
NET PROFIT	59	13.38	81	14.52	37.29	81	14.52	0.00

Figure 12-4

paper and ink sales, we see that the annual increases have been just over 10 percent and 20 percent, respectively. For the purposes of our forecast, let us assume that these two areas continue to grow at their past rates.

Before we enter our projections in the model, take a minute to look at the final three columns of the sheet, columns G, H, and I. Notice that the last column, FORECAST %, currently contains zeroes displayed in $ format. This is the key column that the model uses to forecast next year's income statement. If you compare column H to column E, both labeled % SALES, you will find the numbers identical. The same is true if you compare the actual sales in 1982 with those forecast for 1983. These columns are the same because the model assumes that the forecast year is identical to the previous year's data until you change the numbers in the FORECAST % column for the forecast year. With zeroes in the FORECAST % column, the model says that no change will take place between the last year and the forecast year so all the numbers are identical. You will use the forecast percentage column to alter last year's income statement values by your forecast amount. The forecast amounts will equal the amounts shown in last year's income statement plus or minus the percentage change that you specify. This is easier seen than explained.

To see the model in action, let us enter our assumptions for next year's sales. You use the FORECAST % column to store the percentage you expect sales for each product to either increase or decrease. According to what we know about the Fastsel product line, one set of reasonable sales forecasts would be

Product	Forecast Change
Model I	15%
Model II	40%
Model III	45%
Paper	10%
Ink	20%

To enter this data into the model, move your cursor to I6 and enter 15 ▼ 40 ▼ 45 ▼ 10 ▼ 20 Ⓔ. As you enter each percentage change you will notice that the amounts shown for sales and percent of sales, in column G and H, change to reflect your estimate of percentage increases. By varying the amount of forecast growth, you cause the actual sales figures in your forecast to change accordingly. For example, by assuming an increase in Model I sales of 15 percent, the spread sheet automatically informs you that you will sell $299 worth of Model Is in the coming year as opposed to the $260 you sold last year (remember that these figures are in thousands). If we wanted to forecast a lower level of sales than the previous year, we would use a negative sign to indicate a decrease in sales. For example, if we expected Model I sales to be 10 percent less than the amount we sold last year, we would enter –10 percent in the FORECAST % column.

To complete the sales picture we need to subtract our cost of goods sold (COGS) to find the gross margin. The model can be used to help us forecast this important statistic. By looking at I12 we can see that sales have increased a total of almost 26 percent in our forecast income statement. This growth in sales would probably cause a drop in Fastsel's cost of goods since they can order in greater volume. If there was no change in the COGS, we would enter the amount 25.91 in location I14 to indicate that costs were increasing directly with volume. Since Fastsel will probably get a better discount, however, let us enter **23 (E)** in I14 to indicate a slight drop in the COGS. You can experiment with this percentage to see how your margin will vary.

To complete this example, let us assume that wages will increase by 35 percent and use of long distance will increase by 20 percent in the coming year. To enter this information move your cursor to I20 and enter **35 ▾▾▾ 20 (E)**.

Check your model against Figure 12-5 to see if you have entered it correctly.

Once you have completed both the income and expense sections, you will see your gross and net profit (before tax) for the coming year, according to your sales and expense forecast revealed in line 28. By altering your projected % change estimates, you can create several versions of your forecast income statement, each revealing a different possible future scenario.

Notice that the forecast sales figures we have arrived at using this model agree fairly well with the figures from the SFI model. Using this forecasting model is a good way to doublecheck the validity of your SFI sales estimates.

These models when used together or separately can help keep your business on course.

FURTHER READING

Bolt, Gordon J. *Market and Sales Forecasting—A Total Approach.* New York: Halstead Press Division, John Wiley and Sons, 1972.

Lippitt, Vernon G. *Statistical Sales Forecasting.* New York: Financial Executives Research Foundation, 1969.

"Forecasting Sales," Business Policy No. 106. National Industrial Conference Board. New York, 1964.

Wortman, Leon A. *Successful Small Business Management.* New York: Amacom, 1976.

INCOME STATEMENTS   FORECAST

	1981	% SALES	1982	%SALES	% CHANGE	1983	% SALES	FORECAST %
S A L E S								
MODEL I	210	47.62	260	46.59	23.81	299	42.56	15.00
MODEL II	100	22.68	130	23.30	30.00	182	25.90	40.00
MODEL III	71	16.10	100	17.92	40.85	145	20.64	45.00
PAPER	45	10.20	50	8.96	11.11	55	7.83	10.00
INK	15	3.40	18	3.23	20.00	22	3.07	20.00
TOTAL SALES	441	100.00	558	100.00	26.53	703	100.00	25.91
COST OF GOOD	240	54.42	290	51.97	20.83	357	50.77	23.00
GROSS MARGIN	201	45.58	268	48.03	33.33	346	49.23	29.07
WAGES	120	27.21	160	28.67	33.33	216	30.74	35.00
RENT	15	3.40	18	3.23	20.00	18	2.56	0.00
PROFESSIONAL	4	0.91	5	0.90	25.00	5	0.71	0.00
TELEPHONE	3	0.68	4	0.72	33.33	5	0.68	20.00
TOTAL EXPENS	142	32.20	187	33.51	31.69	244	34.70	30.37
NET PROFIT	59	13.38	81	14.52	37.29	102	14.53	26.05

Figure 12-5

Chapter 13

Budgeting

For many of us the word "budget" is associated with a collection of negative images. Talk of budgeting around the office often means that we will not get the extra staff we need or that the annual company pilgrimage to Reno might be called off. We see government trying to control its massive spending year after year with one ineffectual budget after another. Even when we shop, the "budget" brand occupies a diminutive position, whether among the popcorn or the toilet paper.

In this chapter we will examine some basic principles of budgeting. Specific examples of budgets will be discussed along with the factors that can make a budget succeed or fail. We may even discover why budgeting has received so much bad press.

In the models section we will use VisiCalc to construct detailed budgeting systems—one system for the retailer and one for the manufacturer. VisiCalc's flexibility will be particularly useful in setting up our budget sheets, as well as in analyzing the difference between our budgeted versus actual results.

A budget has two different aspects. The first and most commonly recognized aspect is that the budget is a control over resources, be they man-hours, raw materials, or cash. The second and less often recognized aspect is that of planning. A budget is the quantitative translation of a business plan into day-to-day operating objectives.

In the last chapter we discussed sales forecasting. Forecasting and budgeting are often lumped together. In order to understand and use these tools effectively, they should be clearly differentiated from each other. A forecast is a prediction of future events and their expected impact on business operations. A budget is a detailed plan used to reach specific operating targets. A budget also serves as a management tool. It can be used to control various areas of operations such as production and purchasing. A budget can also act as an early warning system, alerting management to potential problem areas before they get out of hand.

Many companies have seen their most earnest attempts at budgeting fail. Over the years, experienced executives have identified several key areas that help make a budget work. We will examine some of these elements in this chapter. If you have tried using budgets and have experienced dubious results, these hints will help you identify where you may have gone wrong. If you have never tried using a budget, you will be able to see if your business has the requirements necessary to make budgeting successful.

The first requirement for a successful budget is a business with a clearly defined organizational structure. There must be a clear understanding of who is responsible for production, administration, and the other controllable aspects of the business's operation.

The ability to control operations with a budget in turn depends on being able to identify whether an individual's performance is above or below par. Once this is established the person responsible for the specific function can be dealt with directly. No matter how much energy is put into the budgeting process, it will not be able to supply an effective means of control if there are no clear lines of responsibility. There is no point turning the dial of a thermostat if it is not connected to a furnace.

In order to successfully implement a budget there must be a cooperative environment existing between the line managers, the people in the trenches who directly control operations, and the budget administrators. The budget officer is in a somewhat strange position within the corporate hierarchy. He has vast powers that can dramatically affect the company's performance; however, he usually does not have the ability to enforce the budgets. This is where the interest of top management is essential. Unless the executive maintains a high profile in its support of the budgeting process, line management will not have a strong incentive to work closely with the budgeting staff. Periodical letters from the president or vice president of divisions specifically supporting the budgeting process are a good way to show management interest. More important, though, is the need for management to act on results that come from the budget groups—especially when they call for specific action to be taken.

Another key requirement of the budgeting process is that there must be a way to measure results. Budgets can only control a measurable process and so budgets often depend on information supplied by the company's accounting department. This information allows us to keep score so we know if we are winning or losing. Accounting information should be quickly and easily applied to the various budgets without time-consuming conversions, recalculations, or other modifications. It is also important that the accounting information be available within a reasonable time span in terms of the budgeting process. There is no point in telling a production supervisor that two months ago he was 15 percent over budget on overtime in his metal stamping operation. This may seem obvious, but many companies inform their managers of poor performance many months after the fact. Effective budgets must give information to the people they affect in a short enough time span to allow useful corrective action to be taken.

A successful budget needs the support of all those who come under its sphere of control. Middle management must accept and support the assigned production, sales, or spending goals. You achieve this base of support by involving middle management in the budgeting process from the start. In this way, the budgets realistically represent what the individual managers feel they can actually accomplish, and they know what must be done to achieve these goals. Budgets have a better chance of succeeding if the people who have to meet the goals have a say in setting those goals.

You can now take a look at your own business and see if it has the elements necessary to insure successful budgeting. Not all businesses can use budgets to help improve operations. By realistically examining your situation right now, you can save yourself a lot of time and effort should a budgeting approach not suit your business environment.

Most budgets begin with a forecast of future sales. Since all operating expenses are paid out of the revenues generated by sales, the sales forecast sets the tempo for all other areas of your operation. Sales determine not only what a company can spend in the short term, but will also reveal how much income will be generated to service longer-term commitments such as the retirement of debt, the expansion of existing facilities, or the acquisition of other companies.

In this chapter we will specifically examine how manufacturers and retailers can apply budgeting to improve profitability. While both begin the budget process by projecting sales, the specific budgets they use will differ. We will start by first examining the manufacturers' budgets.

For most manufacturers, the sales forecast is in the form of the amount of product units that are expected to be sold over the coming period. These forecast sales figures form the basis of a series of manufac-

174 Applications and Models

turers' budgets. Throughout this chapter we will assume the forecast is over the period of a year.

The figure below represents a typical materials requirements estimate. This is often the first proto-budget spawned by the sales forecast. The materials requirement sheet explodes each product into its separate components and allows calculation of the amount and the cost of materials required to meet sales projections for the year.

MATERIALS REQUIREMENTS ESTIMATE

PRODUCT	PROJECTED UNIT SALES	MATERIAL INVENTORY NUMBER	MATERIAL REQUIRED PER UNIT	TOTAL MATERIAL REQUIRED	MATERIAL COST PER UNIT	TOTAL COST
A	1000	1427-A	3	3000	2.50	7500.00
		824-C	2	2000	1.15	2300.00
		914-L	5.5	5500	0.10	550.00
PRODUCT A TOTALS:			10.5	10500	10.35	10350.00

Figure 13-1

In our example we are calculating the material requirements for a single product. In practice, manufacturers usually produce several different products. In this case they would create a separate materials requirements budget for each product.

Let us look at this example in more detail. The sales department has informed us that projected sales for the coming year call for 1,000 units of product A to be sold. Product A is composed of three different materials. These materials appear in the third column and are listed by their inventory reference numbers. The number of units of each material that composes a single unit of the product is shown in the next column. The next column over shows the total units of each material that are needed to make all 1,000 units of product A. The second to last column shows the cost of each material on a per unit basis. We know the total of each material required and the cost per unit. We can now calculate the total cost of all the materials required to meet the forecast demand. This amount is shown in the final column of the chart.

The next step is to take this materials requirements estimate and translate it into a usable materials budget. Our purpose in applying a budget to materials is to help control our cost of goods manufactured. A materials budget helps alert us to problems in the production cycle as well as insure that we have the raw materials we need to meet our sales demand. The materials budget also helps us avoid holding a large raw materials inventory.

The figure below illustrates the materials budget for product A.

MATERIALS BUDGET MARCH 1982

PRODUCT: A

MATERIAL	BUDGETED USAGE	ACTUAL USAGE	VARIANCE	YEAR - TO - DATE BUDGET	ACTUAL	VARIANCE
1427-A	250	270	1.08	750	786	1.05
824-C	167	172	1.03	501	515	1.03
914-L	458	522	1.14	1374	1526	1.11

Figure 13-2

The materials budget shows at a glance how successful our production people have been at producing our goods to preset standards. Should our monthly use of materials appear different than our budgeted amounts, we can return to our line management, who hopefully helped set the initial budget and find out what is causing the problem. In some cases the corrective action may involve the fine tuning of the initial production standards on which the budget was based. These standards could be unrealistic. Overuse of materials is often caused by equipment or labor problems.

Take a closer look at the materials budget. In order to simplify our example we have assumed that demand for product A is constant throughout the year. Therefore, monthly requirements for materials will be one twelfth of the annual material requirements for product A or about 80 pieces a month. This report shows us the detailed results of the current month as well as the year-to-date results.

After examining the materials required for the coming year, the next budget of interest concerns how much time and money we will spend producing our products through labor expense. After several years of experience manufacturing specific products, certain production standards become known concerning how long it takes to perform a specific job or activity. These standards are usually expressed in man-hours or minutes per unit of production. The labor budget begins by taking projected demand from the sales forecast and multiplying this by the man-hours required to produce the product in order to arrive at the total labor budget projection. Again, we can see not only the results for the operations for March, but we also see how we stand year-to-date. We assume that there are four specific activities that are required to produce Product A: machine labor, trimming, frame assembly, and packing and shipping the product. The column headed "STANDARD TIMES (MINS)" indicates how long these specific activities take. The figure below illustrates a labor budget for Product A, considering we expect to produce 80 units a month.

			LABOR	BUDGET		MARCH 1982	
PRODUCT: A UNITS: 80					*********************************		
TASK	STANDARD TIMES (MINS)	BUDGETED LABOR	ACTUAL LABOR	VARIANCE	YEAR - TO - BUDGET	DATE ACTUAL	VARIANCE
MACHINE PARTS	25	2000	2150	1.08	6000	6150	1.03
TRIM	20	1600	1750	1.09	4800	4950	1.03
ASSEMBLE	35	2800	2850	1.02	8400	8470	1.01
PACK & SHIP	14	1120	1130	1.01	3360	3540	1.05

Figure 13-3

This last example illustrates a direct labor budget. All the activities described in this budget are directly attributable to the manufacturing of Product A. This budget really only tells us part of the labor story since many indirect labor charges are usually associated with the manufacturing of a product. For example, wages paid for supervision, equipment maintenance, training, and cleaning are all costs incurred by the manufacturer but are not directly attributable to any one specific product. This is assuming that there is more than one product being manufactured in the plant. In the case of a company that manufactures only one product, all labor costs can be attributed directly to that product and so all costs can be referred to as direct costs. Most companies produce a variety of products and so have to come to grips with direct versus indirect costs.

What is the advantage of dividing costs into either direct or indirect? In most manufacturing environments products have a life cycle. Products are introduced, they mature, and eventually they go the way of the quill pen, the hula hoop, or the Edsel. Tastes change, technology advances, markets saturate, thus ending the product life cycle. One of the most crucial decisions facing management is to decide when to phase out a specific product line or, alternatively, when to expand production for a product that is gaining increasing acceptance. In order to make these decisions, management must first know exactly what it costs to manufacture a product. This requires knowing both the direct and indirect costs associated with the product. Knowing exact costs, both directly attributable to the product and indirectly associated with it, makes it possible to calculate breakeven points and to determine how profitable the manufacturing of a specific product will be.

The figure below shows a completed labor budget breaking down both indirect and direct labor costs associated with Product A. Assigning indirect costs to a product is not easy. Several of the books listed at the end of this chapter discuss this problem in detail.

LABOR BUDGET MARCH 1982

PRODUCT: A
UNITS: 80

	TASK	STANDARD TIMES (MINS)	BUDGETED LABOR	ACTUAL LABOR	VARIANCE	YEAR - TO - DATE BUDGET	ACTUAL	VARIANCE
DIRECT:	MACHINE PARTS	25	2000	2150	1.08	6000	6150	1.03
	TRIM	20	1600	1750	1.09	4800	4950	1.03
	ASSEMBLE	35	2800	2850	1.02	8400	8470	1.01
	PACK & SHIP	14	1120	1130	1.01	3360	3540	1.05
	SETUP		500	620	1.24	1500	1800	1.20
INDIRECT:	MAINTENANCE		260	275	1.06	780	765	0.98
	TRAINING		100	120	1.20	300	340	1.13
	SUPERVISION		300	300	1.00	900	870	0.97

Figure 13-4

Like the materials budget, the labor budget also measures the pulse of a manufacturing process. Increasing cost of maintenance, for example, can signal equipment that should be scheduled for replacement. Increased training time caused by high turnover can be a sign of personnel problems.

So far our budgets have been set to control the production aspects of manufacturing. What about head office expenses? We will now consider an expense budget for general administrative costs.

Past experience is a great help when it comes to setting expense levels for general and administrative spending. The number of administrative personnel and their salaries are usually known well in advance. Regular expenses incurred in running the general and administrative functions are also known well in advance, because changes such as moving to a new premises or creating a new administrative department are comparatively radical and need to be planned far in advance. The figure below illustrates the format of a typical general and administrative budget.

```
                OFFICE    EXPENSE   BUDGET    4 TH QUARTER 1982

                                                      YEAR  TO   DATE
                         BUDGET   ACTUAL  DIFFERENCE  BUDGET  ACTUAL  DIFFERENCE
MANAGEMENT SALARIES
STAFF SALARIES
PRODUCTION ADMIN.
PERSONNEL ADMIN.
ACCOUNTING
TRAVEL
ADVERTISING
OFFICE SUPPLIES
```

Figure 13-5

This illustration displays a standard budget format. While the current example uses general and administrative expenses, any department that has fixed expenses can utilize this type of budget layout. For example, a sales or advertising department could use this type of budget format to monitor various expenses. This is particularly useful if these areas are treated as separate profit centers. In each case the fixed costs can be budgeted and reports produced monthly, quarterly, or annually, as desired.

The key to this budget, as with all the others we have examined, is the quantitative comparison between what was expected to happen and what actually did happen. Deviations from the expected can be quickly spotted and dealt with.

This concludes our brief examination of applied budgets for the manufacturer. We have only scratched the surface with the few budgets that were introduced. For a more detailed discussion of manufacturers' budgets, especially fixed versus variable budgeting, see the reading list at the end of the chapter.

We can now examine the ways that a retailer can use budgets to improve profitability.

We will illustrate a budget system specially designed to help a retailer monitor one of his most crucial operating areas: his gross profit margin. This is perhaps the single most important operating statistic for many retailers. Any reduction of margin is immediately felt in the store's bottom line. Suppose a business grosses one million dollars in sales a year. If the gross margin is decreased by only 1 percent, profit is reduced by $10,000.

Our budgeting system is composed of four different reports. The first three reports contribute information necessary to calculate the monthly gross margin statistics, and the fourth is the actual margin budget itself.

Controlling operating profit begins with better control of inventory costs and pricing. The first step in the creation of our monthly gross margin budget begins at the point where inventory is received by the business. Two of the most common reasons why a retailer's profit margin declines are loss caused by excessive discounting of goods and the failure to pass along producer price increases. We begin our margin control procedure by creating a receiving journal. A sample receiving journal appears below.

```
                    RECEIVING    JOURNAL     FEB 1982

DATE       SUPPLIER           COST        RETAIL        MARKUP
FEB  3     JOE'S SUPPLY       500.00      850.00          0.41
                .               .           .              .
                .               .           .              .
                .               .           .              .
                .               .           .              .
                .               .           .              .
-------------------------------------------------------------
TOTAL:                       15000.00    25000.00         0.40
```

Figure 13-6

As each shipment of inventory enters the store, we will want to record the day and date the shipment has been received, the supplier, and the invoice number. We will also want to show our cost, retail and markup percent for each shipment we receive.

The receiving journal acts as a barometer for your inventory. Not only do you record receipts but also supplier returns, supplier credits, and any additional markups that affect the value of your inventory.

At the end of the month you will be able to read exactly how the cost and retail value of inventory has changed by looking at the bottom line of the receiving journal. We will need this information later on when we construct our margin budget. The journal will also let you see the markup on each item you have received. This will let you quickly spot declining supplier margins or lines of goods that you have priced inappropriately.

In our specific example we assume that during the month of February the inventory was increased by $15,000 and $25,000 on a cost and retail basis, respectively. The markup of the added goods was 40 percent.

We are now ready to go to the next step in our margin budget system. This second step deals with controlling discounts. The illustration below shows a typical discount register.

DISCOUNT REGISTER FEB 1982

DATE	ITEM	QUANTITY	OLD PRICE	NEW PRICE	DIFFERENCE	EXTENSION
FEB 6	HAND DRILL	5	29.95	19.95	10	50
.	.	.	.	.	.	.
.	.	.	.	.	.	.
.	.	.	.	.	.	.
.	.	.	.	.	.	.
.	.	.	.	.	.	.
TOTALS:						2100

Figure 13-7

The purpose of the discount register is to keep a running total of the amount that you have discounted your inventory. These discounts come from clearances, sales, and other types of price reductions. The amount that an inventory is discounted is a key indicator of how good a job you are doing purchasing and pricing inventory.

There are only two types of transactions we have to be concerned about in our discount register. We will either be discounting existing stock or we will be bringing back discounted stock to regular price levels.

If you stay faithful and keep your discount register current, at the end of the month you will know the total impact discounts have had on the retail value of your inventory. This is shown as the total under the "EXTENSION" column. In our example, the discount register reports that the retail value of the inventory was reduced a total of $2,100 during the month of February. This bottom line total for the month's discounts will be combined with the results from the receiving journal to get to the next step in our margin budget system, the inventory tally sheet.

At the end of each month or each quarter, depending on the period you decide to use, you will transfer the totals from the receiving journal and the discount register to the inventory tally sheet. This will give you a running portrait of your inventory position. The illustration below shows the inventory tally sheet.

In order to use this sheet, a physical inventory needs to be taken on the first month that the margin budget goes into effect. This establishes

INVENTORY TALLY

		COST	RETAIL	MAINTAINED COST %
JANUARY 1 OPENING	INVENTORY	120000	185000	0.65
ADD:	PURCHASES	22000	31000	
LESS:	SALES	15550	24000	
	DISCOUNTS	900	1400	
	SHRINKAGE	155	240	
FEBRUARY OPENING	INVENTORY	125395	190360	0.66
ADD:	PURCHASES	15000	25000	
LESS:	SALES	17000	28000	
	DISCOUNTS	1350	2100	
	SHRINKAGE	185	210	
MARCH 1 OPENING	INVENTORY	121860	185050	0.66

Figure 13-8

the initial inventory level, shown on the sheet as "OPENING INVENTORY." Once this has been done, the receiving journal and the discount register will allow you to calculate the running value of your inventory on a monthly basis. Let us see how the running tally actually works.

Following the calculation of the opening inventory, we record the inventory purchases that occurred during the month. The purchases for the month, at cost and retail, can be obtained from your receiving journal. You transfer the totals from the cost and retail columns over to the appropriate columns in the tally sheet.

To find the opening inventory for the next month, we need to add the inventory purchased during the month and subtract the sales, shrinkage, and discounts to arrive at the inventory available at the start of the next month. So far, we have the additions to inventory at cost and at retail from the receiving journal, and we can total our sales slips to find our monthly sales. Our discount register tells us the total amount that our inventory has been reduced due to discounts, on a retail basis. To take the value of discounts at retail and convert this to cost, we multiply the retail amount by the inventory at cost divided by the inventory at retail. This ratio of inventories at cost to retail gives us our conversion factor for retail to cost. The last bit of information we need to complete the monthly additions and reductions to our inventory is the shrinkage. Since shrinkage can only be known exactly by doing a physical inventory, we will estimate shrinkage using past experience. Usually, some percentage of sales is used to estimate shrinkage. In our example we have decided to estimate shrinkage as about 1 percent of sales. The tally sheet also shows our maintained markup percentage so we can see if we are maintaining the margins we require.

We are now in a position to generate our margin budget. It compares our performance this year with our results last year to determine if we are experiencing any erosion of our gross margin. The real advantage of this system is that you do not have to wait until your year-end to find out if you are having a good year or a bad one. The figure below illustrates a typical monthly gross margin budget.

		GROSS MARGIN BUDGET		
		LAST YEAR	THIS YEAR	DIFFERENCE
JANUARY	NET SALES	13000	24000	11000
	C.O.G.S	8200	15550	7350
	DISCOUNTS	500	900	400
	SHRINKAGE	110	155	45
	GROSS MARGIN	4190	7395	3205
	% MARGIN	0.32	0.31	-0.01
FEBRUARY	NET SALES	15000	28000	13000
	C.O.G.S	9200	17000	7800
	DISCOUNTS	1000	1350	350
	SHRINKAGE	130	185	55
	GROSS MARGIN	4670	9465	4795
	% MARGIN	0.31	0.34	0.03

Figure 13-9

For the retailer, control over gross profit margin is crucial. Even a small reduction of margin can seriously affect profitability. Using this budget will alert you to reductions in your operating margin. If you do notice a problem, you will have the tools you need to find a solution. The gross margin budget, inventory tally sheet, discount register, and receiving journal combine to serve this purpose well. If they are kept current, they not only tell you that you have a problem, but they also tell you where to find it.

We will use VisiCalc to design these four spread sheets in the applications section of this chapter.

So far we have discussed a few examples of budgeting from the manufacturer's and the retailer's perspective. It looks deceptively simple when you view the examples in this chapter and see costs clearly divided into direct and indirect, exact figures for cost of goods sold, or exact prices for raw material costs. The truth is that raw material costs change daily, some costs are not clearly direct or indirect, and often the cost of goods sold cannot be known exactly until year-end.

The figures used in many budgets represent approximations. Budgets are an exact plan that are translated from an approximate scenario of what forecasters think the future holds. A budget should never be thought of as infallible or held as immutable. A good budget should have room to react to events and not be treated as if it were cast in stone.

The "people" side of budgeting is the most crucial part. People make a budget succeed or fail. We will briefly look at the reasons why budgets fail, particularly from the standpoint of how they are put into use. It is hoped that this discussion will prevent some of the forms we have just described from popping up unannounced on a production supervisor's desk or from being used arbitrarily as the basis to assign gross margin goals to the manager of a retail department.

The major reason why budgets do not control the things they were designed to is lack of consultation with the people concerned. People are more likely to participate and to make a plan work if they feel they had a say in how the goals were set. This also helps instill some realism into budgets.

A budget is a feedback mechanism. In order to work properly it should behave like a living thing. It should show managers where they are succeeding and where they are failing. A crucial part of this feedback is timing. The time delay should be short enough between the performance of a task and its evaluation that the budget takes on some realistic meaning.

A continuation of this idea is management's commitment to the budget. As we observed earlier, many of the budgeting personnel do not have line authority. That means that any incentive to follow the budget and meet its goals has to come from senior management. Budget followup from this level of management should be prompt and effective.

Since many budgets are broken down by specific departments, it is important that the budgeted areas within these departments are directly assigned to responsible managers.

Since many budgets depend on standards, the assignment of these standards is crucial. Whether the standards show how much can be spent at a Christmas office party, how many hours it takes to train a worker on a given machine, or how much down-time a piece of equipment should have in a month, they must be carefully considered if the budget is to succeed. The collection and revision of standards should be an ongoing process.

The final reason that we will discuss concerning why budgets fail is perhaps the one that people complain about the most: You cannot change them. Since a budget is a control, it will not work if a simple request can change it. It is up to the budget administrators to make these plans difficult to change or they have no hope of working at all. However, at the other end of the spectrum you have the budget administrators who say that no revisions can be made to an operating budget. The problem is that a budget looks very exact. People tend to interpret this exactness as infallibility. In the business world, change is commonplace. A budget that cannot change quickly becomes fossilized. Many companies guard against this by using the ex-budget request. This is a sticky process one goes through to alter a budget parameter. The name of the game is to not make it impossible but merely difficult to change a budget. Thus, if the need arises, you will have the ability to adjust your budget to suit changing events.

SUMMARY

Making a budget that works requires expertise at handling both people and resources. An effective budget has a dual nature. It is a way to control parts of your business, but even more than that, it allows you to translate your business plans into reality.

Not all companies can effectively use budgets. We examined some of the characteristics that a business should have if it wants to get more out of budgeting than just the creation of extra paperwork.

We examined several ways that manufacturers and retailers use budgets to improve their efficiency and increase their profits. For the manufacturer we looked at how sales projections were used as the basis to build materials, labor, and general and administrative budgets. Designing the labor budget caused us to look into the advantages of separating costs into either the direct or indirect variety. For the retailer we went through four separate steps to create a monthly gross margin budget. This system was designed to watchdog the retailer's operating profit.

Our budget examples could be misleading. Their neatly ordered rows and columns hide a collection of assumptions, simplifications, and just plain educated guesses. We looked at the reasons why well-intentioned (and some not so well-intentioned) attempts at budgeting have failed.

THE MODELS

Now that we have acquired a basic understanding of some of the fundamentals of the budgeting process, we will develop two groups of VisiCalc models. The first group is composed of spread sheets for some of the manufacturers' budgets we described earlier in this chapter. Using these models, a manufacturer can go from a sales forecast to the creation of his own detailed materials and labor budgets. The second group will develop spread sheets for each step of the retailer's gross margin budget. We will illustrate how to use each spread sheet in detail.

Model I: Manufacturer's Budgets

In this section we will develop two Visicalc spread sheets. They are designed to be used as budgets for materials and labor for a manufacturing company. The first model we will examine is the materials budget and is stored under the name MATBUD. After typing in the keystrokes or loading the model from disk, your screen should contain the model shown in Figure 13-10.

Each sheet can be used to analyze the material cost profile of a specific product. Suppose that you are manufacturing a toy racing car that is composed of a chassis, four wheels, and a front and rear chrome bumper. You expect to manufacture 1,000 units a month and you are two months into production. Let us see how to apply the materials budget to this situation.

First, move the cursor to C2 and enter the product description as follows: **RACING CAR** Ⓔ. We want to see what the budget looks like for 1,000 cars. Assuming that it is February, you would move your cursor to C3 and enter **1000 ▼ FEBRUARY** Ⓔ.

We need to make room for the three parts that compose the car. Move your cursor to A10 and enter **/IR/IR** . We only need to insert two rows since we have one already in place. Now replicate a copy of row 9 into rows 10 and 11 so that the formulas we need are in place. Enter **/R BS B9. K9:B10.B11** Ⓔ **RNRRRRRRRR.**

To enter the names of the specific materials required, move your cursor to A9 and enter **WHEELS ▼ BUMPERS ▼ CHASSIS** Ⓔ.

The inventory numbers are optional and we will leave them out of our example. To enter them you would simply type the appropriate inventory codes into column B.

Move your cursor to C9 and enter the number of parts required for each finished car as follows: **4 ▼ 2 ▼ 1** Ⓔ. Notice that the budgeted usage

MATERIALS BUDGET

PRODUCT:
NUMBER OF UNITS:
MONTH:

****

MATERIAL	INVENTORY NUMBER	QUANTITY PER UNIT	BUDGETED USAGE	ACTUAL USAGE	DIFF.	VARIANCE	YEAR - TO - DATE BUDGET	ACTUAL	DIFF.	VARIANCE
			0		0	ERROR			0	ERROR
TOTAL			0	0	0	ERROR	0	0	0	ERROR

Figure 13-10

is automatically calculated. The budgeted usage is equal to the number of units that we entered in location C3 times the number of parts each requires.

The production department has provided the following table which shows the actual results for January and February racing car production:

	January Actual	February Actual	Year To Date Budget	Year To Date Actuals
Wheels	4,050	4,100	8,000	8,150
Bumpers	2,200	2,250	4,000	4,450
Chassis	1,030	1,020	2,000	2,050

Let us begin entering this information into the spread sheet. We start by entering in the actual material usage for February. Move your cursor to E9 and enter **4100 ▼ 2250 ▼ 1020 Ⓔ**. The difference and variance to budget for the month's production is automatically calculated. This brings us current on the monthly production performance.

To complete this spread sheet we enter the figures for the year-to-date budget and actual material usage. Move your cursor to H9 and enter **8000 ▼ 4000 ▼ 2000 ▶ 2050 ▲ 4450 ▲ 8150 Ⓔ**. The model automatically calculates the difference and variance for our year-to-date material usage. This model can be used on a monthly basis to monitor how successful the production management is using raw materials. The budget can help point out problems in the manufacturing process as well.

When you enter your own product information, you will follow the same steps as we did. First, make enough room to store each product component by inserting lines between the border rows. Next, replicate the formulas in these newly created blank lines. Finally, enter your budget and actual information into the sheet. The comparisons will be done for you.

The second budget we will examine is designed to control direct and indirect labor costs. Be sure you have saved a copy of your materials budget model and then enter **/CY** to clear the screen. The keystrokes for the labor budget can be found under LABORB. Once you have created or loaded this model your spread sheet should match Figure 13-11.

This budget is used in much the same way as our materials budget. Continuing with our racing car example, let us assume that there are three steps in the manufacture of the car. First, the parts are assembled, then the car is painted, and finally it is tested to insure it is securely put together. It takes ten minutes to assemble the car, five minutes to paint it, and two minutes to test it. We begin by entering the descriptive information into the model. Move your cursor to C2 and enter **FEBRUARY ▼**

MONTH:
PRODUCT:
NUMBER OF UNITS:

LABOR BUDGET

****

	STANDARD TIME	BUDGETED LABOR	ACTUAL LABOR	DIFF.	VARIANCE	YEAR – TO – DATE			
TASK						BUDGET	ACTUAL	DIFF.	VARIANCE
DIRECT:		0	0	0	ERROR	0	0	0	ERROR
TOTAL	0	0	0	0	ERROR	0	0	0	ERROR

****

	ATTRIBUTED TIME	BUDGETED LABOR	ACTUAL LABOR	DIFF.	VARIANCE	YEAR – TO – DATE			
TASK						BUDGET	ACTUAL	DIFF.	VARIANCE
INDIRECT:		0	0	0	ERROR	0	0	0	ERROR
TOTAL	0	0	0	0	ERROR	0	0	0	ERROR
TOTAL DIRECT AND INDIRECT	0	0	0	0	ERROR	0	0	0	ERROR

Figure 13-11

RACING♭CAR ▼ 1000 Ⓔ. As in the previous budget example, this signifies the product, date, and number of units on which the monthly budget will be based.

As we did before, we make room for the separate tasks by inserting rows between the border rows. Move your cursor to A11 and enter **/IR /IR**. Now replicate the formulas into place: **/R BS B10.K10:B11.B12 Ⓔ RNRRRRRRRR**. Note that the only "N" response is in the second position.

To enter the different tasks and their standard times, move your cursor to B10 and enter **ASSEMBLY ▼ PAINTING ▼ TESTING ▶ 2 ▲ 5 ▲ 10 Ⓔ**.

The actual labor figures can now be entered into this spread sheet as was done for the materials budget.

The second part of the model is used in the same way except that the labor figures will refer to indirect costs.

Once the data has been entered for both the direct and indirect sections, the total results can be seen at the bottom of the sheet.

Model II: Retailer's Budgets

This system of four related spread sheets monitors the margin of a retailer on a monthly basis. The system will keep you up to date on the profitability of your business. You will not have to wait until year-end to see if you are making any money.

We will begin with the first step in the margin budget—the receiving journal. If you have not read the first part of this chapter on the retailers' budgeting system, you should do so now. Load or type in the RJOURNAL model. It should look like Figure 13-12.

As the month passes and new stock is delivered, you record additions to stock. Each new line you insert represents information about a new delivery. We will illustrate the use of this model and the others in this section by examining how a shoe retailer might use these spread sheets.

To indicate that this receiving journal records January information, move your cursor to B4 and enter **JANUARY Ⓔ**.

Let us say that on January 3 our shoe store receives a delivery of stock from the Jones Shoe Company. The delivery is 12 pair of men's runners at a cost of $140. The invoice number is LL510 and the shipping charge comes to $20. The retail value of this shipment is $225. To enter this information into the receiving journal, move your cursor to A8 and enter **JAN♭3 ▶ JONES♭SHOE♭CO ▶ LL510 ▶ 140 ▶ 20 ▶▶ 225 Ⓔ**. Notice that your landed cost and markup are automatically calculated.

MONTHLY   RECEIVING   JOURNAL
****

FOR :

DATE	SUPPLIER	INVOICE #	INVOICE COST	TRANSPORTATION	LANDED COST	RETAIL	MARKUP
					0.00		ERROR
TOTAL:			0.00	0.00	0.00	0.00	ERROR

Figure 13-12

Budgeting 191

In order to keep a complete record of everything that happens to the inventory during the month, there are several other types of transactions that we need to record in our receiving journal. In fact, if our receiving journal is to do its job we need to record all the transactions that affect the value of our inventory. This information will be used later to help us keep track of the value of our total inventory on a monthly basis.

Suppose that a specific product has sold extremely well at a given price and you decide that you have underpriced the goods. For example, you might mark up five pair of gray women's pumps an additional $5 each. In this case, you will be adding to the retail value of your inventory.

To enter this additional markup into the journal, you must first make room between the dashed border lines. Move your cursor to A9 and enter /IR/IR/IR. We are inserting several lines here because we will need the extra space later. Now we enter the additional markup information by moving the cursor to A9 and entering **JAN∅10 ▸PARIS∅CO. ▸MARKUP∅5 ▸GRAY∅PUMPS ▸"$5∅EACH ▸▸25 Ⓔ**. Since labels are considered to be zero for calculation purposes, you can use the invoice, invoice cost, and transportation columns to record the description of your additional markup.

Another transaction that affects the value of your inventory is returns to suppliers. In this case we will need to subtract both the retail and the cost value of the merchandise from our inventory. Let us say that four pair of women's jogging shoes were delivered with defective soles. Suppose the order was from Runner's Incorporated and had a retail value of $80 and our cost was $55. We also paid $15 shipping charge. We would enter this information into our model by placing the cursor at A10 and entering **JAN∅12 ▸RUNNER'S∅INC. ▸A2323∅RET ▸-55 ▸-15 ▸▸-80 Ⓔ**. All the costs must be entered as negative numbers because the return reduces the retail and cost value of your inventory. The RET is added after the invoice number to signify that the merchandise was returned.

The final type of transaction that is recorded in our receiving journal is a supplier credit. Say that on January 14 you received a $50 credit from the Hot Foot Company, due to an incorrect charge on a previous invoice. This shipment has already been recorded in the receiving journal and appears in your inventory at cost and retail values. The credit will reduce only the cost of your inventory, so we would move the cursor to A11 and enter the credit transaction as follows: **JAN∅14 ▸HOT∅FOOT∅CO ▸ W510∅CR▸-50 Ⓔ**. The CR is added after the invoice number to remind us that this is a supplier credit.

We need to replicate the formulas that calculate landed cost and the markup into the rows we have just entered. To do this, enter the following keystrokes: **/R BS F8 Ⓔ F9.F11 Ⓔ RR /R BS H8 Ⓔ H9.H11 Ⓔ RRR**.

Once you have replicated the formulas into place, you will notice a markup is calculated for the supplier return, the credit, and the additional markup that appears in column H. These individual markups are not factored into the total markup shown at the bottom of the model but they are inaccurate. To remove them from the model, move your cursor to H9 and enter **0 ▾ 0 ▾ 0 Ⓔ**.

This completes the use of the receiving journal. If you keep it current, you will be able to see all the additions and reductions to the value of your inventory at both cost and retail for the month. This information will be used later in our margin budget.

The second step in assembling our margin budget is the discount register. This spread sheet will track all the changes in the value of your inventory directly related to discounts. First, be sure you have a saved copy of the receiving journal. Then enter **/CY** to clear the screen. You can now enter or load the discount register which appears under the title DISCOUNT. It should look like Figure 13-13.

There are only two types of transactions that you enter on this sheet. You either mark down an item or you cancel a markdown returning the price to its original value. First enter the month by moving your cursor to B3 and typing **JANUARY Ⓔ**.

Suppose that on January 15 we decided that some slow-moving stock must be discounted to help clear the way for new inventory. Perhaps it was during happy hour at the Shoe Dealers' Trade Show in Cincinnati. Could that have been when our shoe buyer decided to go with the three pairs of simulated red lizard skin pumps? Well business is a learning experience and now it's time to see if our retailer can get some of this stuff cleared out of the store. Three pairs of shoes originally priced at $110 each will be marked down to $60. Moving the cursor to A7 we would make the following entries in our discount register: **JAN▸15 ▸RED▸LIZARD ▸PUMPS▸3▸ARTISTIC▸SHOES▸110▸60 Ⓔ**. The difference in price and the total reduction in inventory due to the markdown are automatically calculated in the last two columns of the sheet.

On the next day the retailer decides that he does not want the store looking like a bargain basement. He decides to take the five pair of hiking boots that had been on special and mark them back up to regular price. To add this to the spread sheet, you first insert a new row between the border rows by moving your cursor into row 8 and entering **/IR**. Now replicate the formulas with the following keystrokes: **/R BS C7.H7:C8 Ⓔ RRRR** . Next, you would move the cursor to A8 and enter **JAN▸16 ▸HIKING▸BOOTS▸5▸"▸WILD▸BOOTS▸INC▸50▸65 Ⓔ**. The discount spread sheet automatically shows the canceled markdown by showing a reduction in inventory value.

DISCOUNT REGISTER
****

FOR:

DATE	ITEM	QUANTITY	SUPPLIER	OLD PRICE	NEW PRICE	DIFFERENCE	EXTENSION	COMMENTS
						0.00	0.00	

TOTAL: 0.00

Figure 13-13

By keeping the discount register up to date, you will have a record of all the stock you have had to discount during the month. We will need this information to help track our gross margin on a monthly basis. This spread sheet can also help you spot suppliers whose goods often need to be discounted.

We can now move on to the next step in the margin budget. We will use the information from the discount register and the receiving journal to keep a running tally of our inventory.

Be sure you have a copy of the discount register saved and enter /**CY** to clear the screen. The keystrokes for the next spread sheet are stored under TALLY. After loading the sheet or typing it in, your sheet should look like Figure 13-14.

Let us examine this model in detail. Down column A are labels for the 12 months. Each month begins with an opening inventory. Purchases for the month are added to this figure and then sales, discounts, and shrinkage are deducted. You end up with the opening inventory for the next month. This process is repeated each month to give you an ongoing portrait of your inventory. The procedure is done for inventory at cost and retail. The maintained cost percentage is also calculated each month, reflecting the current profit represented by your inventory.

Let us continue with our shoe store example and see how the inventory tally sheet works in practice. Suppose a physical inventory was taken on January 1. The retail value of the inventory turned out to be $1.4 million and the value at cost, $800,000. We begin by moving our cursor to C6 and entering the opening inventory as follows: **800000 ▶ 1400000 Ⓔ**. If you look at E6, you will see the maintained cost percentage of your inventory is automatically displayed. Let us assume that during January there were $20,000 worth of shoes purchased at cost, and the recorded retail value of this new inventory was $30,000. Where would this information come from? It can be read off the bottom line of the receiving journal. At the end of the month this spread sheet will tell us the net additions that were made to the inventory at cost and retail. To enter this information into the model, move your cursor to C7 and enter **20000 ▶ 30000 Ⓔ**.

The next figures we need to enter are for the monthly sales at retail and cost. From the sales slips, let us assume that the shoe store retail sales for January were $15,000. Move your cursor to D8 and enter **15000 Ⓔ**. The cost equivalent automatically appears in column C.

The formula below shows how retail sales are converted to their approximate equivalent in sales at cost.

Sales at Cost = Retail Sales*
Maintained Cost %

```
                        INVENTORY  TALLY
                        **********************
                                                    MAINTAINED
                                      COST   RETAIL   COST %
JANUARY 1
OPENING     INVENTORY                                  ERROR
    ADD:    PURCHASES
    LESS:   SALES       ERROR
            DISCOUNTS   ERROR
            SHRINKAGE   ERROR
FEBRUARY 1
OPENING     INVENTORY   ERROR    0             ERROR
    ADD:    PURCHASES
    LESS:   SALES       ERROR
            DISCOUNTS   ERROR
            SHRINKAGE   ERROR
MARCH 1
OPENING     INVENTORY   ERROR    0             ERROR
    ADD:    PURCHASES
    LESS:   SALES       ERROR
            DISCOUNTS   ERROR
            SHRINKAGE   ERROR
APRIL 1
OPENING     INVENTORY   ERROR    0             ERROR
    ADD:    PURCHASES
    LESS:   SALES       ERROR
            DISCOUNTS   ERROR
            SHRINKAGE   ERROR
MAY 1
OPENING     INVENTORY   ERROR    0             ERROR
    ADD:    PURCHASES
    LESS:   SALES       ERROR
            DISCOUNTS   ERROR
            SHRINKAGE   ERROR
JUNE 1
OPENING     INVENTORY   ERROR    0             ERROR
    ADD:    PURCHASES
    LESS:   SALES       ERROR
            DISCOUNTS   ERROR
            SHRINKAGE   ERROR
JULY 1
OPENING     INVENTORY   ERROR    0             ERROR
    ADD:    PURCHASES
    LESS:   SALES       ERROR
            DISCOUNTS   ERROR
            SHRINKAGE   ERROR
AUGUST 1
OPENING     INVENTORY   ERROR    0             ERROR
    ADD:    PURCHASES
    LESS:   SALES       ERROR
            DISCOUNTS   ERROR
            SHRINKAGE   ERROR
SEPTEMBER 1
OPENING     INVENTORY   ERROR    0             ERROR
    ADD:    PURCHASES
    LESS:   SALES       ERROR
            DISCOUNTS   ERROR
            SHRINKAGE   ERROR
OCTOBER 1
OPENING     INVENTORY   ERROR    0             ERROR
    ADD:    PURCHASES
    LESS:   SALES       ERROR
            DISCOUNTS   ERROR
            SHRINKAGE   ERROR
NOVEMBER 1
OPENING     INVENTORY   ERROR    0             ERROR
    ADD:    PURCHASES
    LESS:   SALES       ERROR
            DISCOUNTS   ERROR
            SHRINKAGE   ERROR
DECEMBER
OPENING     INVENTORY   ERROR    0             ERROR
    ADD:    PURCHASES
    LESS:   SALES       ERROR
            DISCOUNTS   ERROR
            SHRINKAGE   ERROR
```

Figure 13-14

A retail value is converted to its approximate cost equivalent by multiplying it by the maintained cost percentage. This cost percentage is calculated using the cost and retail value of the entire inventory including purchases.

Next, we get the total month's discounts at retail from the total line of our discount register. Suppose this turned out to be $500. Move your cursor to D9 and enter **500** Ⓔ. This allows the discounts at cost to automatically be displayed. The formula used to convert retail to cost is the same as the one used above.

The final information we need to enter into the inventory tally sheet is the estimated reduction in inventory at cost and retail due to shrinkage. Since shrinkage can only be known after a physical inventory is taken, we will have to estimate its amount. Let us assume shrinkage is roughly 1 percent of monthly sales. Move your cursor to D10 and enter **150** Ⓔ for the shrinkage estimate. Its cost equivalent is automatically displayed in C10.

This completes the changes in inventory for January. The new opening balance for February 1 is automatically calculated as is the new maintained markup.

We can now proceed to our final spread sheet in the margin budget system.

Be sure you have saved a copy of the inventory tally model. After you have done so, enter **/CY** to clear the screen.

The keystrokes for the budget margin model can be found under the title MARGIN. After typing in or loading the model from disk, check that your sheet matches the packed model in Figure 13-15.

To use this sheet you enter the net sales, cost of goods sold, discounts, and shrinkage for the month. The gross margin and percent margin is calculated for you. You can also see the difference in results between the current year and the previous year.

The table below shows the January results for our shoe retailer for this year and last year.

	Last Year	This Year
Sales	12,000	15,000
COGS	5,500	6,420
Discounts	800	500
Shrinkage	120	150

You can enter this information into the model by moving your cursor to C5 and entering **12000▶15000 ▼ 6420◀5500 ▼ 800▶500 ▼ 150◀ 120** Ⓔ.

If you have entered this information correctly, you should see that the gross margin has increased by $2,350, which is an increase of 42

GROSS MARGIN BUDGET

		LAST YEAR	THIS YEAR	DIFFERENCE	% CHANGE
JANUARY	NET SALES			0	ERROR
	C.O.G.S			0	ERROR
	DISCOUNTS			0	ERROR
	SHRINKAGE			0	ERROR
	GROSS MARGIN	0	0	0	ERROR
	% MARGIN	ERROR	ERROR	ERROR	ERROR
FEBRUARY	NET SALES			0	ERROR
	C.O.G.S			0	ERROR
	DISCOUNTS			0	ERROR
	SHRINKAGE			0	ERROR
	GROSS MARGIN	0	0	0	ERROR
	% MARGIN	ERROR	ERROR	ERROR	ERROR
MARCH	NET SALES			0	ERROR
	C.O.G.S			0	ERROR
	DISCOUNTS			0	ERROR
	SHRINKAGE			0	ERROR
	GROSS MARGIN	0	0	0	ERROR
	% MARGIN	ERROR	ERROR	ERROR	ERROR
APRIL	NET SALES			0	ERROR
	C.O.G.S			0	ERROR
	DISCOUNTS			0	ERROR
	SHRINKAGE			0	ERROR
	GROSS MARGIN	0	0	0	ERROR
	% MARGIN	ERROR	ERROR	ERROR	ERROR
MAY	NET SALES			0	ERROR
	C.O.G.S			0	ERROR
	DISCOUNTS			0	ERROR
	SHRINKAGE			0	ERROR
	GROSS MARGIN	0	0	0	ERROR
	% MARGIN	ERROR	ERROR	ERROR	ERROR
JUNE	NET SALES			0	ERROR
	C.O.G.S			0	ERROR
	DISCOUNTS			0	ERROR
	SHRINKAGE			0	ERROR
	GROSS MARGIN	0	0	0	ERROR
	% MARGIN	ERROR	ERROR	ERROR	ERROR

Figure 13-15

percent over last year. Similarly, the percentage of margin to sales has increased 14 percent over last year. This improvement in margin could be due to better purchasing, which has resulted in less need to discount.

Using these four models on a monthly basis keeps you current on the profitability of your business. The inventory tally sheet and the

198   Applications and Models

	NET SALES			0	ERROR
	C.O.G.S			0	ERROR
JULY	DISCOUNTS			0	ERROR
	SHRINKAGE			0	ERROR
	GROSS MARGIN	0	0	0	ERROR
	% MARGIN	ERROR	ERROR	ERROR	ERROR
	NET SALES			0	ERROR
	C.O.G.S			0	ERROR
AUGUST	DISCOUNTS			0	ERROR
	SHRINKAGE			0	ERROR
	GROSS MARGIN	0	0	0	ERROR
	% MARGIN	ERROR	ERROR	ERROR	ERROR
	NET SALES			0	ERROR
	C.O.G.S			0	ERROR
SEPTEMBER	DISCOUNTS			0	ERROR
	SHRINKAGE			0	ERROR
	GROSS MARGIN	0	0	0	ERROR
	% MARGIN	ERROR	ERROR	ERROR	ERROR
	NET SALES			0	ERROR
	C.O.G.S			0	ERROR
OCTOBER	DISCOUNTS			0	ERROR
	SHRINKAGE			0	ERROR
	GROSS MARGIN	0	0	0	ERROR
	% MARGIN	ERROR	ERROR	ERROR	ERROR
	NET SALES			0	ERROR
	C.O.G.S			0	ERROR
NOVEMBER	DISCOUNTS			0	ERROR
	SHRINKAGE			0	ERROR
	GROSS MARGIN	0	0	0	ERROR
	% MARGIN	ERROR	ERROR	ERROR	ERROR
	NET SALES			0	ERROR
	C.O.G.S			0	ERROR
DECEMBER	DISCOUNTS			0	ERROR
	SHRINKAGE			0	ERROR
	GROSS MARGIN	0	0	0	ERROR
	% MARGIN	ERROR	ERROR	ERROR	ERROR

Figure 13-15 (cont'd)

margin budget watch for erosion of profits. If you do have a problem, the receiving journal and discount register can help you locate the cause. The receiving journal can tell you if you are pricing your inventory correctly. The discount register will tell you how much profit you are losing through markdowns. It can also point out if there are any suppliers that habitually end up on your discount register. As a group, these models help you protect your business margin and let you manage for greater profit.

FURTHER READINGS

Boer, Germain. *Direct Cost and Contribution Accounting.* New York: John Wiley and Sons, 1974.

Simini, Joseph P. *Cost Accounting Concepts for NonFinancial Executives.* New York: Amacom, 1976.

Sweeny, Allen, and Wisner, John N., Jr. *Budgeting for NonFinancial Executives.* New York: Amacom, 1975.

Chapter 14

Cash Management

The key to successful cash management is to always have cash when you need it, but to never have too much on hand. If you have too little cash, you risk angering your creditors. Idle cash, on the other hand, earns nothing until you invest it, so too much cash means that your profits are less than they could be. In this chapter we will design two VisiCalc spread sheets that will help you walk this financial tightrope and find your own efficient level of operating cash.

Cash is like any other asset, even though it occupies a special place in many of our hearts. Improved control, faster turnover, and more efficient use result in added profits.

Improved cash control begins with understanding how cash moves in and out of your business. Most companies have a characteristic cash flow pattern. Retailers often record 40-60 percent of their sales in the last quarter of the year. Suppliers of building materials record their greatest shipments in the spring. While some businesses have a much more predictable cash cycle than others, most can benefit from a closer examination of their cash cycle. In baseball, coaches keep a "Book" which records where opposing batters tend to hit the ball. By using the book during the game a coach can place his fielders in the areas where a batter is most likely to hit. Historical patterns are no guarantee of success, but they often can supply a competitive edge.

We will be using VisiCalc to track historic revenue and expense patterns. This will help characterize the historic cash flow picture, making it easier to predict future cash requirements. Knowing when and how much cash you require helps to minimize idle cash while helping you avoid panic cash shortages. This can supply you with a competitive edge of your own.

There are many ways a business benefits from cash flow forecasts. Perhaps the most important benefit is that proper cash planning keeps you from running out of cash. In the short-term, this means having enough money for payrolls, rent, interest payments, and other operating necessities.

By foreseeing future cash requirements, the forecast helps you plan your borrowing requirements. This can actually help you get the money you need. Most bankers, when approached by businesses for interim financing, react favorably when greeted with a well-thought-out cash plan. From the cash plan the potential lender will be able to see where the loan will be used and how it will be repaid. More important, the lender will see that he is dealing with a business person who is a careful planner. This can not only help you get the funds you need, but also help improve the terms and reduce the cost of the loan.

In the past, an effective loan presentation often required a management consultant or accountant. These professionals have access to computer-generated cash flows and other tools which help dress up a loan application. Now you can have the advantages of these reports by using VisiCalc and your own computer. The cash flow models we develop in this chapter could be used to help you get your next loan.

Another benefit gained from short-term cash forecasting is better management of your excess cash. The challenge is to make the most efficient use of your excess cash. In order to choose the best short-term investments, you need to know how much money you have to invest and how long it can stay invested. This allows the yield from your short-term investments to be as large as possible given your expected cash flow.

There are two methods commonly used to forecast future cash needs. The first and simplest method uses previous cash flow patterns to project future cash needs. This method, called the Receipts and Disbursements Method, is used to forecast cash requirements for periods of up to one year. To project cash requirements, past receipts and disbursements are totaled and these totals are used as a basis for cash projections. The second method we will discuss is the Adjusted Net Income Method. This tool is used to project cash flows over periods of a year or more. The Adjusted Net Income Method begins with projections of expected income, and then adjusts this level of income to reflect the results of both operating and nonoperating factors. This method is also referred to as the Source and Application of Funds Method. We will discuss both of these methods in detail and examine the advantages and disadvantages of each. Two VisiCalc spread sheets will be built that will allow you to apply both of these forecasting methods to your specific business.

The Cash Flow or Receipts and Disbursement Method is the most commonly used cash forecasting method. It is the easiest to use and understand, and it allows you to exercise tight control over your short-term cash needs.

You begin by collecting historic expense and receipt information. That means looking through your journal entries or digging through your records shoe box, whichever more closely fits. Let us assume that a monthly cash flow projection is required. In this case you would go back over the preceding four to six months and examine the receipts and disbursements made during this period. Depending on the type of business you have, you may find that you need to collect more historic information. If your business is growing rapidly, or if it has large seasonal fluctuations, you may also have to analyze the cash forecast either by season or by quarter. The object of the exercise is to characterize the historic ebb and flow of cash through your business.

Periodic expenses will be easy to project. Items such as rent, utilities, insurance, and other types of expenses are easy to account for because they are paid regularly, and changes in these expenses are usually known in advance. Unfortunately, not all of our expense items are as simple to project. Two factors common to most businesses are difficult to forecast: collections and material costs.

Collections are difficult to project because client payment patterns can fluctuate at random due to a variety of reasons. For example, as interest rates increase collections tend to slow because clients try to keep their own funds earning interest for as long as possible. General business conditions also play an important role in collection periods. Lean times tend to lengthen collection periods, while a buoyant business climate tends to speed up collections. It is not an easy task to forecast collections, yet a useful cash flow needs an accurate forecast of collections.

The simplest approach to projecting collections is to gather recent data on collections and project it forward. Suppose that the collections have averaged $100,000 a month over the last three months, and sales are expected to remain roughly the same over the next month or two. You could then forecast collections for the next 30 days at $100,000. This is fine for businesses that are relatively stable, but it will not work for companies that are growing rapidly or that have highly seasonal sales patterns. For these businesses, adjustments must be made to reflect their specific sales and collections patterns.

In many cases forecasts of collections will require a group effort, combining management from the marketing and finance departments. Each of these managers holds an important piece of the collections puzzle. The finance department knows the amount of outstanding credit. The marketing department projects sales. Together they have access to the information needed to create a reasonable collections forecast.

If a company has diverse operating sites, the local credit or finance manager will usually be responsible for forwarding collection estimates to headquarters. These estimates are then consolidated into the complete collections picture for the company.

Some companies forecast collections on an individual account basis. This is particularly helpful when a company has a small number of clients which account for a large percentage of sales. When a company has too many accounts to forecast on an individual basis, one common method to use is to group accounts by business type. Companies use account designations such as "trade" or "government" for this purpose. The projections can then be broken down for each type of client making the projected collections more accurate.

The second area that complicates cash flow projections involves the cost of materials. Materials can be taken in the broader sense to include services as well.

Your costs of labor, raw materials, and energy are constantly fluctuating, and it seems that they fluctuate up a lot more often than down. Trying to forecast these costs is difficult. Many changes in price levels are impossible to predict. Those due to shortages, strikes, or changes in government policy are beyond your control. Nevertheless, we need to take our best educated guess about future material costs if we want to create a realistic cash flow.

The job of estimating materials cost is made easier if it is divided into smaller parts. First, the sales forecast is used to prepare a detailed analysis of the materials and labor required to meet the projected product demand. Each of these expenses is then broken down and each component estimated individually. Your recent payment history can help estimate these costs.

Given the difficulty of projecting costs, the cash flow forecast should be in a form that can easily be changed to reflect new price levels. VisiCalc is particularly good at helping us cope with these types of changes. By building flexible models we can quickly change our estimates to reflect the effects of constantly changing price levels on the profitability of our business.

The Receipts and Disbursements Method is used when tight cash control and a detailed forecast are desired. After all, this forecast uses information from your own books so it should create a complete picture. There can be problems, however, when applying this method directly to a rapidly growing business or to one that has strong seasonal elements in its cash flow. If your company falls into one of these categories, you will have to make some changes to the standard receipts and disbursements approach. Here, your skill as an estimator will have a major impact on the accuracy of a forecast, because the past is not necessarily a reliable guide. Our Receipts and Disbursements model contains a forecast versus actual element which lets you keep track of how correct your estimates have been. This feedback can make you a better forecaster, especially where these "difficult-to-forecast" categories are concerned.

A major weakness of the Receipts and Disbursements Method is that it does not take into account changes in receivables, debt, inventory levels, or other noncash items. As a result, while the Receipts and Disbursements Method gives an excellent short-term view of cash flow, the big picture can be missed. For example, suppose that the interest rates rise. Your collections will slow down because people will try to hold their cash as long as possible. Even longer than usual! The collection receipts will only hint at this slowing of collection rates. The problem occurs after six to eight months of slow collections. Your projection of accounts receivable becomes too low. The decrease in collections slowly accumulates and all of a sudden will shout for attention. This could cause you to be left embarrassingly short of cash. Similarly, if sales slow you may have more and more cash tied up in slow-moving inventory because production will keep piling goods higher and higher. The decrease in collections from slowed sales will increase your need for cash, but it will not be immediately apparent from your Receipts and Disbursements Forecast where you need to exercise better control.

The second cash forecasting method we will discuss, the Adjusted Net Income Method, will help us guard against this problem. This cash projection technique reflects changes in the assets that make up your working capital, allowing your cash flow forecast to reflect nonoperating factors.

The first step in using the Adjusted Net Income Method is to forecast future income. You can do this by examining historical sales and expense trends and projecting these into the coming period. Once the level has been set, you then adjust it in two ways. First, all noncash expenses are identified. These noncash expenses include depreciation, amortization, and deferred tax and can be added back into your forecast as sources of cash, since you do not pay out cash for these expenses. The second set of adjustments comes from nonoperating factors such as capital expenditures and changes in working capital items such as inventories or receivables and debt repayments.

This method of forecasting is usually used by large companies and is based on converting accounting data from an accrual to a cash basis. If this sounds too complex, then you are probably fine confining your cash forecasts to the Receipts and Disbursements Method discussed above.

Due to the scope of the net income approach, it can be used to forecast cash requirements for any period ranging from one to twenty years.

This method has the advantage of showing a comprehensive picture of a company's total cash position. This is very useful as a base for longer-range planning, but it is only useful if you are keeping accounting records and producing regular financial statements. The Receipts and Disbursements Method captures all the detail needed for businesses that do not go to this expense. It may be all that is required for short-term forecasts of cash flows, provided no major changes to the business are anticipated over the forecast period.

A company can make good use of both these cash forecasting techniques. They complement each other, one offering a good look at short-term needs while the other provides a long-term view of cash needs. Using both methods together has another advantage; each serves as a way to check on the accuracy of the other.

Long-range cash forecasting differs substantially from the short-term methods we have discussed so far. Long-term plans such as major business expansion through merger and acquisition, new product development, purchase of new plant and equipment, and other capital-intensive projects need to be considered. Unlike the short-term systems which reveal specific detail, the long-term forecast attempts to show general cash requirements for the company over the next three to five years. Many companies use forecasts for periods of ten years or longer. It is no wonder that many executives refer to the exercise of long-term forecasting as "crystal balling."

One major benefit of long-range cash planning is that it helps to control major borrowing. A cash plan will show how much money is required, how much cash a company will internally generate to cover the borrowing over the loan period and how long it will take to repay the loan. This type of analysis is not only necessary for successful planning, but as we saw in the case of short-term financing, it increases the probability of getting the loan and may help you get a more favorable rate.

While the benefits of long-range cash forecasting are important, the level of difficulty involved in looking three or five years into the future should not be minimized. Suppose that several years ago you were asked to look into the future. Would you have foreseen problems with nuclear power, the explosive growth of the microcomputer industry, or the problems faced by car manufacturers? The long-range forecaster has to think about future changes in consumer tastes, possible interest rate levels, government regulations, and the effects of competition, to name only a few key factors. Not an enviable task.

Many forecasters use computers to help with this formidable task. By assessing more data than previously possible and analyzing hundreds of different future scenarios, the computer has helped deliver forecasting from the realm of the witch doctor's tent into the executive's office.

For some managers, computer-aided forecasts have an aura of infallibility. The principle of GIGO (garbage in, garbage out) should be understood by all managers who find themselves confronted with reams of computer forecasts. In the final analysis all projections are a product of human judgment. Someone decides which forecasting methods to use, which data to examine, and how to display the final results. Erroneous judgment means erroneous results, even if they shine forcefully out of a computer terminal or appear solemnly arrayed in the rows and columns of a management consultant's report.

In spite of the difficulties and potential dangers, most companies project their cash needs over a long term.

When you start looking at how you manage cash, you will begin to see how different areas of your business affect how efficiently you can control company cash. For example, the way you handle your inventories, collections, and payables will have a major effect on how well your cash management goals are achieved. We will briefly discuss some of these areas and how they can help you manage cash.

An average of 30-40 percent of an industry's total assets are carried in inventories. The way you manage inventories can have a profound effect on your cash situation. With careful sales forecasting you can avoid overproduction and free up cash that would normally have been used to carry excess inventory.

The way you collect receivables is also an important part of your cash management program. Some companies use special methods to reduce the time it takes cash to travel from the customer's bank into the corporate account. From the time a customer writes a check to when the check is actually charged against the customer's account, the check is said to "float." Companies try to reduce float. The time that a check spends in the mail is usually the major contributor to float. Another contributor is the time the bank takes to process the check once it has been received.

One way companies reduce mail float is through the use of a lock box. The customer sends his checks to a locked post office box that is located in the area of the company's bank. The bank sends out staff periodically to empty the box and to deposit the checks in the corporate account. In some cases, when the dollar amounts are large enough, the box may be emptied several times a day.

Another way companies speed up collections is to use regional banks for deposits in the area where the collection occurs. These deposits are then forwarded to a central bank by electronic funds transfer. This allows the company to use the bank's extensive branch network to improve collection speeds.

Better control of payables is another way to improve cash management. The most direct way to improve results is to take advantage of discounts when they are offered by your suppliers. This may seem obvious, but if the company has a large, decentralized operation it is hard to insure that all the purchasing officers take advantage of discounts. Often these regional managers would rather hold cash than pay to receive discounts.

Centralizing funds can also help increase payables efficiency. If a company has various operating locations, pooling money at a central site can improve cash management. This avoids large sums of cash being tied up in a large number of remote checking accounts.

Your cash management objectives can be affected by indirect factors such as inventories, collections, and payables. While the ways these areas affect your cash levels are not as obvious as the amount of cash you keep in a checking account, they need to be considered when planning your overall cash management strategy.

SUMMARY

Improving the way you manage cash depends on knowing how much money you need and when you need it. You start by examining your business's historic cash flow patterns. The Receipts and Disbursements Method helps you do this by examining historic cash and expense patterns. This short-term forecasting method lets you spot periods of cash surplus or shortage and take necessary action. You can plan short-term borrowing to cover shortages or invest funds if there is a surplus. For most small- to medium-size businesses, this simple method can handle your cash forecasting needs.

To get an overview of cash demand over a longer period of time you can use the Adjusted Net Income Method of cash forecasting. This Method projects the sources and the applications of funds, both cash and noncash. This method is necessary for larger companies that have sums of money allocated to depreciation, depletion, amortization, deferred tax, and other noncash accounts.

These two forecasting methods combine to give both a long-term and short-term view of cash needs. The difficulty of looking several years into the future cannot be minimized, and we need to be on guard against the air of infallibility that computers can lend to even the most absurd conclusions.

Once you start watching your cash flow, you will begin to notice how different parts of your business affect cash levels. Efficient cash management depends on how you collect from your customers, how you pay your suppliers, and how well you manage your inventories. Your total cash management program will depend on many interrelated factors.

THE MODELS

The two models discussed in this section are designed to help you forecast your cash requirements. The first model uses the Receipts and Disbursements Method as a short-term cash forecasting tool. It is the simpler of the methods to use and lets you project your cash needs in detail. For most small- to medium-sized businesses this model will cover your cash forecasting needs. The second model uses the Adjusted Net Income approach to cash forecasting. This method forecasts cash needs over the long-term and does not offer the detail that the Receipts and Disbursements Method provides. It is usually used by larger companies who want an overview of corporate cash requirements several years into the future.

Model I: Receipts and Disbursements Cash Forecast

The keystrokes for this spread sheet are in the appendix under RANDD. If you key in the spread sheet, be sure to save it under this name before proceeding further. If you have the disk, you can load the model directly using the name RANDD. Either way, your screen should contain the spread sheet shown in Figure 14-1.

Looking across the top of the spread sheet you see that there are three columns labeled FORECAST, ACTUAL, and %VARIANCE. If you want to forecast cash on a monthly basis, then one quarter of forecasts will fit on each spread sheet. If you need to forecast weekly cash needs, you can store three weeks of forecasts on each sheet. You are free to use this model over any time period you require. In our current example we will be doing a quarterly cash forecast.

You begin by entering your cash projections in the FORECAST column. The sheet records your cash forecasts for the various receipt and

RECEIPTS & DISBURSEMENTS FORECAST
****

	FORECAST	ACTUAL	%VARIANCE	FORECAST	ACTUAL	%VARIANCE	FORECAST	ACTUAL	%VARIANCE
BEGINNING BAL									
CASH	0.00	NA	NA	0.00	NA	NA	0.00	NA	NA
MARKETABLE SE	0.00	NA	NA	0.00	NA	NA	0.00	NA	NA
TOTAL	0.00	NA	NA	0.00	NA	NA	0.00	NA	NA
CASH RECEIPTS									
CASH SALES	0.00	NA	NA	0.00	NA	NA	0.00	NA	NA
A/R COLLECTIO	0.00	NA	NA	0.00	NA	NA	0.00	NA	NA
SALE OF FIXED	0.00	NA	NA	0.00	NA	NA	0.00	NA	NA
INVESTMENT IN	0.00	NA	NA	0.00	NA	NA	0.00	NA	NA
OTHER	0.00	NA	NA	0.00	NA	NA	0.00	NA	NA
TOTAL	0.00	NA	NA	0.00	NA	NA	0.00	NA	NA
CASH DISBURSE									
PAYROLL	0.00	NA	NA	0.00	NA	NA	0.00	NA	NA
TAXES PAID	0.00	NA	NA	0.00	NA	NA	0.00	NA	NA
SUPPLIER INVO	0.00	NA	NA	0.00	NA	NA	0.00	NA	NA
OPERATING EXP	0.00	NA	NA	0.00	NA	NA	0.00	NA	NA
INTEREST PAYM	0.00	NA	NA	0.00	NA	NA	0.00	NA	NA
ADVERTISING	0.00	NA	NA	0.00	NA	NA	0.00	NA	NA
DEBT REPAYMEN	0.00	NA	NA	0.00	NA	NA	0.00	NA	NA
INSURANCE	0.00	NA	NA	0.00	NA	NA	0.00	NA	NA
DIVIDENDS	0.00	NA	NA	0.00	NA	NA	0.00	NA	NA
CAPITAL EXPEN	0.00	NA	NA	0.00	NA	NA	0.00	NA	NA
OTHER	0.00	NA	NA	0.00	NA	NA	0.00	NA	NA
TOTAL	0.00	NA	NA	0.00	NA	NA	0.00	NA	NA
ENDING BALANC									
OPENING CASH	0.00	NA	NA	0.00	NA	NA	0.00	NA	NA
PLUS RECEIPTS	0.00	NA	NA	0.00	NA	NA	0.00	NA	NA
LESS DISBURSE	0.00	NA	NA	0.00	NA	NA	0.00	NA	NA
NET CHANGE	0.00	NA	NA	0.00	NA	NA	0.00	NA	NA

Figure 14-1

disbursement categories. Later, when you know what the actual cash requirements were for the forecast period, you enter these results in the ACTUAL column. VisiCalc automatically reports the percentage that your estimates differed from your actual cash needs. The formula used for this calculation is:

$$\% \text{ Variance} = (\text{Actual} - \text{Forecast})/\text{Forecast}$$

This allows you to monitor how accurate your cash projections have been in the past. By keeping this spread sheet up to date you will have a record of your cash forecasts and an analysis of how far the predicted levels were from the actual levels. This will help you to refine your cash forecasts, making you a better manager.

The formula used to calculate %VARIANCE is the reason that NA appears down many of the columns in the empty model. If this were not done, the formulas that have a zero divide in the %VARIANCE column would display ERROR in each location. By using the @NA we avoid having to look at the error message while we wait to enter data in the ACTUAL column. Once you have entered all your actual as well as forecast data the NAs will disappear.

The sheet is divided into four different areas: BEGINNING BALANCE, CASH RECEIPTS, CASH DISBURSEMENTS, and ENDING BALANCE. Each of these areas is used to record a different element of your cash forecast.

You start by collecting the records of past receipts and disbursements. This lets you see your business's cash history. You should go back far enough so that any significant cash patterns in your business will show up. Separate the receipts and disbursements and then categorize them by type.

Once you have done this preliminary work, you can start entering your information into the sheet. We will begin by looking at the top of the sheet which contains the opening cash balance information.

To enter your forecast for the beginning cash balance, move your cursor to B8 and type in the appropriate amount. Suppose that you forecast an opening cash balance of $10,000. You would enter this amount directly into B8. With your cursor at B8, enter **10000 Ⓔ**.

What about marketable securities? Suppose that you do not have any. You can delete this line by placing your cursor anywhere in line 9 and entering **/DR**. This will not affect any of our stored formulas because we use the border rows to mark the beginning and ending ranges of our functions. If you do have marketable securities, you would enter an appropriate amount in B9, but for now, delete the row.

Let us move on to the receipts section of the quarterly cash forecast. You can move your cursor down the FORECAST column and enter the forecast amounts for the various receipt categories. The total receipts will be calculated for you. As in the example we just completed you go down the forecast column one category at a time and enter amounts where appropriate and delete the rows you do not need. If you need more categories than the model has in this section, you have two options. You can move your cursor over a category label that you do not need and simply change the name, or you can insert a new row and replicate an adjacent row into the vacant row. You need to do this if you run out of space in a given section.

In our current example, suppose that you expect to receive $15,000 from cash sales, and collect $20,000 from your credit customers during the first quarter. To enter this forecast information, move your cursor to B15 and enter **15000** ▼ **20000** Ⓔ. Now, since these are all the sources of cash, we need to delete all the other rows in the cash receipts section. Move your cursor into row 17 and enter **/DR/DR/DR**. Your cursor should now be on the border row and the total receipts, $35,000, should appear below your cursor.

As you use this model, you must delete the lines for which you have no forecast data. If these empty lines are left in place, the NAs contained at various locations in the line would propagate through the model, obscuring the other calculations.

You can see that by going down the FORECAST column you can enter your cash projections for the various categories. To keep this example simple we will only complete the BEGINNING BALANCE and CASH RECEIPTS sections of this model. You handle the CASH DISBURSEMENTS section in the same way.

If you need to insert a new row in any of the model sections, you use two steps. First, you insert a new row using the /IR command. Next, you replicate a nearby row into the empty row that you have just created. The keystrokes that accomplish this are /R BS B#.J#:B## Ⓔ RRRRRRRRR. The single "#" is filled in by the source row number while the "##" represents the target row number.

Once you have entered your projections for cash in and cash out of your business and deleted the lines that do not apply to you, the ENDING BALANCE section is used. This section summarizes the bottom line results of your cash forecast. By examining this last section you can see the impact of your cash projections.

Your projected cash requirements can be used as a base for many of your cash management decisions. You can spot short-term borrowing needs if you are short of cash, or plan short-term investments if you are forecasting a cash surplus.

When you know the actual results for the forecast period you can go back and update the cash forecast model with actual cash data. Here, the model will really help you by letting you know how good or bad your forecast was and by flagging items that require attention.

Suppose that after a month has passed you discover that your period opening balance was actually $11,500, your cash sales were $18,000, and your collections were $16,000. You enter these results by moving your cursor to C8 and entering **11500 ⓔ >C15 ⓔ 18000 ▼ 16000 ⓔ**. The % VARIANCE displays how far off your forecast was.

You can go through this forecast exercise each quarter, month, or week, and gradually you will build up an historic track record of cash forecasts. You will slowly sharpen your cash forecasting skills and make better use of your cash resources.

Model II: Adjusted Net Income Forecast

This forecast is used to get a general overview of your company's cash needs one or more years into the future. Larger companies will usually use this type of cash projection.

The model is stored under the name SANDAP. With VisiCalc loaded you can enter the keystrokes for this model found in the appendix. If you have the model disk, you can load it directly. Be sure you keep an empty copy of this model for future use. It should look like Figure 14-2.

This model is divided into three sections: the sources of funds, the uses of funds, and a summary of the operating cash results.

To use this model, move your cursor to the appropriate row and column and enter your projected sources and uses of funds. VisiCalc lets you see how this will affect your operating cash requirements.

This model is particularly easy to use since you need only move your cursor to the specific month and enter the projected source or use of funds. For example, to enter forecast net income for January, you move your cursor across row 8 to column C and enter the expected amount. By proceeding across the row you can enter the forecast amounts for the other months. If you find that a monthly basis is an inappropriate time frame to use for your forecasts, you can change the labels across row 5 to weeks, years, or quarters. By proceeding down the various sources of funds, you can build a complete picture of all places you expect to contribute funds throughout the year.

By repeating this process for the various categories listed under uses of funds, you can add all the places that will require cash during the year.

Monthly totals for the sources and uses of funds are automatically calculated, and the annual total for each specific source and use category is displayed in column O.

ADJUSTED NET INCOME FORECAST

	JAN	FEB	MAR	APR	MAY	JUN	JUL	AUG	SEP	OCT	NOV	DEC	ANNUAL
SOURCES OF FUNDS													
NET INCOME													0
DEPRECIATION													0
AMORTIZATION													0
DEFERRED TAX													0
ACCOUNTS PAYABLE													0
SHORT-TERM BORROWI													0
OTHER													0
TOTAL	0	0	0	0	0	0	0	0	0	0	0	0	0
USES OF FUNDS													
ACCOUNTS RECEIVABL													0
INVENTORIES													0
CAPITAL EXPENDITUR													0
L-T-D REPAYMENT													0
DIVIDENDS													0
OTHER													0
TOTAL	0	0	0	0	0	0	0	0	0	0	0	0	0
OPERATING CASH													
BEGINNING BALANCE		0	0	0	0	0	0	0	0	0	0	0	
PLUS SOURCES	0	0	0	0	0	0	0	0	0	0	0	0	
LESS USES	0	0	0	0	0	0	0	0	0	0	0	0	
ENDING BALANCE	0	0	0	0	0	0	0	0	0	0	0	0	

Figure 14-2

To complete the cash flow portrait you need to enter the beginning balance for the first month. Once this opening cash balance is entered, it will be automatically carried forward to each successive month. The beginning cash balance is the first row in the Operating Cash Section. When you first load the model, it will be in location C33.

When you have entered all the cash forecasts, VisiCalc will display the total sources, uses, and ending cash balance in the operating cash summary at the bottom of the model. When this section is printed out it acts as a convenient summary of the final forecast results.

If you find that some of these categories do not apply to your business, simply remove that particular row. To do this, place your cursor in the row and type **/DR.** You can delete any row in the sources or uses sections, but as usual, leave the border rows alone.

By altering the estimates that you key into these models, you can generate a whole family of cash flow scenarios. Because you have used VisiCalc to record your estimates, you can easily change your spread sheets to reflect any new information. This will let you measure the impact these changes will have on your cash situation.

FURTHER READINGS

Hunt, Alfred. *Corporate Cash Management With Electronic Funds Transfer.* New York: Amacom, 1978.

Milling, Bryan E. *Cashflow Problem Solver: Procedures and Rationale for the Independent Businessman.* Radnor, PA: Chilton, 1981.

Pflomm, Norman E. *Managing Company Cash,* Business Policy Study No. 99. National Industrial Conference Board. New York, 1961.

Chapter 15

Portfolio Management

There is a way to make a lot of money in the stock market; unfortunately it is the same way to lose a lot of money in the stock market.

Peter Passell

Unfortunately, this chapter does not contain the key to making a fortune in the stock market. As the quotation from Mr. Passell suggests, there is no easy path to stock market riches. One thing is certain, however: Millions of us buy and sell stocks every day. It is estimated that currently one in every six American adults owns stocks valued in total at over $800 billion.

In this chapter we will build several VisiCalc models that will help improve the way we manage our investment portfolios. The selection of stocks is a tricky business. In this chapter we are only attempting to offer an overview of portfolio management and securities in general. Before you make any investment decisions, we suggest you discuss your ideas with an investment professional.

There are three main elements that will concern you when it comes to managing your investment portfolio. The first is the selection of the investments that will initially compose your portfolio. The next, and most challenging element is to strive to keep your investments current and your portfolio filled with the most profitable investments that you can. The final task is keeping track of the administrative and bookkeeping aspects of your investments. You must check to see that dividends are received, rights and warrants are either exercised or sold, and all interest income that you are entitled to is actually collected. You will also want to monitor your tax exposure.

Of these three areas, we will find that VisiCalc is particularly useful for keeping our portfolios current as well as helping with the paperwork. The models at the end of this chapter are concerned with these two on-going areas of portfolio management.

Portfolio management begins with the initial selection of securities. Before you can begin selecting securities, you have to define your own investment objectives. This is a good opportunity to examine your future plans and goals in the financial, career, and total life sense. The objective is to discover what kind of an investor you are. Portfolios are flexible; they can be constructed to suit investors of any temperament. They usually represent a balance between income and growth; income representing the more conservative end of the strategy spectrum while growth is the more aggressive. Finding your particular blend of investments takes experience. It is our firm belief that professional guidance is indispensable, especially for the less experienced investor. By taking the time now to examine your own personal investment goals, you will be in a better position to get the most out of any professional advice that you seek. No advisor can really offer you any help until you have been able to tell him about your particular investment goals.

Below is a list of topics which you should think about before you talk to any investment professional. Some areas, such as number of dependents and age, are easy for you to answer. Other areas, such as how you feel about assuming risk or the income level you want to experience during retirement, may take more soul searching.

Investment Profile

Physical	*Emotional*
Age	Temperament
Dependents	Interest
Income	Time
Financial Resources	Ability
Tax Situation	Future Income Level Desired
Current Level of Debt	

The left-hand column will help you outline your physical characteristics; these topics are relatively self-explanatory. They will help you paint your own self-portrait as far as your earning capability, growth prospects, financial commitments, etc., are concerned.

The right-hand column deals with your emotional make-up. Your temperament refers to your reaction to assuming risk. For some people, the risk associated with owning common stocks causes too much stress. For these people, the creation of a more stable portfolio that stresses income and maintenance of capital is required. Other people thrive on risk and enjoy aggressive investment strategies. Discovering which of these investors you most closely resemble will help you select the investments that are best suited to your needs. Many people gain a new personal clarity from this process of self-definition.

The emotional side of the investment profile will also help you determine the role you will play in the selection of investments. Do you have the time to keep yourself up to date on the ever-changing investment market? Do you have training in economics, statistics, or other related areas that can help you in the analysis of investments? By answering these questions you can determine how much and what type of help you will need to build your personal investment portfolio.

Once you begin to understand your investment goals you can begin to think about what types of securities fit your profile. There are basically three types of securities available to the investor: common stock, preferred stock, and debentures. We will discuss each type briefly and see how they combine to determine a portfolio's aggressive or defensive character. This discussion is meant to be a simple introduction to securities. Readers who want more information are directed to the reading list at the end of this chapter.

Common stock, the first type of security we will examine, represents ownership in a company. Corporations issue shares and receive equity capital in return. The company then uses this capital for its various operations. Each common shareholder is entitled to participate in corporate earnings after prior claims such as interest, dividends owed to preferred shareholders, and taxes have been paid. This participation in earnings occurs in two ways. First, the success of a company often translates into a higher price for its stock. This means the common shareholders' investment grows in value. Second, companies usually put some of their profits back in the shareholders' pockets by paying dividends periodically. These dividends can be in the form of cash or additional stock. A common shareholder has the right to elect members to the board of directors as well as vote on company policy. The common shareholder is also entitled to attend annual meetings and receive a copy of the company's annual report.

When compared with preferred stocks and bonds, common stocks offer an investor the greatest potential for capital gain. With this added profit potential comes added risk. There is no guarantee that the value of the company's stock will increase or that dividends will be paid. The success or failure of the company will usually control the market value of the stock, while the board of directors will decide if and when dividends will be paid. When a company has a poor year, it may very well elect to pass on paying dividends, deciding instead to retain this cash for future use. Should a company go bankrupt, the common shareholders have to wait in line behind the bond and preferred shareholders to recover their investment. If there are not enough assets to go around, the common shareholders run the most risk of being left out in the cold.

The preferred shareholder occupies a position between the bond holder and the common shareholder as far as a claim to a company's assets is concerned. The preferred shareholder is entitled to a fixed rate of return paid out in the form of dividends. While the preferred shareholders are always assured that their dividends will be paid before the common shareholders get theirs, they do not participate in the growth of the company over and above the fixed dividend. They forgo the possibility of future profits in order to be assured of a prior claim to dividends. Things usually must get pretty bad before preferred dividends are not paid. Missing a preferred dividend harms a company's general credit rating and impairs its ability to raise funds through equity financing in the future.

Preferred shares come in many varieties. They are usually cumulative, which means that any dividends that are missed accumulate and must be paid off before a common dividend is paid. Also, once the dividend is missed the preferred shareholders can usually appoint members to the board of directors. There are many good reasons why companies do not like to miss preferred dividend payments.

Participating preferred shares have limited rights to share in the earnings of a company over and above the specified dividend rate. An example of this type of stock is the Loblaw Groceteria $.50 participating preferred issue. When the common stock has earned $.50 per share, the participating feature takes effect. Any dividends beyond this $.50 level are divided equally between the common and preferred shareholders.

Another variety of the preferred stock is the convertible preferred. This allows the preferred shareholder to convert his stock into common shares of the company, at a specified price, giving the preferred shareholder the opportunity to participate directly in corporate growth. For instance, the $2.12 convertible preferred shares of Pitney Bowes are convertible into the company's common stock on a 1 for 1.47 basis; each convertible share held can be converted into 1.47 shares of the underlined common stock.

Because of the current tax laws, a private investor will usually receive a higher rate of return on a quality corporate bond than from a preferred stock. This is because 85 percent of the dividends from a U.S. company are tax exempt when held by another U.S. company. That means if you are U.S. Steel, it is very attractive to have some of your cash sitting in A.T.&T. preferred stock. They earn a nice return on the investment since 85 percent of this income is tax free. As a result, companies will pay more for a preferred stock because a great deal of the income earned is tax exempt.

Bonds and debentures make up the third category of securities. When you buy a bond or debenture you are actually making a loan to the issuer. A bond differs from a debenture in that a bond is a secured promise to pay, backed up by a specific asset. A debenture, however, relies solely on the credit rating of the company that issues it. Both of these securities pay out interest over a specified term. After the term is over it is up to the borrower to repay the principal or face amount of the security.

An interesting example of companies that issue bonds are the railways. They make use of equipment trust bonds as a way to finance railcars. The railroad will pay 20 percent down on a railcar, and the balance is financed by the sale of bonds which are secured by the equipment itself. The title of the rolling stock is held by a trustee who leases it to the railway for a rental period sufficient to pay the interest and the debt on the rolling stock. That means a bond holder may one day be held up at a railway crossing by the very piece of equipment that secures his loan.

Other forms of bonds differ mainly in the collateral used to secure the loan. Mortgage bonds, as the name implies, pledge actual land or buildings as security. Collateral trust bonds are not secured by property but by the physical pledge of other securities.

Corporate debentures are unsecured loans. Both bonds and debentures are guaranteed to repay the principal at maturity and to pay interest on a regular basis, as long as corporate funds are available. Neither bonds nor debentures participate in the growth of a company. Fixed income securities come with a wide variety of options designed to attract investors. In times of high inflation investors do not want to be locked in to earning a fixed rate of interest over a long period of time. Because of this some debentures are retractable. The retractable debenture is initially a long-term note, usually 20 years, but gives the investor the option to redeem the certificate at an earlier date. In times of rapidly changing interest rates, this allows the investor to avoid being locked into a low-yielding investment.

The opposite of the retraction feature is the extension feature. This gives the investor the opportunity to extend the maturity date beyond the initial term of the bond. Both of these securities are referred to as having variable maturities, since the investor has the option of either lengthening or reducing the term.

Many debentures come with a conversion option. This allows the owner to convert the debenture into a specified amount of the issuer's common stock at a specified price. For example, Eastman Kodak has a convertible debenture that pays 4.5 percent interest. At any time the bond holder can convert the bonds into common stock. The cost is $96 for each common share purchased.

The warrant is another way companies make their debt issues more attractive to the public. Warrants are attached to some debentures. They allow the investor to purchase a specific amount of common stock at a specific price. Warrants must be exercised by a specific date, after which they expire.

The chart below summarizes our simple introduction to securities.

	Guaranteed Rate of Return	*Guaranteed* Principal	*Capital Appreciation*
Bonds & Debentures	Yes	Yes	No
Preferred Stock	Yes	No	Some
Common Stock	No	No	Yes

*Guaranteed provided funds are available.

This last section has given you a general idea of the types of securities that are available in the marketplace. Let us examine how these various securities can be combined to create portfolios which suit different investor's objectives.

Securities can be categorized as contributing either income or growth to an investor's portfolio. Income-producing securities represent a more defensive, conservative investment strategy, while growth stocks represent a more aggressive investment stance. By selecting the appropriate balance of growth and income stocks, you can customize your portfolio to meet your particular investment objectives. A professional portfolio manager can offer expert help when it comes to fine tuning the growth and income elements of your portfolio.

Growth stocks are identified by their superior earnings records compared to other stocks within their industry. Growth companies consistently outperform the stock market averages as well as the economy in general. Perhaps the easiest way to see what types of stocks are considered growth stocks is to examine the growth industries of previous decades.

In the 1950s several industries experienced fantastic growth. At the start of the decade only 10 percent of the households in America had a television set. Even the most pessimistic investor believed that the television boom would not stop until everyone in America owned a set. Stock in Admiral rose from $7 a share to over $80 in less than two years, while Zenith more than doubled from $30 to $70 in the first six months of 1950. This spectacular growth took place while the stock market in general was in the doldrums. Later in the decade, the launch of Sputnik shocked America. The prices of the aerospace industry stocks, such as Douglas Aircraft, General Dynamics, and Lockheed, grew over 25 percent in the last quarter of 1957. Over the last half of the decade more stable, but no less impressive growth, was recorded by Standard Oil, General Motors, American Telephone & Telegraph, and General Electric. Most of these stocks doubled while others more than doubled from 1955-1960.

The 1960s saw a virtual kaleidoscope of industries vying for the investors' attention. The growth of leisure-related industries—electronics, computer-leasing, soft drink, and retail companies—created periods of excellent growth. Investors fought to participate in the bright future of these companies. Perhaps the companies that attracted investors with the strongest lure were the large conglomerates. The massive expansion of I.T.&T, Gulf and Western, and Textron through acquisition had many investors paying huge earnings multiples for stock in these companies.

During the 1970s the stock market was in the doldrums, yet several companies experienced remarkable growth. The fast food giant, McDonalds, experienced fantastic growth in this period. The same growth was experienced by computer companies such as Texas Instruments and Hewlett Packard. Fears about oil supplies contributed to the growth of companies like Standard and Mobil Oil.

In many cases these growth industries were pioneering new products and technologies. They captured the investor's imagination. Through aggressive management, their modest resources were parlayed into vast business empires.

How do you spot growth stocks? They show better earnings than the rest of the pack. You will have to pay a premium for these stocks. Their future looks bright so investors are willing to pay more today on the promise of participating in future growth. Since many of these industries are in the formative stages, growth companies tend to plow earnings back into the company to finance expansion and fund their large research and development commitments. This makes the yield on growth stocks lower because less earnings are targeted to pay dividends.

A good growth company should show an above average rate of return on invested capital. This indicates that management is effectively handling its capital resources and signals that the market actually desires the company's product or service. This superior rate of return should also be combined with a steady growth in sales volume. Both of these indicators carry more weight if they are observed over a period of several years.

Another ingredient to look for in a growth stock is capable and aggressive management. A growth company must be managed by people willing to assume calculated business risks. These companies are pioneering in new industries and creating new products. There is no well-worn path to success.

The most important factor involved in finding good growth stocks is to select the right industry. Being aware of the needs of the buying public as well as judging the impact of changing technology is of major importance when finding the right growth stock.

Selecting growth stocks is a difficult task. You must see the potential in these companies before other investors. If you do not, you run the risk of paying such a high price for the stock that future growth prospects are already discounted by the price.

Growth stocks will provide your portfolio with a bulwark against inflation. The goal of these investments is not to protect the principal amount of your investment, but rather to provide you with some real capital appreciation. These stocks will comprise the aggressive section of your portfolio.

At the other end of the investment spectrum we find the income stocks. They are selected to provide the portfolio with regular income and are intended to offer capital protection. Selecting stocks that provide income is an easier task than selecting winning growth stocks. Stocks that are good candidates for the income-conscious investor are stocks in mature companies within well-established industries. These companies have an established track record as well as a well-defined and stable market for their products.

An important feature to look for in an income stock is the dividend record. Does the company have a reasonably long history of paying out dividends to shareholders? Does this record hold up even in times of adverse business conditions? These are important considerations. If you will be relying on the income from these dividends, perhaps during retirement, you will want to see management approve dividend payments, even if the earnings for that particular year were less than expected. In addition to the consistent payment of dividends, you will also want to see the dividends grow. An attractive dividend rate today will have to increase to stay attractive in the future.

You should also check whether the company has actually earned the dividends that they are paying out. Did the company pay dividends out of the earnings generated by its operations, or were the dividends paid out of retained earnings or some other nonoperational source? Dividends not paid for by earnings are a danger signal. Sooner or later the retained earnings will be exhausted.

There are many factors that go into evaluating the quality of a security. Examining a company's cash flow, return on equity, and profit margins, as well as many other factors, is important in determining whether you want to invest in a company. This chapter is only intended as an introduction to some of the general features of the securities market. If you want to learn more, you may like to examine the reading list at the end of this chapter.

Income and growth stocks each have their place in the portfolio. Generally speaking, the younger the investor the greater the proportion of growth to income securities in the portfolio. Since this younger investor will not be retiring for a long time, investment in growth stocks is important to provide the portfolio with real growth in the face of inflation. Preservation of principal is less important as he has many years of earnings ahead. As he grows older, there is a gradual shift away from a more aggressive, growth-oriented portfolio, to one better suited to provide income in the retirement years. In this older investor's income-oriented portfolio, safety of principal and continuance of income are stressed.

Once you have done your soul searching and defined your investment goals and selected your initial stocks, you will be concerned at that point with two ongoing aspects of portfolio management: (1) adjusting your initial selection of stocks so that your portfolio continues to be composed of good quality securities, and (2) managing the daily administration of the portfolio.

Adjusting your portfolio mix entails watching the overall combination of stocks that comprise your portfolio. The administrative responsibilities include verifying that you are receiving all the income you are entitled to from dividends, interest, or other sources. This also means keeping track of stock splits, rights, expiring options, and the other time-sensitive elements of your securities. These jobs are done by the various investment houses for your convenience, but many investors wisely keep track of this information themselves. This is done for the same reasons that you reconcile your monthly bank statement. It is always a good idea to "watch the watcher." VisiCalc will help us in both these ongoing areas of portfolio management.

The first area we will examine is how to keep your investments healthy. Several principles have been identified as contributing to the successful management of stock portfolios. While there is no sure key to success, the general principles of portfolio management discussed below do provide food for thought. They have been used successfully by many investors.

The first and best known investment management principle is diversification. The principle of diversification says "Don't put all your eggs in one basket." Forces that generate major declines in a stock's value are often industry-wide. This causes stocks in similar industries to advance as well as decline together. For example, high interest rates will have a negative effect on industries related to home building, such as lumber and construction product manufacturers. Defense industries and microcomputer manufacturers, on the other hand, are less sensitive to interest rates. By diversifying you protect yourself from holding only stocks of a specific industry. Should some unforeseen event occur that severely harms a specific industry, you can avoid a disaster by holding stock in a variety of industries. Owning the stock of three different automotive companies is not diversification. Events that affect one company adversely will, if they are industry specific, affect all three in the same negative way. The same can be said about steel and automotive stocks. Since the steel industry depends heavily on orders from car manufacturers, if car production sags, so will—to a degree—steel production. Because the two industries are related, they do not offer the same level of diversification as two totally unrelated industries.

By examining your portfolio by industry type you can detect overinvestment in a specific industry. Diversification represents a good middle-of-the-road strategy for the average investor. While you will not make a million overnight, you will avoid the undesirable possibility of suffering a major loss because the one stock you have invested in proceeds to drop like a rock.

The principles of diversification can be applied to other areas of the portfolio. By staggering the maturity dates on your bonds for example, you will avoid all your bonds coming due at a time when purchasing new bonds and debentures is unfavorable because of low interest rates. You can also stagger bond interest, payment dates, and preferred stock dividends throughout the year. This lets you receive a steady income.

Some investors take the diversification principle too far. They purchase a bewildering variety of stocks, usually holding only a small number of shares in each company. This creates several problems. First, it becomes difficult to keep up to date on all the different issues you hold. Second, if you are holding many different stocks, chances are that you can afford to purchase only a few shares in each company. If you purchase stock in amounts of less than 100 shares, you are dealing in what stockbrokers refer to as "odd" or "broken" lots. When you buy in odd lots you pay more in commission costs and you usually do not receive as favorable a price as those investors who are dealing in round lots (multiples of 100 shares). So, in the end, you pay more and cannot exercise the same control over your investments as a more focused investor.

One way to avoid the problem of overdiversification is to limit yourself to holding no more than 10-15 different stocks. This way you can watch your selected stocks more carefully and, at the same time, enjoy reduced commission costs.

Another advantage you will gain from deciding on a maximum number of different stocks to carry is that, once you reach this limit, you will have to sell a stock first before you buy a new one. For investors who have a tendency to buy and sell on the spur of the moment, sticking with a selected number of stocks will help avoid impulse decision-making.

For example, suppose that you have decided that you will limit yourself to a maximum of ten different stocks. If you decide you want to add a new security to your portfolio, you will first have to reduce your holdings by one stock, assuming you are at your limit of ten stocks. Which one do you sell? For many, the decision will be to take a profit on one of their stocks, hoping that some of the poorer performers will eventually turn around. Investors of this school of thought often say "You can't go broke taking a profit." What will happen if you continue this strategy over the years? You will have shifted the balance of your portfolio to the losers—not a good way to plan for the future. Stock market analysts seldom agree on anything. One thing they do agree on is that the inability to take a loss is one of the greatest reasons why many investors lose in the market. No one is right all the time. By taking a loss today you can put the mistake behind you and go forward that much wiser. By carrying your losses forward you eventually erode your portfolio. Before adding a new security to your portfolio, ask yourself which of the securities you currently own is no longer contributing to your overall investment goals. This is the one to sell. Thus, the second principle of portfolio management: When it comes time to sell, look first at your losers. This allows you to continually move to a position of strength.

One of the VisiCalc models we will develop in this chapter will help monitor the composition of our portfolio. The model will allow us to see what percentage of our total portfolio is invested in each specific industry. As the value of our security holdings change, we will be able to see how the overall balance of our portfolio is affected.

The final area of portfolio management we want to discuss is daily administration.

Your securities require ongoing attention. Like all investments, your securities are subject to the ever-swirling tides of change. Interest is paid on debentures, warrants are issued and eventually expire, stocks split, and dividends are paid. We will discuss the time-sensitive features of each security. This will lay the groundwork for a VisiCalc sheet that tracks the various important financial dates.

Both bonds and debentures pay interest regularly. The payment dates should be recorded along with the amount due. Tracking payments will not only insure that you receive the income you are entitled to, but will also help improve your cash planning. You will also want to keep track of the maturity dates of your fixed income securities. This is the date that the issuer will repay the principal amount of your bond or debenture. These dates warn you when lump sum principal payments are due.

The preferred shareholder is interested in the dividend payment dates. If you own convertible stock, then the conversion terms and associated dates should also be recorded. The portfolio model that we develop later in this chapter will allow you to use as much or as little space as you need to record this information.

The same type of information should be recorded for your rights and warrants. The expiry dates are crucial for these investments, as an expired right or warrant is worthless.

SUMMARY

Before you can select stocks for a portfolio, you must first discover what type of investor you are. Knowledge of the types of securities available as well as their investment characteristics is important in constructing a portfolio tuned to suit your special needs. Like the primary colors on a painter's palette, different combinations of growth and income stocks can be used to create an entire spectrum of portfolio types, suited to various different investors.

VisiCalc helps in two ongoing areas of portfolio management: keeping your portfolio tuned and helping you control the paperwork. By displaying your portfolio so that composition by industry can be seen, you can measure your level of diversification. By tracking dividend payments, maturity dates, tax liabilities, and other administrative details, VisiCalc can help you control your investment paperwork, while insuring that you get all the benefits to which you are entitled.

THE MODELS

In this section we will develop four different models designed to help you manage your investment portfolio. They display your portfolio holdings, record your investment transactions, project income, and record all dividend and interest payments received. Each model will be described in detail. Specific examples will be given so that you can see how to enter your own investment data into each sheet.

Model I: The Portfolio

This model displays your entire investment holdings. It is designed to let you see the overall composition of your portfolio. Your investments are divided into two different parts: a Bond section and a Stock section. Figure 15-1 shows the packed form of the portfolio report.

To learn how to use this model, type in the keystrokes in the appendix for this chapter under the title "PORT," or if you have purchased the model disk, load the model called "PORT" from the disk.

Throughout these models we will be using the sample portfolio of a 45-year-old office equipment sales manager. We will begin by entering his bonds into the spread sheet and then we will enter his stocks.

Suppose he holds the following debt issues, listed at face value:

-$5,000 Gulf Oil 13.75% debentures due September 15, 2009. His unit cost was $99.95 for each $100.

-$1,000 Tandy Corporation 10.00% debentures due December 31, 1991. His unit cost was $81.72 for each $100.

-$1,100 McDonnell Douglas Co. $4.75 convertible debentures due July 1, 1991. The conversion rate is $30.61 for each common share. His unit cost was $92.00 for each $100.

-$500 Chase Manhattan Bank $4.875 convertible debentures due May 1, 1993. The conversion rate is $55.00 for each common share. His unit cost was $88.25 for each $100.

This completes the list of all the portfolio's debentures. Let us turn our attention to the model so we can begin to enter the investment information.

We will divide the bonds into two groups: Corporate and Corporate Convertible. First, let us enter the corporate debentures that are "straight," i.e., they have no conversion privilege. Move the cursor to A8 so that you are over the label SECURITY. Now enter **CORPORATE** Ⓔ in this location. We have now replaced the general label by one that matches the type of securities we want to add.

Next, we need to create more space in which to work. Move the cursor to A9 and enter **/IR/IR/IR/IR/IR**; this inserts five new lines. We need to replicate the dummy line that contains the formulas and formats that we need. Since the first line of the model will be across row 9 and

BOND SECTION
****

PAR VALUE	SECURITY	UNIT COST	BOOK VALUE	MARKET PRICE	MARKET VALUE	% OF TOTAL	INTEREST	ANNUAL INCOME	YIELD
SECURITY			0.00		0.00	ERROR		0.00	
TOTAL	BONDS		0.00		0.00	ERROR		0.00	

STOCK SECTION
****

NUMBER OF SHARES	SECURITY	UNIT COST	BOOK VALUE	MARKET PRICE	MARKET VALUE	% OF TOTAL	DIVIDEND	ANNUAL INCOME	YIELD
SECURITY			0.00	0.00	0.00	ERROR	0.00	0.00	0.00
TOTAL	STOCKS		0.00		0.00	ERROR		0.00	
PORTFOLIO TOTALS			0.00		0.00	ERROR		0.00	

Figure 15-1

the dummy line is in row 14, we use the following replicate command: **/R BS A14.J14:A9 Ⓔ RRRRRNRR.** This will replicate the dummy line into row 9. Notice that the replication command produces prompts for Relative or No Change at the columns for BOOK VALUE, MARKET VALUE, % OF TOTAL, and ANNUAL INCOME. You can easily make a mistake when you use the replicate command if you are not careful to get the Rs and Ns in the right order. All the responses to the replicate prompt are Rs except for the second coordinate of the formula contained in the % OF TOTAL column. As the columns pass during the replicate command, watch for the % OF TOTAL column. This way you will be ready to enter the sole "N" response at the right time.

As you continue to replicate dummy rows, you will find that it gets easier. In the beginning, though, it is best to take your time when you replicate.

Now we can enter the data on the Gulf Oil debenture. Move the cursor to A9 and enter **5000▶GULF♭OIL♭13.75%▶99.95▶▶85.75▶▶▶13.75 ▶▶16.00 Ⓔ**. We have entered the par amount of the debenture, the description, our purchase price, the current market price, the interest rate, and the yield. The current market price and the yield can be found in *Barrons* or the *Wall Street Journal*.

The model has calculated the book value, market value, and annual income for this security. The book value tells us what we paid for the debenture, while the market value tells us what it is worth today. The % OF TOTAL column reveals how much of our total holdings are represented by this security. The current value of the portfolio is used for the percent of total calculation. So far we have entered only the one debenture and it composes 100 percent of our portfolio. This number will change as we add new securities.

To complete our description of the Gulf Oil debenture we should include the due date. Let us add this on the line below. Place the cursor at B10 and enter **DUE♭09/09 Ⓔ**.

We can now add the second corporate bond. The first step is to replicate the dummy line into row 12. We leave a line between the securities to make the spread sheet easier to read. Enter the following: **/R BS A14.J14:A12 Ⓔ RRRRRNRR.** Now move your cursor to A12 and enter the information on the Tandy debenture as follows: **1000▶TANDY♭ CORP♭10.00%▶81.72▶▶72.25▶▶▶10 ▶▶14.00 Ⓔ**. Add the expiry information at B13 as follows: **DUE♭12/91 Ⓔ**.

This completes the corporate bonds. Notice that if you move the cursor down column A, you will get to the TOTAL BOND line. At this point it shows that the total book value for these bonds is 5814.70, the market value is 5010.00, combined they make up 100 percent of the portfolio, and they will contribute 787.50 in income.

Now let us move on to the convertible bonds.

We will first create some more room in which to operate. With the cursor anywhere in row 14, enter the following: **/IR/IR/IR/IR/IR/IR /IR/IR/IR/IR.** You have inserted ten new rows. The dummy row is now in row 24.

The new heading for the next set of securities is placed in A15 and B15. Move your cursor to A15 and enter **CORPORATE▸"▸CONVERTIBLE Ⓔ.**

On the next line add the data for the McDonnell Douglas convertible debenture. First, replicate the dummy line as follows: **/R BS A24.J24: A16 Ⓔ RRRRRNRR.** Now add the data **1100▸MCDONNELL▸DOUGLAS▸ $4.75▸92.00▸▸96.00▸▸▸4.75▸▸@NA Ⓔ.** The yield is not shown for a corporate convertible debenture, due to the unknown effects of the underlying common stock. As a result we enter "@NA" in the yield column.

To complete the background information we need to add the redemption date as well as the conversion features. Move your cursor to B17. We will place this information in B17 and B18 as follows: **DUE▸07/91 ▾ CONV▸@$30.61/SHARE Ⓔ.** This completes the McDonnell Douglas information.

We will leave a line between the securities and replicate the dummy line into line 20 as follows: **/R BS A24.J24:A20 Ⓔ RRRRRNRR.** With your cursor at A20, the data on the final convertible security can be entered as follows: **500▸CHASE▸MANHATTAN▸BANK▸$4.875▸88.25▸▸102.50▸▸▸ 4.875▸▸@NA Ⓔ.** Move your cursor to B21 and enter the supplementary information as follows: **DUE▸05/93 ▾ CONV▸@$55.00/SHARE Ⓔ.**

This completes the bond section of the spread sheet. By examining the total line you can see that the bond section has a total book value of $7,267.95, and a market value of $6,578.50. Since we have not added any stocks yet, the bonds comprise 100 percent of the portfolio. The expected annual income from these investments is $864.13.

For those of you who hold mortgages as part of your portfolio you can record them in the bond section as well. Simply record the face value of the mortgage in the par value column, then record the cost and market value as 100. The effective interest rate is then entered into the interest column as well as in the yield column. The annual income is automatically calculated.

Now we can turn our attention to the stock section of the portfolio.

The same principles apply to this section of the sheet as applied to the first. You insert rows to make room for securities and enter the appropriate information. This process is repeated until all the securities are entered.

Let us look at the stocks that our sales manager has invested in over the last few years. The list below describes his entire stock holdings and the average costs per share.

- 100 shares of Colgate-Palmolive $3.50 cumulative preferred shares at $34.50 per share.
- 100 shares of General Dynamics $4.25 cumulative convertible preferred shares at $70.25 per share.
- 300 shares of General Dynamics common at $12.50 per share.
- 100 shares of Northrop Corporation at $40.25 per share.
- 200 shares of Hewlett-Packard Company at $24.25 per share.
- 100 shares of Texas Instruments at $110.50 per share.
- 300 shares of CBS Incorporated at $61.00 per share.
- 100 shares of Warner Communications at $15.25 per share.
- 200 shares of Tandy Corporation at $37.60 per share.
- 100 shares of Sears at $28.10 per share.

This completes the stock profile. We know all the holdings and their average cost so we can proceed to enter the information into the stock section of the portfolio spread sheet.

To understand more about the portfolio composition we will divide up the stocks into two major sections: Preferred and Common. The preferred stocks will be further divided into Preferred and Preferred Convertible. The common stocks will be displayed under the headings Aerospace, Data Processing, Entertainment, and Merchandising.

To make the data entry easier we will fix the column headings of the stock section into place. This will let us refer to the headings as we enter data. Scroll down the screen so that the "NUMBER OF" label in column A is at the top of the screen. Move the cursor to A34; this should be the second line from the top of the screen. Enter **/TH.** This will freeze the column headings in place.

With your cursor on A39, insert eight new lines as follows: **/IR/IR /IR/IR/IR/IR/IR/IR.** The dummy line that we will be replicating is now in row 47. Change the general SECURITY label at A37 to PREFERRED. Now we will replicate the dummy row into row 38. There will be a slight difference between replicating this row and the one used in the bond section. Use the following keystrokes: **/R BS A47.J47:A38 Ⓔ RRRRRN RRRR.** We need to specify two more Rs in this replication because we have an extra formula in the yield column. As in the bond section you still need to watch for the % OF TOTAL column. It signals that an "N" response is required to the replicate prompt. Remember that it is the

234 Applications and Models

second coordinate in the formula that requires an "N" response. In the bond section we have to manually enter the bond yield. The calculation of bond yield to maturity depends on too many factors to be included in this model. The yield of a stock, however, is much easier to calculate. It is the dividend divided by the current price of the stock. It is this formula that creates the extra replicate prompts.

With your cursor at A38, enter the information for Colgate as follows: **100▶COLGATE-PALMOLIVE▶34.50▶▶29.50▶▶▶3.50 Ⓔ**. Add the following descriptive information in B39: **"$3.50⌼CUMULATIVE Ⓔ**. If you would like to turn off the automatic recalculation feature to speed up the data entry, you can do so by entering /**GRM**.

We can now enter the General Dynamics convertible preferred, but first we should insert the appropriate heading. Move your cursor to A41 and enter **PREFERRED▶"⌼CONVERTIBLE Ⓔ**. Replicate the dummy line into row 42 as follows: /**R BS A47.J47:A42 Ⓔ RRRRRNRRRR**. The stock data is entered as follows: **100▶GENERAL DYNAMICS▶70.25▶▶89.50▶▶▶4.25 Ⓔ**. Move the cursor to B43 and enter **"$4.25⌼CUM⌼CONV⌼@2.27⌼COMMON/PREF⌼SHARE Ⓔ**. Each preferred share can be converted into 2.27 common shares at the owner's request.

This completes the preferred shares. We still need to enter the common stock data.

Insert six rows between row 44 and row 45 by placing your cursor in row 44 and entering these keystrokes: /**IR/IR/IR/IR/IR/IR**. With the cursor at A45, enter **COMMON▶"⌼STOCKS Ⓔ**.

Enter the heading for the first type of common stock at A46: **AEROSPACE Ⓔ**. Now we need to replicate the dummy line that is currently in row 53 into row 47. Use the following keystrokes: /**R BS A53.J53:A47 Ⓔ RRRRRNRRRR**. With your cursor at A47, enter the first stock as follows: **300▶GENERAL DYNAMICS▶12.50▶▶24.10▶▶▶.72 Ⓔ**.

At this point you should be able to add the other securities in our sales manager's portfolio to our spread sheet. Figure 15-2 shows the completed portfolio. Take the time to fill in the remaining common stocks and check to see that your answers agree with the ones shown below. You can get the market prices and dividends from the illustration. Be sure that you enter **!** so that the model calculates all of your input data. We do this because we have turned off the automatic recalculation feature.

This model is designed to give you an overview of how your portfolio is composed. By dividing your securities into industry groups, you can see the diversification of your investments. You can also model the impact that a stock purchase would have on the diversification of your portfolio. To do this, simply enter the stocks and their prices to your

BOND SECTION

PAR VALUE	SECURITY	UNIT COST	BOOK VALUE	MARKET PRICE	MARKET VALUE	% OF TOTAL	INTEREST	ANNUAL INCOME	YIELD
CORPORATE 5000	GULF OIL 1 DUE 09/09	99.95	4997.50	85.75	4287.50	5.82	13.75	687.50	16.00
1000	TANDY CORP DUE 12/91	81.72	817.20	72.25	722.50	0.98	10.00	100.00	14.00
CORPORATE CONVERTIB 1100	MCDONNELL DUE 07/91 CONV @$30.	92.00	1012.00	96.00	1056.00	1.43	4.75	52.25	NA
500	CHASE MANH DUE 05/93 CONV @$55.	88.25	441.25	102.50	512.50	0.70	4.88	24.38	NA
			0.00		0.00	0.00		0.00	
TOTAL	BONDS		7267.95		6578.50	8.93		864.13	

Figure 15-2

```
                                    STOCK            SECTION
                        ****************************************************

NUMBER OF                     UNIT      BOOK    MARKET   MARKET    % OF              ANNUAL
 SHARES   SECURITY            COST     VALUE    PRICE    VALUE     TOTAL  DIVIDEND   INCOME    YIELD

PREFERRED
 100      COLGATE-PA          34.50   3450.00   29.50   2950.00    4.00    3.50      350.00   11.86
          $3.50 CUMU
PREFERRED CONVERTIB
 100      GENERAL DY          70.25   7025.00   89.50   8950.00   12.15    4.25      425.00    4.75
          $4.25 CUM
COMMON    STOCKS
AEROSPACE
 300      GENERAL DY          12.50   3750.00   24.10   7230.00    9.82    0.72      216.00    2.99
 100      NORTHROP C          40.25   4025.00   45.25   4525.00    6.14    1.80      180.00    3.98
DATAPROCES
 200      HEWLETT-PA          24.25   4850.00   40.75   8150.00   11.06    0.24       48.00    0.59
 100      TEXAS INST         110.50  11050.00   79.75   7975.00   10.83    2.00      200.00    2.51
ENTERTAINM
 300      CBS                 61.00  18300.00   44.00  13200.00   17.92    2.80      840.00    6.36
 100      WARNER COM          15.25   1525.00   58.50   5850.00    7.94    1.00      100.00    1.71
MERCHANDIS
 200      TANDY CORP          37.60   7520.00   33.00   6600.00    8.96    0.00        0.00    0.00
 100      SEARS               28.10   2810.00   16.50   1650.00    2.24    0.00        0.00    0.00

                                         0.00              0.00    0.00    0.00        0.00    0.00
                                     --------          --------  ------              -------
TOTAL     STOCKS                     64305.00          67080.00   91.07              2359.00

                                     ========          ========  ======              =======
PORTFOLIO TOTALS                     71572.95          73658.50  100.00              3223.13
```

Figure 15-2 *(Continued)*

Portfolio Management

portfolio and VisiCalc will tell you how the purchase affects your investment blend.

Model II: Transactions

Keeping track of your stock investments is important for several reasons, not the least being that the government can throw you in jail if you do not pay your taxes. Recording of capital gains and losses is required of all investors. But keeping track of your historic trading performance can also help make you a better investor. Learning from past mistakes can keep you from repeating them.

The keystrokes that compose this model are in the appendix under TRANS. If you key in the model or load it from the model disk, your packed sheet should look like the picture below.

The security transaction sheet is designed to help you track your historic trading activity for each separate security.

Let us return to our sales manager. We know from his portfolio that he owns 300 shares of General Dynamics common stock that was purchased at an average cost of $12.50 per share. Actually, the stock has been accumulated over several years. The trading history of his General Dynamics common stock looks like this:

-Bought 100 shares on February 14/76 for $9.50 each.

-Bought 100 shares on June 01/76 for $12.70 each.

-Bought 100 shares on June 25/78 for $15.30 each.

The 300 shares were purchased on three separate occasions. We will illustrate how to enter each of these transactions into the transaction spread sheet.

Move the cursor so that row 6, the top line of the transaction sheet, is at the top of the screen. We will fix these rows in place so they will be in sight as we enter the data. Move the cursor to A7 and type **/TH.** This will fix the column headings in place.

Move the cursor to A9. As we did before, we will overwrite the general label SECURITY and enter the title GENERAL DYNAMICS COM.. Enter this label at A9 using the following keystrokes: **GENERAL♭DY-NAMICS♭COM.** ⒠. We need to make enough room to record the stock transactions to date. With your cursor at A11, insert three rows: **/IR/IR /IR.** Due to the nature of the formulas in this model it is important to replicate the dummy row from the top down. First, let us fill row 10 with the February transaction data. With your cursor at B10, enter **FEB♭14/76➤100 ➤9.50** ⒠.

SECURITY TRANSACTION RECORD
****

DATE	AMOUNT BOUGHT	PRICE	AMOUNT SOLD	PRICE	SHARES HELD	AVERAGE COST	L/S? (1/0)	L.TERM GAIN/LOSS	S.TERM GAIN/LOSS	NET GAIN/LOSS
SECURITY										
	0				0	0.00		0.00	0.00	0.00
TOTALS										
	0		0					0.00	0.00	0.00

DATE	AMOUNT BOUGHT	PRICE	AMOUNT SOLD	PRICE	SHARES HELD	AVERAGE COST	L/S? (1/0)	L.TERM GAIN/LOSS	S.TERM GAIN/LOSS	NET GAIN/LOSS
SECURITY										
	0				0	0.00		0.00	0.00	0.00
TOTALS										
	0		0					0.00	0.00	0.00

Figure 15-3

Move your cursor further along row 10 and you will notice that the number of shares you currently hold and their average costs are calculated for you. This will seem more apparent as we enter the next transaction.

Move the cursor to B11 and enter **JUN∆01/76➤100 Ⓔ /FI➤12.70 Ⓔ**. Now that you have entered the transaction data you need to replicate the formulas into the rest of the row so that the desired calculations will be performed. We want to replicate the formulas into the range G11 through L11 from their source range of G10 through L10. All the coordinates of the replicate will be relative. This means that you will respond with "R" to each replicate response. There will be 20 "R" responses required in all. Enter **/R BS G10.L10:G11 Ⓔ**.

After the calculations have been performed for this second transaction, move the cursor across row 11 and notice that the number of shares owned appears as 200 and their average cost is now $11.10.

Add the final transaction by placing your cursor at B12 and entering **JUN∆25/78➤100 Ⓔ /FI➤15.30 Ⓔ**. Now, replicate the dummy row into place: **/R BS G11.L11:G12 Ⓔ**; be sure to respond with all the required "Rs."

The transaction picture for General Dynamics is complete.

Let us tackle a slightly more detailed example. Our sales manager has been more active in his buying and selling of Tandy stock. The trading history is listed below:

- Bought 100 shares for $5.20 each on June 05/72.
- Bought 200 shares for $5.00 each on October 10/72.
- Sold 300 shares for $3.90 each on April 05/73.
- Bought 100 shares for $5.50 each on August 01/75.
- Bought 200 shares for $11.20 each on April 15/76.
- Bought 200 shares for $10.00 each on February 12/77.
- Bought 300 shares for $9.30 each on March 03/78.
- Sold 800 shares for $13.80 each on August 24/79.
- Bought 200 shares for $37.60 each on June 11/81.

We record these transactions in the same way as we did for the previous stock. The difference now is that we will see what happens when he sells stock. Move the cursor down to the second transaction entry sheet on the page. With your cursor at A22, replace the general title with **TANDY∆CORP. Ⓔ**. We have nine transactions to enter, so with your cursor in row 24, enter **/IR/IR/IR/IR/IR/IR/IR/IR/IR**. This inserts the nine rows we need.

240 Applications and Models

Again, we will want to fix the column heading. First, enter **/TN** to reset the screen. Now scroll the screen so that row 19 is at the top of the screen. With your cursor in row 20, enter **/TH** to fix the labels in place.

Let us begin entering transactions. Move your cursor to B23 and enter **JUN♭05/72▶100▶5.20 ▾ ◀◀OCT♭10/72▶200 Ⓔ/FI▶5.00 Ⓔ**. Replicate the formulas into row 24 as follows: **/R BS G23. L23:G24 Ⓔ RRRRR RRRRRRRRRRRRRRR.** The first two purchases have been recorded. The model informs us that he owns 300 shares at an average cost of $5.07 per share.

Now we enter the first sell transaction. Move the cursor to B25 and enter **APR♭05/73▶▶▶300 Ⓔ /FI▶3.90 Ⓔ**. We now have a capital loss to record. Replicate the formula in the line above as follows: **/R BS G24.L24: G25 Ⓔ RRRRRRRRRRRRRRRRRRRR.** Now move the cursor over to column I. This column tells the model whether you want the transaction to be recorded as a long- or short-term capital gain. If you enter a "1" in this column, the gain or loss will be transferred into the long-term column; if you enter a "0", the result will be sent to the short-term column. Since he has held the stock for less than one year, enter **0 Ⓔ** at I25 to record the short-term loss. Notice that the loss of $350 appears in the short-term column.

We will now illustrate how to enter the next four transactions at once. Move your cursor to B26 and enter **AUG♭01/75▶100 Ⓔ /FI▶5.50 ▾ ◀◀APR♭15/76▶200 Ⓔ /FI▶11.20 ▾ ◀◀FEB♭12/77▶200 Ⓔ /FI▶10 ▾ ◀◀ MAR♭03/78▶300 Ⓔ /FI▶9.30 Ⓔ**. Now when we replicate the formulas we can specify a target as well as a source range. This is faster since we avoid entering all those "Rs" for each new line. Enter **/R BS G25.L25: G26.G29 Ⓔ**. Now, after you have entered the "Rs", the line replicates itself across all four rows.

The last two transactions include a buy and a sell. We could have included them with the last four transactions, doing six rows at once, but the added practice using this sheet will be helpful.

Move the cursor to B30 and enter **AUG♭24/79▶▶▶800 Ⓔ /FI▶13.80 ▾◀◀◀◀JUN♭11/81▶200 Ⓔ /FI▶37.60 Ⓔ**. Now replicate the formulas into these last two rows: **/R BS G29.L29:G30.G31 Ⓔ**. After entering the "Rs", move your cursor across to I30 and enter **1,** to indicate that he records a long-term gain. Put your cursor at I26 and type **/B ▾ /B ▾ /B ▾ /B ▾▾ /B Ⓔ**.

Check to see that your model matches the one pictured below.

Using this model will give you a historic perspective on your security transactions. By entering hypothetical sales, you can determine tax consequences.

Each time you load TRANS you will find two separate grids. Each one will hold the data on a different security. Once you fill them with data be sure to save the model under a different name. For example,

```
               SECURITY      TRANSACTION       RECORD
               ******************************************
```

	DATE	AMOUNT BOUGHT	PRICE	AMOUNT SOLD	PRICE	SHARES HELD	AVERAGE COST	L/S? (1/0)	L.TERM GAIN/LOSS	S.TERM GAIN/LOSS	NET GAIN/LOSS
GENERAL DY											
	FEB 14/76	100	9.50			100	9.50		0.00	0.00	0.00
	JUN 01/76	100	12.70			200	11.10		0.00	0.00	0.00
	JUN 25/78	100	15.30			300	12.50		0.00	0.00	0.00
TOTAL		300		0					0.00	0.00	0.00

	DATE	AMOUNT BOUGHT	PRICE	AMOUNT SOLD	PRICE	SHARES HELD	AVERAGE COST	L/S? (1/0)	L.TERM GAIN/LOSS	S.TERM GAIN/LOSS	NET GAIN/LOSS
TANDY CORP											
	JUN 05/72	100	5.20			100	5.20		0.00	0.00	0.00
	OCT 10/72	200	5.00			300	5.07		0.00	0.00	0.00
	APR 05/73			300	3.90	0	5.07	0	0.00	-350.00	-350.00
	AUG 01/75	100	5.50			100	5.50		0.00	0.00	-350.00
	APR 15/76	200	11.20			300	9.30		0.00	0.00	-350.00
	FEB 12/77	200	10.00			500	9.58		0.00	0.00	-350.00
	MAR 03/78	300	9.30			800	9.48		0.00	0.00	-350.00
	AUG 24/79			800	13.80	0	9.48	1	3460.00	0.00	3110.00
	JUN 11/81	200	37.60			200	37.60		0.00	0.00	3110.00
TOTAL		1300		1100					3460.00	-350.00	

Figure 15-4

242 Applications and Models

if you own two entertainment stocks you can load the TRANS model, fill up two grids, and save it under the name TRANSENT. This denotes that the saved model contains transactions from your entertainment stocks. By using the same titles in the transaction model groupings as you used in the portfolio model, you will have a convenient cross-reference system. A similar example would be entering in the transactions of the aerospace stocks in the model TRANSAER. You do not have to fill up both grids on the sheet. If there is only one security in a group, you can leave the other grid empty for later use.

Model III: Portfolio Cash Flow

Many of the investments in your portfolio produce income through the year. The Portfolio Cash Flow model projects the income that you expect to receive from your investments for the coming year. If you rely on your investment for income, this model will help you monitor your income. If you plan on reinvesting the income generated by your investments, this model will help you plan future stock purchases.

The model is stored under the name PORTFLOW. When you have loaded or typed it in, your screen should look like Figure 15-5.

Suppose that our sales manager wants to project the annual income generated by his investments. Let us begin with the bond section of his holdings.

He owns $5,000 of Gulf Oil debentures which pay 13.75 percent interest. Annually, this amounts to $687.50. These debentures pay interest twice a year, in July and December. Half of this interest, $343.75, is paid in July and the other half in December.

Let us insert several rows in our cash flow model. With your cursor in row 5, enter **/IR/IR/IR/IR/IR.** Place the label **GULF♭OIL♭13.75'S♭09** Ⓔ in A5.

We can use VisiCalc to do the actual interest rate calculation for us. Move the cursor to H5 to enter July's income. You can do the calculation directly in the cell as follows: **(5000*.1375)/2** Ⓔ. Now move your cursor to M5 and enter the same formula for December's income: **(5000*.1375)/2** Ⓔ.

Similarly, the income from the other debentures can be entered as follows:>A6 Ⓔ **TANDY♭CORP♭10'S♭91** ▶**(1000*.1)/2** Ⓔ >H6 Ⓔ **(1000*.1)/2** Ⓔ >A7 Ⓔ **MCDONNELL♭DOUGLAS♭4.75'S♭91** ▶**(1100*.0475)/2** Ⓔ >H7 Ⓔ **(1100*.0475)/2** Ⓔ >A8 Ⓔ **CHASE♭MANHATTAN♭CORP♭4.875'S♭93** Ⓔ >F8 Ⓔ **(500*.04875)/2** Ⓔ >K8 Ⓔ **(500*.04875)/2** Ⓔ.

These keystrokes record all the expected income from the bond section of the portfolio. The only formula that needs to be replicated

PORTFOLIO PROJECTED INCOME

SECURITY	JAN	FEB	MAR	APR	MAY	JUN	JUL	AUG	SEPT	OCT	NOV	DEC	ANNUAL
													0.00
MONTHLY TOTAL	0.00	0.00	0.00	0.00	0.00	0.00	0.00	0.00	0.00	0.00	0.00	0.00	
CUM. TOTAL	0.00	0.00	0.00	0.00	0.00	0.00	0.00	0.00	0.00	0.00	0.00	0.00	

Figure 15-5

is in column M. This calculates the annual totals for the specific securities. To replicate this formula, move your cursor to N10 and type **/R ⓔ N5.N8 ⓔ RR.** You can now see how much income the individual securities contribute during the year.

To insure that the model is working correctly, all you need to do is check that the row, column, and cumulative totals are displaying the correct results.

This model offers you several views of your cash flow. If you look across row 5, you see that a total income of $687.50 is generated by the Gulf debenture during the year. The annual contribution from each investment is displayed in column N. The model also shows your cash flow on a monthly basis. We can see that so far the income is not distributed evenly throughout the year. The final perspective we gain on the cash flow is the cumulative income generated by the investments. By looking at the line labeled cumulative total, we can see our retained income at any point during the year.

The dividend income from the preferred and common stock is added in the same way. First, insert the number of empty lines that you require. Next, enter the name of the security in column A. Move the cursor across to the appropriate months and enter the amount of income that you expect to receive. The model will do the rest.

VisiCalc is especially useful for this type of model since many investments, particularly stocks, often return either more or less than the expected income amount. When this happens you can easily adjust the actual income received. If you like you can keep two versions of this model. One holds your projected cash flow while the second holds the actual cash that you received.

Model IV: The Income Record Model

The final model in this chapter records income received from your investments. The model allows you to record the payment date as well as the amount received.

Load or enter the model called DIVRECS. Your model should look like Figure 15-6.

As in the previous model we insert lines as we need them. We will illustrate how to enter data into this model using a stock and a debenture from our sample portfolio.

Let us assume that it is September. We will first record the income received from the Gulf Oil debenture. We know that it pays interest in July and in December. In September we would have only received the July payment. To record this, move your cursor to A7 and enter

```
             INCOME RECORD
             ******************

                                  INTEREST/
    SECURITY        DATE    AMOUNT DIVIDEND    TIMES    TOTAL
    =========================================================
                                                        ERROR
    ---------------------------------------------------------
    TOTAL INC=====================================      ERROR
    =========================================================
```

Figure 15-6

GULF♭OIL♭DEB►JULY♭5►5000►.1375►2 Ⓔ. The amount collected from the July payment is displayed in column F. Column E is labeled TIMES; this refers to the number of times that the income is paid out during the year. In the case of the Gulf Oil debenture, that number is 2 since it pays its interest in two installments, once in July and once in December. This is the case for most bonds and debentures. Stocks usually pay dividends on a quarterly basis.

Our sample stock will be Warner Communications. There are 100 shares of this stock in the portfolio. The annual dividend is $.68 per share. Warner pays dividends quarterly, on the second month of each quarter. In September the payments for February, May, and August would have been received. Let us insert several lines so we can enter this income information. With your cursor in row 8, enter **/IR/IR/IR.** Now, let us replicate line 7 into lines 8 to 10 in the following manner: **/R BS B7.F7:B8.B10 Ⓔ RRR.** Now, with your cursor at A8, enter the dividend information as follows: **WARNER♭COMMUNICATIONS►FEB♭10►100►.68►4 ▼ 4◄.68◄ 100◄MAY♭12 ▼ AUG♭10►100►.68►4 Ⓔ.**

If you prefer, you can use a separate grid for each security you own; in that way, you will have an individual record of each security's payment history. The advantage to grouping the securities together onto one grid is that you can see what your income has been over the course of a year. This helps when it comes to completing your tax return.

As with the other models in this section, once you have replicated the dummy formulas for the first time you can delete the dummy row and use one of the existing rows as the source for your replicate command.

FURTHER READINGS

Graham, Benjamin, Dodd, D.L., & Cuttle, Sidney. *Security Analysis: Principles and Techniques.* 4th ed. New York: McGraw-Hill, 1962.

Hayes, Douglas A. *Investments: Analysis and Management.* 2nd ed. New York: The MacMillan Co., 1969.

Sauvain, Harry. *Investment Management.* 3rd ed. Englewood Cliffs, N.J.: Prentice-Hall, 1967.

SAVE TIME AND MONEY. The VisiCalc models developed in this book are available in disk form for use with your own personal computers. All the keystrokes that make up the packed models are already entered for you. Just load the model and you are ready to begin tailoring it to suit your own needs. Order your models disk today, you pay only $39.95 for all 17 models.

....

Please send me the packed models disk at the price of $39.95 for the following computer:

IBM PC☐   APPLE II☐   Radio Shack Model II☐   Radio Shack Model III☐

☐ VISA   ☐ master charge   ☐ AMERICAN EXPRESS Card   ☐ Check (U.S. Funds)

CARD NO. _____

SIGNATURE _____ EXPIRES _____

NAME (please print) _____

ADDRESS _____

CITY _____ STATE _____ ZIP _____

Make check or money order payable to CONSUMERS BUSINESSWARE.

Mail to:
Consumers Businessware
2521 Kitchener St.
Vancouver, B.C.
V5K 3C7

Please allow six to eight weeks for processing.

....

Please send me the packed models disk at the price of $39.95 for the following computer:

IBM PC☐   APPLE II☐   Radio Shack Model II☐   Radio Shack Model III☐

☐ VISA   ☐ master charge   ☐ AMERICAN EXPRESS Card   ☐ Check (U.S. Funds)

CARD NO. _____

SIGNATURE _____ EXPIRES _____

NAME (please print) _____

ADDRESS _____

CITY _____ STATE _____ ZIP _____

Make check or money order payable to CONSUMERS BUSINESSWARE.

Mail to:
Consumers Businessware
2521 Kitchener St.
Vancouver, B.C.
V5K 3C7

Please allow six to eight weeks for processing.

Appendix

CREDIT CONTROL

CREDIT

\>A1 Ⓔ CREDIT ➤ANALYSIS Ⓔ

\>I1 Ⓔ /FRCURRENT ♭ TO: Ⓔ

\>A3 Ⓔ /FR/R Ⓔ B3.Q3 Ⓔ NAME ➤ADDRESS ➤HOME# ➤BUS.#
➤ACCT# ➤LIMIT ♭ ➤BILLING♭DATE ➤INVOICE# ➤ DATE ➤BALANCE
➤CREDIT ➤CURRENT ➤">30 ♭ DAYS ➤">60 ♭ DAYS ➤">90 ♭ DAYS
➤BAD♭DEBT ➤COMMENTS Ⓔ

\>A4 Ⓔ /-= Ⓔ /R Ⓔ B4.R4 Ⓔ

\>B5 Ⓔ /FR ➤/FR ➤/FR ➤/FR ➤ ➤/FR

\>H6 Ⓔ /FR ➤/FR ➤@SUM(L6.06)-K6 ➤0 ➤0 ➤0 ➤0 ➤0 ➤0 Ⓔ

\>A7 Ⓔ /-= Ⓔ /R Ⓔ B7.R7 Ⓔ

\>A8 Ⓔ /-= Ⓔ /R Ⓔ B8.D8 Ⓔ

248 Appendix

>E8 Ⓔ TOTALS: ►@SUM(F4.F7) ► ► ► ►@SUM(J4.J7) Ⓔ /R Ⓔ K8.P8 Ⓔ RR

>A9 Ⓔ /-= Ⓔ /R Ⓔ B9.R9 Ⓔ

>L11 Ⓔ /FR/R Ⓔ M11.P11 Ⓔ

>L11 Ⓔ CURRENT ►">30♭DAYS ►">60♭DAYS ►">90♭DAYS ►BAD♭ DEBTⒺ

>L12 Ⓔ /-- Ⓔ /R Ⓔ M12.P12 Ⓔ

>J13 Ⓔ /FR"%♭AGED♭AN ►/FLALYSIS: ►(L8/J8)*100 Ⓔ /R Ⓔ M13.P13 Ⓔ RN

>I14 Ⓔ /FRLARGEST ►/FROUTST ►/FLANDING: ►@MAX(L4.L7) Ⓔ /R Ⓔ M14.P14 Ⓔ RR

>H16 Ⓔ /FRALLOWANCE ►/FR"♭FOR♭BAD ►/FRDEBT♭%♭ES ►/FLTIMATE: ►/FG.01 ►/FG.02 ►/FG.08 ►/FG.2 ►/FRTOTAL Ⓔ

>I17 Ⓔ /FRALLOWANCE ►/FRFOR♭BAD ►/FL"♭DEBT: ►/F$+L8*L16 Ⓔ/R Ⓔ M17.017 Ⓔ RR ► ► ► ►@SUM(L17.017) Ⓔ

>E19 Ⓔ /FR/R Ⓔ F19.H19 Ⓔ ANNUAL♭ ►PROJECTED ►CREDIT ►SALES: ►/F$@NA Ⓔ

>F20 Ⓔ /FRAVERAG ►/FLE♭COLLECTION ►/FRPERIOD: ►/FI(J8/I19)*365 Ⓔ

>G21 Ⓔ /FRINTEREST ►/FRRATE: Ⓔ

>G22 Ⓔ /FRCARRYING ►/FRCOST: ►/F$(J8*I21)/12 Ⓔ

/GC12 Ⓔ

/GF$

CREDREC

>A1 Ⓔ /FRCREDIT ►/FRTO: Ⓔ

>A4 Ⓔ /FR/R Ⓔ B4.L4 Ⓔ NAME ➤ACCT# ➤LIMIT ➤Y-T-D ➤DAYS
➤INVOICE# ➤CURRENT ➤">30 ␣DAYS ➤">60 ␣DAYS ➤">90 ␣DAYS
➤BAD DEBT ➤COMMENTS Ⓔ

>A5 Ⓔ /-= Ⓔ /R Ⓔ B5.M5 Ⓔ

>B6 Ⓔ /FR ➤➤@SUM(G9.J9) Ⓔ

>E7 Ⓔ /FI ➤/FR ➤0 ➤0 ➤0 ➤0 Ⓔ

>A8 Ⓔ /-= Ⓔ /R Ⓔ B8.M8 Ⓔ

>A9 Ⓔ /-= Ⓔ /R Ⓔ B9.E9 ➤ ➤ ➤ ➤ ➤TOTALS: ➤@SUM(G5.G8) Ⓔ /R Ⓔ H9.K9 Ⓔ RR

>A10 Ⓔ /-= Ⓔ /R Ⓔ B10.M10 Ⓔ

>A13 Ⓔ /FRAVERAGE␣C ➤/FLOLLECTION ➤/FRPERIOD:
➤/FI@AVERAGE(E5.E8) Ⓔ

/GF$

FINANCIAL STATEMENT ANALYSIS

RATIOS

>C2 Ⓔ FINANCIAL ➤"␣STATEMEN ➤T␣ANALYSI ➤S Ⓔ

>A3 Ⓔ INCOME ␣ST ➤ATEMENT Ⓔ

>A5 Ⓔ I␣N␣C␣O␣M ➤"␣E Ⓔ

>A6 Ⓔ /-* ➤/-* Ⓔ

>A7 Ⓔ /-- Ⓔ /R Ⓔ B7.L7 Ⓔ

>A8 Ⓔ NET␣SALES ▼ OTHER␣INC ➤OME Ⓔ

>A10 Ⓔ /-- Ⓔ /R Ⓔ B10.L10 Ⓔ

250 Appendix

>A11 Ⓔ TOTAL INC ►OME ►@SUM(C7.C10) Ⓔ /R Ⓔ D11.L11 Ⓔ RR

>A12 Ⓔ /-- Ⓔ /R Ⓔ B12.L12 Ⓔ

>A14 Ⓔ E X P E N ►"S E S Ⓔ

>A15 Ⓔ /-* ►/-* Ⓔ

>A17 Ⓔ COST OF G ►OODS SOLD Ⓔ

>A18 Ⓔ "* GROSS P ►ROFIT ►+C11−C17 Ⓔ /R Ⓔ D18.L18 Ⓔ RR

>A19 Ⓔ /-- Ⓔ /R Ⓔ B19.L19 Ⓔ

>A20 Ⓔ GEN. SALE ►S & ADMIN Ⓔ

>A21 Ⓔ DEPRECIAT ►ION Ⓔ

>A22 Ⓔ RESEARCH ►"& DEVEL. Ⓔ

>A23 Ⓔ /-- Ⓔ /R Ⓔ B23.L23 Ⓔ

>A24 Ⓔ TOTAL OPE ►RATING EX ►@SUM(C19.C23) Ⓔ /R Ⓔ D24.L24 Ⓔ RR

>A25 Ⓔ /-- Ⓔ /R Ⓔ B25.L25 Ⓔ

>A26 Ⓔ "* NET OPE ►R. INCOME ►+C18−C24 Ⓔ /R Ⓔ D26.L26 Ⓔ RR

>A27 Ⓔ INTEREST ►EXPENSE Ⓔ

>A28 Ⓔ "* INCOME ►BEF. TAX ►+C26−C27 Ⓔ /R Ⓔ D28.L28 Ⓔ RR

>A29 Ⓔ TAXES Ⓔ

>A30 Ⓔ "* NET BEF ►" MIN & EX ►+C28−C29 Ⓔ /R Ⓔ D30.L30 Ⓔ RR

>A31 Ⓔ MINORITY ►INTEREST Ⓔ

>A32 Ⓔ EXTRAORDI ►NARY ITEM Ⓔ

>A33 ⓔ DISCONTIN ►UED ь ITEM ⓔ

>A35 ⓔ "*ьNETьINC ►OME ►+C30+C31+C32+C33 ⓔ /R ⓔ D35.L35 ⓔ RRRR

>A37 ⓔ "#ьPREFьSH ►".ь(000'S) ⓔ

>A38 ⓔ "#ьCOM.ьSH ►".ь(000'S) ⓔ

>A39 ⓔ COM.ьMARK ►ETьPRICE ►/F$/R ⓔ D39.L39 ⓔ

>A40 ⓔ /-* ⓔ /R ⓔ B40.L40 ⓔ

>A41 ⓔ STATEMENT ►"ьOFьRETAI ►NEDьEARNI ►NGS ⓔ

>A43 ⓔ RETAINED ►INCOME ⓔ

>A44 ⓔ "*ANNUALьN ►ETьINCOME ►+C35 ⓔ /R ⓔ D44.L44 ⓔ R

>A45 ⓔ "*TOTьRET. ►"ьINCOME ►+C43+C44 ⓔ /R ⓔ D45.L45 ⓔ RR

>A47 ⓔ DIVIDENDS ►"ьPAID: ⓔ

>A48 ⓔ PREFERRED ▼ COMMON ⓔ

>A50 ⓔ "*ьTOTAL ьD ►IVIDENDS ►+C48+C49 ⓔ /R ⓔ D50.L50 ⓔ RR

>A52 ⓔ "*ьBALANCE ►"ьYEARьEND ►+C45-C50 ⓔ /R ⓔ D52.L52 ⓔ RR

>A53 ⓔ /-* ⓔ /R ⓔ B53.L53 ⓔ

>A54 ⓔ BALANCEьS ►HEET ⓔ

>A56 ⓔ CURRENTьA ►SSETS: ⓔ

>A57 ⓔ /-- ⓔ /R ⓔ B57.L57 ⓔ

>A58 ⓔ CASH ⓔ

>A59 ⓔ SECURITIE ►S ⓔ

>A60 ⓔ RECEIVABL ►ES ⓔ

>A61 Ⓔ INVENTORY Ⓔ

>A62 Ⓔ DEFERRED ➤TAXES Ⓔ

>A63 Ⓔ OTHER CUR ➤".↳ASSETS Ⓔ

>A64 Ⓔ /-- Ⓔ /R Ⓔ B64.L64 Ⓔ

>A65 Ⓔ TOTAL ↳CUR ➤RENT ➤@SUM(C57.C64) Ⓔ /R Ⓔ D65.L65 Ⓔ RR

>A66 Ⓔ /-- Ⓔ /R Ⓔ B66.L66 Ⓔ

>A68 Ⓔ FIXED ↳ASS ➤ETS: Ⓔ

>A69 Ⓔ /-- Ⓔ /R Ⓔ B69.L69 Ⓔ

>A70 Ⓔ PROPERTY ➤PLANT,EQUITY Ⓔ

>A71 Ⓔ LESS↳ACC. ➤"↳DEPRECIATION Ⓔ

>A72 Ⓔ OTHER↳FIX ➤ED↳ASSETS Ⓔ

>A73 Ⓔ /-- Ⓔ /R Ⓔ B73.L73 Ⓔ

>A74 Ⓔ TOTAL↳FIX ➤ED↳ASSETS ➤@SUM(C69.C73) Ⓔ /R Ⓔ D74.L74 Ⓔ RR

>A75 Ⓔ /-- Ⓔ /R Ⓔ B75.L75 Ⓔ

>A77 Ⓔ INTANGIBL ➤E↳ASSETS: Ⓔ

>A78 Ⓔ /-- Ⓔ /R Ⓔ B78.L78 Ⓔ

>A79 Ⓔ GOODWILL Ⓔ

>A80 Ⓔ OTHER Ⓔ

>A81 Ⓔ /-- Ⓔ /R Ⓔ B81.I81 Ⓔ

>A82 Ⓔ TOTAL ↳INT ➤".↳ASSETS ➤@SUM(C78.C81) Ⓔ /R Ⓔ D82.L82 Ⓔ RR

>A83 Ⓔ /-- Ⓔ /R Ⓔ B83.L83 Ⓔ

>A84 Ⓔ "*␣TOTAL␣A ➤SSETS ➤+C65+C74+C82 Ⓔ /R Ⓔ D84.L84 Ⓔ RRR

>A87 Ⓔ CURR.␣LIA ➤BILITIES: Ⓔ

>A88 Ⓔ /-- Ⓔ /R Ⓔ B88.L88 Ⓔ

>A89 Ⓔ ACCOUNTS ➤PAYABLE Ⓔ

>A90 Ⓔ NOTES␣PAY ➤ABLE Ⓔ

>A91 Ⓔ LOANS␣PAY ➤ABLE Ⓔ

>A92 Ⓔ INCOME␣TA ➤X␣PAYABLE Ⓔ

>A93 Ⓔ /-- Ⓔ /R Ⓔ B93.L93 Ⓔ

>A94 Ⓔ TOTAL␣CUR ➤RENT␣L. ➤@SUM(C88.C93) Ⓔ /R Ⓔ D94.L94 Ⓔ RR

>A95 Ⓔ /-- Ⓔ /R Ⓔ B95.L95 Ⓔ

>A97 Ⓔ DEBT: Ⓔ

>A98 Ⓔ /-- Ⓔ /R Ⓔ B98.L98 Ⓔ

>A99 Ⓔ LONG-TERM ➤".␣DEBT Ⓔ

>A100 Ⓔ OTHER␣L.T ➤".␣DEBT Ⓔ

>A101 Ⓔ OTHER␣L.T ➤".␣DEBT Ⓔ

>A102 Ⓔ /-- Ⓔ /R Ⓔ B102.L102 Ⓔ

>A103 Ⓔ TOTAL␣L.T ➤".␣DEBT ➤@SUM(C98.C102) Ⓔ /R Ⓔ D103.L103 Ⓔ RR

>A104 Ⓔ /-- Ⓔ /R Ⓔ B104.L104 Ⓔ

>A106 Ⓔ OTHER␣LIA ➤BILITIES Ⓔ

>A107 Ⓔ /-- Ⓔ /R Ⓔ B107.L107 Ⓔ

>A108 (E) DEFERRED ➤TAXES (E)

>A109 (E) OTHER LIA ➤BILITIES (E)

>A110 (E) OTHER LIA ➤BILITIES (E)

>A111 (E) /-- (E) /R (E) B111.L111 (E)

>A112 (E) TOTAL OTH ➤ER ➤@SUM(C107.C111) (E) /R (E) D112.L112 (E) RR

>A113 (E) /-- (E) /R (E) B113.L113 (E)

>A114 (E) "*TOTAL L. ➤T. LIABIL ➤+C103+C112 (E) /R (E) D114.L114 (E) RR

>A116 (E) "*TOTAL LI ➤ABILITIES ➤+C94+C114 (E) /R (E) D116.L116 (E) RR

>A119 (E) OWNERS EQ ➤UITY: (E)

>A120 (E) /-- (E) /R (E) B120.L120 (E)

>A121 (E) PREFERRED (E)

>A122 (E) PREFERRED (E)

>A123 (E) COMMON (E)

>A124 (E) COMMON (E)

>A125 (E) CAPITAL S ➤URPLUS (E)

>A126 (E) RETAINED ➤EARNINGS (E)

>A127 (E) LESS TREA ➤S. STOCK (E)

>A128 (E) /-- (E) /R (E) B128.L128 (E)

>A129 (E) TOT. OWNE ➤RS EQUITY ➤@SUM(C120.C128) (E) /R (E) D129.L129 (E) RR

>A130 Ⓔ /-- Ⓔ /R Ⓔ B130.L130 Ⓔ

>A132 Ⓔ "*TOT&LIA. ➤ "&&OWN&EQU ➤+C116+C129 Ⓔ /R Ⓔ D132.L132 Ⓔ RR

>A134 Ⓔ /-# Ⓔ /R Ⓔ B134.L134 Ⓔ

>C135 Ⓔ ANALYSIS ➤SECTION Ⓔ

>A137 Ⓔ LIQUIDITY ➤": Ⓔ

>A138 Ⓔ WORKING&C ➤APITAL ➤/F$(C65/C94) Ⓔ /R Ⓔ D138.L138 Ⓔ RR

>A139 Ⓔ QUICK&ASS ➤ET ➤/F$(C65-C61)/C94 Ⓔ /R Ⓔ D139.L139 Ⓔ RRR

>A141 Ⓔ L.T.&SOLV ➤ENCY: Ⓔ

>A142 Ⓔ DEBT-EQUI ➤TY ➤/F$+C103/C129 Ⓔ /R Ⓔ D142.L142 Ⓔ RR

>A143 Ⓔ TIMES&INT ➤".&EARNED ➤/F$+C28/C27 Ⓔ /R Ⓔ D143.L143 Ⓔ RR

>A144 Ⓔ ASSET&COV ➤ERAGE ➤/F$(C84-C82-C94-C108)/C103 Ⓔ /R Ⓔ D144.L144 Ⓔ RRRRR

>A146 Ⓔ EFFICIENC ➤Y: Ⓔ

>A147 Ⓔ INVENTORY ➤"&TURNOVER ➤/F$+C17/C61 Ⓔ /R Ⓔ D147.L147 Ⓔ RR

>A148 Ⓔ ACCTS.&RE ➤C.&TURNOV ➤/F$(C60*365)/C8 Ⓔ /R Ⓔ D148.L148 Ⓔ RR

>A149 Ⓔ SALES/WOR ➤KING&CAP. ➤/F$+C8/(C65-C94) Ⓔ /R Ⓔ D149.L149 Ⓔ RRR

>A150 Ⓔ SPECIFIC Ⓔ

>A152 Ⓔ PROFITABI ➤LITY Ⓔ

> A153 Ⓔ GROSS⌷PRO ➤F.⌷MARGIN ➤/F$(((C8−(C17+C21))/C8)*100 Ⓔ /R Ⓔ D153.L153 Ⓔ RRRR

> A154 Ⓔ NET⌷PROF. ➤"⌷MARGIN ➤/F$(C30/C8)*100 Ⓔ /R Ⓔ D154.L154 Ⓔ RR

> A155 Ⓔ RETURN⌷ON ➤"⌷COMMON ➤/F$((C30+C31−C48)/(C129−C121−C122))*100 Ⓔ /R Ⓔ D155.L155 Ⓔ RRRRRR

> A156 Ⓔ EARNINGS ➤PER⌷SHARE ➤/F$(C30+C31−C48)/C38 Ⓔ /R Ⓔ D156.L156 Ⓔ RRRR

> A157 Ⓔ PRICE/EAR ➤NINGS ➤/F$+C39/C156 Ⓔ /R Ⓔ D157.L157 Ⓔ RR

> A158 Ⓔ /−# Ⓔ /R Ⓔ B158.L158 Ⓔ

FORECASTING

SFI

> B1 Ⓔ /FR S⌷F⌷I⌷ ➤/FRFORECAST ➤/FRPERIOD: Ⓔ

> C3 Ⓔ PRODUCT: ➤/FR /R Ⓔ E3.O3 Ⓔ 1 ➤2 ➤3 ➤4 ➤5 ➤6 ➤7 ➤8 ➤9 ➤10 ➤ ➤TOTAL Ⓔ

> A4 Ⓔ /−= Ⓔ /R Ⓔ B4.O4 Ⓔ

> A5 Ⓔ SALESMAN ➤ ➤ ➤ 0 ➤0 ➤0 ➤0 ➤0 ➤0 ➤0 ➤0 ➤0 ➤ ➤ @SUM(C5.N5) Ⓔ

> A6 Ⓔ /−= Ⓔ /R Ⓔ B6.O6 Ⓔ

> A8 Ⓔ /FLSUMMARY ➤ ➤ ➤/FR /R Ⓔ E8.M8 Ⓔ 1 ➤2 ➤3 ➤4 ➤5 ➤6 ➤7 ➤8 ➤9 ➤10 Ⓔ

> C9 Ⓔ TOTAL ➤@SUM(D4.D6) Ⓔ /R Ⓔ E9.M9 Ⓔ RR

> C10 Ⓔ AVERAGE ➤@AVERAGE(D4.D6) Ⓔ /R Ⓔ E10.M10 Ⓔ RR

> C11 Ⓔ LARGEST ➤@MAX(D4.D6) Ⓔ /R Ⓔ E11.M11 Ⓔ RR

Appendix 257

>A13 Ⓔ /FRRECOMMEN ➤/FLDATION Ⓔ

/GFI

/GC8 Ⓔ

INCOME

>A1 Ⓔ /FRINCOME ➤"⌴STATEMENTS Ⓔ

>H1 Ⓔ /FRFORECAST Ⓔ

>B3 Ⓔ /FR/R Ⓔ C3.I3 Ⓔ YEAR ➤"%⌴SALES ➤YEAR ➤"%⌴SALES ➤"%⌴CHANGE ➤YEAR ➤"%⌴SALES ➤FORECAST⌴% Ⓔ

>A4 Ⓔ S⌴A⌴L⌴E⌴S ▼ /-- Ⓔ /R Ⓔ B5.I5 Ⓔ

>A6 Ⓔ A ➤0 ➤/F$(B6/B13)*100 ➤0 ➤/F$(D6/D13)*100 ➤/F$((D6−B6)/B6)*100 ➤+D6*(1+(I6/100)) ➤/F$(G6/G13)*100 ➤/F$0 Ⓔ /R BS B6.I6:B7.B11 Ⓔ RNRNRRRRRN

>A7 Ⓔ B ▼ C ▼ D ▼ E ▼ F ▼ /-- Ⓔ /R Ⓔ B12.I12 Ⓔ

>A13 Ⓔ TOTAL⌴SALES ➤@SUM(B5.B12) ➤/F$(B13/B13)*100 ➤@SUM(D5.D12) ➤/F$(D13/D13)*100 ➤/F$((D13−B13)/B13)*100 ➤@SUM(G5.G12) ➤/F$(G13/G13)*100 ➤/F$((G13−D13)/D13)*100 Ⓔ

>A14 Ⓔ /-- Ⓔ /R Ⓔ B14.I14 Ⓔ

>A15 Ⓔ COST⌴OF⌴GOODS⌴SOLD ➤0 ➤/F$(B15/B13)*100 ➤0 ➤/F$(D15/D13)*100 ➤/F$((D15−B15)/B15)*100 ➤+D15*(1+(I15/100)) ➤/F$(G15/G13)*100 ➤/F$0 Ⓔ

>A17 Ⓔ GROSS⌴MARGIN ➤+B13−B15 ➤/F$(B17/B13)*100 ➤+D13−D15 ➤/F$(D17/D13)*100 ➤/F$((D17−B17)/B17)*100 ➤/FI(G13−G15) ➤/F$(G17/G13)*100 ➤/F$((G17−D17)/D17)*100 Ⓔ

>A19 Ⓔ E⌴X⌴P⌴E⌴N⌴S⌴ ➤E⌴S Ⓔ

>A20 Ⓔ /-- Ⓔ /R Ⓔ B20.I20 Ⓔ

>A21 Ⓔ WAGES ➤0 ➤/F$(B21/B13)*100 ➤0 ➤/F$(D21/D13)*100 ➤/F$((D21−B21)/B21)*100 ➤+D21*(1+(I21/100)) ➤/F$(G21/G13)*100 ➤/F$0 Ⓔ /R BS B21.I21:B22.B31 Ⓔ RNRNRRRRRN

258 Appendix

>A22 RENT ▼ UTILITIES ▼ PROFESSIONAL⌂SERVICES ▼ TAXES ▼ DEPRECIATION ▼INTEREST ▼TELEPHONE ▼BAD⌂DEBTS ▼THEFT ▼ MISC ▼ /-- Ⓔ /R Ⓔ B32.I32 Ⓔ

>A33 Ⓔ TOTAL⌂EXPENSES ➤@SUM(B20.B32) ➤/F$(B33/B13)*100 ➤@SUM(D20.D32) ➤/F$(D33/D13)*100 ➤/F$((D33-B33)/B33)*100 ➤@SUM(G20.G32) ➤/F$(G33/G13)*100 ➤/F$((G33-D33)/D33)*100 Ⓔ

>A34 Ⓔ /-- Ⓔ /R Ⓔ B34.I34 Ⓔ

>A36 Ⓔ NET⌂PROFIT ➤+B17-B33 ➤/F$(B36/B13)*100 ➤+D17-D33 ➤/F$(D36/D13)*100 ➤/F$((D36-B36)/B36)*100 ➤+G17-G33 ➤/F$(G36/G13)*100 ➤/F$((G36-D36)/D36)*100 Ⓔ

/GC12 Ⓔ

/GFI

BUDGETING

MATBUD

>E1 Ⓔ MATERIALS ➤ ➤BUDGET Ⓔ

>B2 Ⓔ PRODUCT: Ⓔ

>A3 Ⓔ NUMBER ⌂OF ➤UNITS: Ⓔ

>B4 Ⓔ MONTH: Ⓔ

>H5 Ⓔ /-* ➤/-* ➤/-* ➤/-* Ⓔ

>B6 Ⓔ INVENTORY ➤QUANTITY ➤BUDGETED ➤ACTUAL ➤ ➤ ➤ ➤YEAR⌂-⌂TO⌂ ➤/FL"-⌂DATE Ⓔ

>A7 Ⓔ MATERIAL ➤NUMBER ➤PER⌂UNIT ➤USAGE ➤USAGE ➤DIFF. ➤VARIANCE ➤BUDGET ➤ACTUAL ➤DIFF. ➤VARIANCE Ⓔ

>A8 Ⓔ /-- Ⓔ /R Ⓔ B8.K8 Ⓔ

>D9 Ⓔ /FI+C9*C3 ➤ ➤/FI+E9-D9 ➤/F$+F9/D9 ➤ ➤ ➤+I9-H9 ➤/F$+J9/H9 Ⓔ

Appendix 259

\>A10 Ⓔ /-- Ⓔ /R Ⓔ B10.K10 Ⓔ

\>A11 Ⓔ TOTAL ➤ ➤ ➤@SUM(D8.D10) ➤@SUM(E8.E10)
➤@SUM(F8.F10) ➤/F$+F11/D11 ➤@SUM(H8.H10) Ⓔ /R Ⓔ I11.J11 Ⓔ
RR ➤ ➤ ➤/F$+J11/H11 Ⓔ

\>A12 Ⓔ /-- Ⓔ /R Ⓔ B12.K12 Ⓔ

/GFR

/GC10 Ⓔ

LABORB

\>E1 Ⓔ LABOR ➤ ➤BUDGET Ⓔ

\>B2 Ⓔ MONTH: Ⓔ

\>B3 Ⓔ PRODUCT: Ⓔ

\>A4 Ⓔ NUMBER␢OF ➤UNITS: Ⓔ

\>H6 Ⓔ /-* ➤/-* ➤/-* ➤/-* Ⓔ

\>C7 Ⓔ STANDARD ➤BUDGETED ➤ACTUAL ➤ ➤ ➤ ➤YEAR␢-TO␢
➤/FL"-␢DATE Ⓔ

\>B8 Ⓔ TASK ➤TIME ➤LABOR ➤LABOR ➤DIFF. ➤VARIANCE ➤BUDGET
➤ACTUAL ➤DIFF. ➤VARIANCE Ⓔ

\>A9 Ⓔ /-- Ⓔ /R Ⓔ B9.K9 Ⓔ

\>A10 Ⓔ DIRECT: ➤ ➤ ➤+C10*C4 ➤ ➤+E10-D10 ➤/F$+F10/D10 ➤ ➤
➤+I10-H10 ➤/F$+J10/H10 Ⓔ

\>A11 Ⓔ /-- Ⓔ /R Ⓔ B11.K11 Ⓔ

\>A12 Ⓔ TOTAL ➤ ➤@SUM(C9.C11) Ⓔ /R Ⓔ D12.F12 Ⓔ RR ➤ ➤ ➤
➤/F$+F12/D12 ➤@SUM(H9.H11) Ⓔ /R Ⓔ I12.J12 Ⓔ RR ➤ ➤
➤/F$+J12/H12 Ⓔ

\>A13 Ⓔ /-- Ⓔ /R Ⓔ B13.K13 Ⓔ

/R BS A6.K6:A16 Ⓔ

/R BS A7.K7:A17 Ⓔ

>C17 Ⓔ ATTRIBUTED Ⓔ

/R BS A8.K8:A18 Ⓔ

/R BS A9.K9:A19 Ⓔ

/R BS A10.K10:A20 Ⓔ RNRRRRRRRR

>A20 Ⓔ INDIRECT: Ⓔ

/R BS A11.K11:A21 Ⓔ

/R BS A12.K12:A22 Ⓔ RRRRRRRRRRRRRRRRR

/R BS A13.K13:A23 Ⓔ

>A24 Ⓔ TOTALbDIRE ➤/FLCT Ⓔ

>A25 Ⓔ ANDbINDIRE ➤/FLCT ➤+C22+C12 Ⓔ /R Ⓔ D25.F25 Ⓔ RR ➤ ➤
➤ ➤/F$+F25/D25 ➤+H22+H12 Ⓔ /R Ⓔ I25.J25 Ⓔ RR ➤ ➤ ➤/F$+J25/H25 Ⓔ

>A26 Ⓔ /R BS A23.K23:A26 Ⓔ

/GFR /GC10 Ⓔ

RJOURNAL

>B1 Ⓔ MONTHLY ➤/FRRECEIVINGb ➤/FRJOURNAL Ⓔ

>B2 Ⓔ /-* ➤/-* ➤/-* Ⓔ

>A4 Ⓔ /FRFOR: Ⓔ

>A6 Ⓔ DATE ➤SUPPLIER ➤/FLINVOICE# ➤/FLINVOICEbCOST
➤/FRTRANSPORTATION ➤/FRLANDEDbCOST ➤/FRRETAIL
➤/FRMARKUP Ⓔ

>A7 Ⓔ /-- Ⓔ /R Ⓔ B7.H7 Ⓔ

>C8 Ⓔ /FR ➤ ➤ ➤+E8+D8 ➤ ➤/F$(G8−F8)/G8 Ⓔ

Appendix 261

>A9 Ⓔ /-- Ⓔ /R Ⓔ B9.H9 Ⓔ

>A10 Ⓔ TOTAL: ▶/-- ▶/-- ▶@SUM(D7.D9) Ⓔ /R Ⓔ E10.G10 Ⓔ RR ▶
▶ ▶ ▶(G10-F10/G10) Ⓔ

>A11 Ⓔ /-- Ⓔ /R Ⓔ B11.H11 Ⓔ

/GF$ /GC14 Ⓔ

DISCOUNT

>E1 Ⓔ /FLDISCOUNT ▶REGISTER Ⓔ

>E2 Ⓔ /-* ▶/-* Ⓔ

>A3 Ⓔ /FRFOR: Ⓔ

>E4 Ⓔ /FROLD ▶/FRNEW Ⓔ

>A5 Ⓔ /FLDATE ▶ITEM ▶/FLQUANTITY ▶/FRSUPPLIER ▶/FRPRICE
▶/FRPRICE ▶/FRDIFFERENCE ▶/FREXTENSION ▶/FRCOMMENTS Ⓔ

>A6 Ⓔ /-- Ⓔ /R Ⓔ B6.J6 Ⓔ

>C7 Ⓔ /FL ▶ ▶ ▶ ▶+E7-F7 ▶+G7*C7 Ⓔ

>A8 Ⓔ /-- Ⓔ /R Ⓔ B8.J8 Ⓔ

>A9 Ⓔ TOTAL: ▶/-- Ⓔ /R Ⓔ C9.G9 Ⓔ >H9 Ⓔ @SUM(H6.H8) Ⓔ

>A10 Ⓔ /-- Ⓔ /R Ⓔ B10.J10 Ⓔ

/GF$ /GC12 Ⓔ

TALLY

>C1 Ⓔ INVENTORY ▶/FLTALLY Ⓔ

>C2 Ⓔ /-* ▶/-* Ⓔ

>E4 Ⓔ MAINTAINED Ⓔ

>A5 Ⓔ JANUARY␣1 ▶ ▶/FRCOST ▶/FRRETAIL ▶/FRCOST␣% Ⓔ

>A6 Ⓔ OPENING ►INVENTORY ► ► ►/F$(C6+C7)/(D6+D7) Ⓔ

>A7 Ⓔ /FRADD:♭ ►PURCHASES Ⓔ

>A8 Ⓔ /FRLESS:♭ ►SALES ►+E6*D8 ▼ +E6*D9 ▼ +E6*D10 Ⓔ

>B9 Ⓔ DISCOUNTS ▼ SHRINKAGE Ⓔ

>A11 Ⓔ FEBRUARY♭1 Ⓔ

>A12 Ⓔ OPENING ►INVENTORY ►+C6+C7−C8−C9−C10 ►+D6+D7−D8−D9−D10 ►/F$(C12+C13)/(D12+D13) Ⓔ

>A13 Ⓔ /FRADD:♭ ►PURCHASES Ⓔ

>A14 Ⓔ /FRLESS:♭ ►SALES ►+E12*D14 ▼ +E12*D15 ▼ +E12*D16 Ⓔ

>B15 Ⓔ DISCOUNTS ▼ SHRINKAGE Ⓔ

/R BS A6.A16:A18 Ⓔ

/R BS B6.B16:B18 Ⓔ

/R BS C12.C16:C18 Ⓔ RRRRRRRRRR

/R BS C12.C16:C24 Ⓔ RRRRRRRRRR

/R BS D12.D16:D18 Ⓔ RRRRR

/R BS D12.D16:D24 Ⓔ RRRRR

/R BS E6.E16:E18 Ⓔ RRRRRRRR

>A17 Ⓔ MARCH♭1 Ⓔ

>A23 Ⓔ APRIL♭1 Ⓔ

/R BS A12.A29:A30 Ⓔ

/R BS B12.B29:B30 Ⓔ

/R BS C12.C29:C30 Ⓔ (33 R'S)

/R BS D12.D29:D30 Ⓔ (15 R'S)

/R BS E12.E29:E30 Ⓔ (12 R's)

>A29 Ⓔ MAYߋ1 Ⓔ

>A35 Ⓔ JUNEߋ1 Ⓔ

>A41 Ⓔ JULYߋ1 Ⓔ

/R BS A18.A47:A48 Ⓔ

/R BS B18.B47:B48 Ⓔ

/R BS C18.C47:C48 Ⓔ (55 R'S)

/R BS D18.D47:D48 Ⓔ (25 R'S)

/R BS E18.E47:E48 Ⓔ (20 R's)

>A47 Ⓔ AUGUSTߋ1 Ⓔ

>A53 Ⓔ SEPTEMBERߋ1 Ⓔ

>A59 Ⓔ OCTOBERߋ1 Ⓔ

>A65 Ⓔ NOVEMBERߋ1 Ⓔ

>A71 Ⓔ DECEMBERߋ1 Ⓔ

/GFI   /GC11 Ⓔ

MARGIN

>D1 Ⓔ GROSSߋMARGIN ►"ߋBUDGET Ⓔ

>C3 Ⓔ /FRLASTߋYEAR ►/FRTHISߋYEAR ►/FRDIFFERENCE ►/FR"%ߋCHANGE Ⓔ

>B5 Ⓔ NETߋSALES ▼ C.O.G.S. ▼ DISCOUNTS ▼ SHRINKAGE ▼ GROSSߋMARGIN ▼ "%ߋMARGIN Ⓔ

>A7 Ⓔ JANUARY Ⓔ

>C9 Ⓔ +C5–C6–C7–C8 ▶+D5–D6–D7–D8 Ⓔ

>C10 Ⓔ /F$+C9/C5 ▶/F$+D9/D5 ▶/F$+D10–C10 Ⓔ

>E5 Ⓔ +D5–C5 Ⓔ /R Ⓔ E6.E9 Ⓔ RR

>F5 Ⓔ /F$(D5–C5)/C5 Ⓔ /R Ⓔ F6.F10 Ⓔ RRR

/R BS B5.B10:B12 Ⓔ

/R BS C5.C10:C12 Ⓔ RRRRRR

/R BS D5.D10:D12 Ⓔ RRRRRR

/R BS E5.E10:E12 Ⓔ (12 R'S)

/R BS F5.F10:F12 Ⓔ (18 R'S)

/R BS B5.B17:B19 Ⓔ

/R BS C5.C17:C19 Ⓔ (12 R'S)

/R BS D5.D17:D19 Ⓔ (12 R'S)

/R BS E5.E17:E19 Ⓔ (24 R'S)

/R BS F5.F17:F19 Ⓔ (36 R'S)

>A14 Ⓔ FEBRUARY Ⓔ

>A21 Ⓔ MARCH Ⓔ

>A28 Ⓔ APRIL Ⓔ

/R BS B5.B31:B33 Ⓔ

/R BS C5.C31:C33 Ⓔ (24 R'S)

/R BS D5.D31:D33 Ⓔ (24 R'S)

/R BS E5.E31:E33 Ⓔ (48 R'S)

/R BS F5.F31:F33 Ⓔ (72 R'S)

>A35 Ⓔ MAY Ⓔ

>A42 Ⓔ JUNE Ⓔ

>A49 Ⓔ JULY Ⓔ

>A56 Ⓔ AUGUST Ⓔ

/R BS B33.B59:B61 Ⓔ

/R BS C33.C59:C61 Ⓔ (24 R'S)

/R BS D33.D59:D61 Ⓔ (24 R'S)

/R BS E33.E59:E61 Ⓔ (48 R'S)

/R BS F33.F59:F61 Ⓔ (72 R'S)

>A63 Ⓔ SEPTEMBER Ⓔ

>A70 Ⓔ OCTOBER Ⓔ

>A77 Ⓔ NOVEMBER Ⓔ

>A84 Ⓔ DECEMBER Ⓔ

/GFI   /GC12 Ⓔ

CASH MANAGEMENT

RANDD

>A1 Ⓔ /FLRECEIPTSɃ& ➤/FLDISBURSEMENTS ➤/FL"ɃFORECAST Ⓔ

>A2 Ⓔ /-* Ⓔ /R Ⓔ B2.C2 Ⓔ

>B4 Ⓔ /FR /R Ⓔ C4.J4 Ⓔ FORECAST ➤ACTUAL ➤"%VARIANCE ➤FORECAST ➤ACTUAL ➤"%VARIANCE ➤FORECAST ➤ACTUAL ➤"%VARIANCE Ⓔ

>A6 ⒠ BEGINNING⌴BALANCES ⒠

>A7 ⒠ /-= ⒠ /R ⒠ B7.J7 ⒠

>A8 ⒠ CASH ▸0 ▸@NA ▸((C8-B8)/B8) ▸0 ▸@NA ▸((F8-E8)/E8) ▸0 ▸@NA ▸((I8-H8)/H8) ⒠

>A9 ⒠ MARKETABLE⌴SECURITIES ⒠ /R BS B8.J8:B9 ⒠ RRRRRRRR

>A10 ⒠ /-- ⒠ /R ⒠ B10.J10 ⒠

>A11 ⒠ TOTAL ▸@SUM(B7.B10) ▸@SUM(C7.C10) ▸((C11-B11)/B11) ▸@SUM(E7.E10) ▸@SUM(F7.F10) ▸((F11-E11)/E11) ▸@SUM(H7.H10) ▸@SUM(I7.I10) ▸((I11-H11)/H11) ⒠

>A12 ⒠ /-- ⒠ /R ⒠ B12.J12 ⒠

>A14 ⒠ CASH⌴RECEIPTS ⒠

>A15 ⒠ /-= ⒠ /R ⒠ B15.J15 ⒠

>A16 ⒠ CASH⌴SALES ▸0 ▸@NA ▸((C16-B16)/B16) ▸0 ▸@NA ▸((F16-E16)/E16) ▸0 ▸@NA ▸((I16-H16)/H16) ⒠ /R BS B16.J16:B17.B20 ⒠ RRRRRRRR

>A17 ⒠ A/R⌴COLLECTIONS ▾ SALE⌴OF⌴FIXED⌴ASSETS ▾ INVESTMENT⌴INCOME ▾ OTHER ▾ /-- ⒠ /R ⒠ B21.J21 ⒠

>A22 ⒠ TOTAL ▸@SUM(B15.B21) ▸@SUM(C15.C21) ▸((C22-B22)/B22) ▸@SUM(E15.E21) ▸@SUM(F15.F21) ▸((F22-E22)/E22) ▸@SUM(H15.H21) ▸@SUM(I15.I21) ▸((I22-H22)/H22) ⒠

>A23 ⒠ /-- ⒠ /R ⒠ B23.J23 ⒠

>A25 ⒠ CASH⌴DISBURSEMENTS ▾ /-= ⒠ /R ⒠ B26.J26 ⒠

>A27 ⒠ PAYROLL ▸0 ▸@NA ▸((C27-B27)/B27) ▸0 ▸@NA ▸((F27-E27)/E27) ▸0 ▸@NA ▸((I27-H27)/H27) ⒠

>A28 ⒠ TAXES⌴PAID ⒠ /R BS B27.J27:B28.B37 ⒠ RRRRRRRR ▾ SUPPLIER⌴INVOICES ▾ OPERATING⌴EXPENSES ▾ INTEREST⌴PAYMENTS ▾ ADVERTISING ▾ DEBT⌴REPAYMENT ▾ INSURANCE ▾ DIVIDENDS ▾ CAPITAL⌴EXPENDITURES ▾ OTHER ▾ /-- ⒠ /R ⒠ B38.J38 ⒠

Appendix 267

>A39 Ⓔ TOTAL ➤@SUM(B26.B38) ➤@SUM(C26.C38)
➤((C39–B39)/B39) ➤@SUM(E26.E38) ➤@SUM(F26.F38) ➤((F39–E39)/E39)
➤@SUM(H26.H38) ➤@SUM(I26.I38) ➤((I39–H39)/H39) Ⓔ

>A40 Ⓔ /-- Ⓔ /R Ⓔ B40.J40 Ⓔ

>A42 Ⓔ ENDING⌴BALANCE ▼ /-= Ⓔ /R Ⓔ B43.J43 Ⓔ

>A44 Ⓔ OPENING⌴CASH ➤+B11 ➤+C11 ➤((C44–B44)/B44) ➤+E11
➤+F11 ➤((F44–E44)/E44) ➤+H11 ➤+I11 ➤((I44–H44)/H44) Ⓔ

>A45 Ⓔ PLUS⌴RECEIPTS ➤+B22 ➤+C22 ➤((C45–B45)/B45) ➤+E22 ➤+F22
➤((F45–E45)/E45) ➤+H22 ➤+I22 ➤((I45–H45)/H45) Ⓔ

>A46 Ⓔ LESS⌴DISBURSEMENTS ➤+B39 ➤+C39 ➤((C46–B46)/B46) ➤+E39
➤+F39 ➤((F46–E46)/E46) ➤+H39 ➤+I39 ➤((I46–H46)/H46) Ⓔ

>A47 Ⓔ NET⌴CHANGE ➤+B44+B45–B46 ➤+C44+C45–C46
➤((C47–B47)/B47) ➤+E44+E45–E46 ➤+F44+F45–F46 ➤((F47–E47)/E47)
➤+H44+H45–H46 ➤+I44+I45–I46 ➤((I47–H47)/H47) Ⓔ

>A48 Ⓔ /-- Ⓔ /R Ⓔ B48.J48 Ⓔ

/GC13 Ⓔ

/GF$
                    SANDAP

>E2 Ⓔ /FRADJUSTED ➤/FR NET⌴⌴ ➤/FRINCOME⌴ ➤/FRFORECAST Ⓔ

>E3 Ⓔ /-* Ⓔ /R Ⓔ F3.H3 Ⓔ

>C5 Ⓔ /FR /R Ⓔ D5.O5 Ⓔ JAN ➤FEB ➤MAR ➤APR ➤MAY ➤JUN ➤JUL
➤AUG ➤SEP ➤OCT ➤NOV ➤DEC ➤ANNUAL Ⓔ

>A6 Ⓔ SOURCES⌴O ➤F⌴FUNDS Ⓔ

>A7 Ⓔ /-= Ⓔ /R Ⓔ B7.O7 Ⓔ

>A8 Ⓔ NET⌴INCOM ➤E ▼ ◄DEPRECIAT ➤ION ▼ ◄AMORTIZAT ➤ION ▼
◄ DEFERRED⌴ ➤TAX ▼ ◄ACCOUNTS ➤PAYABLE ▼ ◄SHORT-TER
➤M⌴BORROWING ▼ ◄ OTHER Ⓔ

>O8 Ⓔ @SUM(C8.N8) Ⓔ /R Ⓔ O9.O14 Ⓔ RR

268 Appendix

>A15 Ⓔ /-- Ⓔ /R Ⓔ B15.O15 Ⓔ

>A16 Ⓔ TOTAL ► ►@SUM(C7.C15) Ⓔ /R Ⓔ D16.O16 Ⓔ RR

>A17 Ⓔ /-- Ⓔ /R Ⓔ B17.O17 Ⓔ

>A19 Ⓔ USES␢OF ►FUNDS Ⓔ

>A20 Ⓔ /-= Ⓔ /R Ⓔ B20.O20 Ⓔ

>A21 Ⓔ ACCOUNTS␢ ►RECEIVABLE ▼ ◄ INVENTORI ►ES ▼
◄ CAPITAL␢E ►XPENDITURES ▼ ◄ L-T-D␢REP ►AYMENT ▼
◄ DIVIDENDS ▼ OTHER Ⓔ

>O21 Ⓔ @SUM(C21.N21) Ⓔ /R Ⓔ O22.O26 Ⓔ RR

>A27 Ⓔ /-- Ⓔ /R Ⓔ B27.O27 Ⓔ

>A28 Ⓔ TOTAL ► ►@SUM(C20.C27) Ⓔ /R Ⓔ D28.O28 Ⓔ RR

>A29 Ⓔ /-- Ⓔ /R Ⓔ B29.O29 Ⓔ

>A31 Ⓔ OPERATING ►"␢CASH Ⓔ

>A32 Ⓔ /-= Ⓔ /R Ⓔ B32.O32 Ⓔ

>A33 Ⓔ BEGINNING ►"␢BALANCE ► ►+C36 Ⓔ /R Ⓔ E33.N33 Ⓔ R

>A34 Ⓔ PLUS␢SOUR ►CES ►+C16 Ⓔ /R Ⓔ D34.N34 Ⓔ R

>A35 Ⓔ LESS␢USES ► ►+C28 Ⓔ /R Ⓔ D35.N35 Ⓔ R

>A36 Ⓔ ENDING␢BA ►LANCE ►+C33+C34-C35 Ⓔ /R Ⓔ D36.N36 Ⓔ
RRR

>A37 Ⓔ /-= Ⓔ /R Ⓔ B37.O37 Ⓔ

PORTFOLIO MANAGEMENT

PORT

>D1 Ⓔ BOND ►/FRSECTI ►/FLON Ⓔ

Appendix 269

>C2 ⓔ /-* ⓔ /R ⓔ D2.G2 ⓔ

>C4 ⓔ /FR /R ⓔ D4.I4 ⓔ

>C4 ⓔ UNIT ➤BOOK ➤MARKET ➤MARKET ➤"%⌀OF ➤ ➤ANNUAL ⓔ

>A5 ⓔ /FLPAR⌀VALUE ➤/FR /R ⓔ C5.J5 ⓔ SECURITY ➤COST ➤VALUE ➤PRICE ➤VALUE ➤TOTAL ➤INTEREST ➤INCOME ➤YIELD ⓔ

>A6 ⓔ /-- ⓔ /R ⓔ B6.J6 ⓔ

>A8 ⓔ SECURITY ▼ /FL

>D9 ⓔ (A9*C9)/100 ➤ ➤(A9*E9)/100 ➤(F9/F30)*100 ➤ ➤(A9*H9)/100 ⓔ

>A10 ⓔ /-- ⓔ /R ⓔ B10.J10 ▼ TOTAL ➤BONDS ⓔ

>D11 ⓔ @SUM(D6.D10) ➤ ➤@SUM(F6.F10) ➤@SUM(G6.G10) ➤ ➤@SUM(I6.I10) ⓔ

>A12 ⓔ /-- ⓔ /R ⓔ B12.J12 ⓔ

>D15 ⓔ STOCK ➤/FRSECT ➤/FLION ⓔ

>C16 ⓔ /-* ⓔ /R ⓔ D16.G16 ⓔ

>A18 ⓔ /FR /R ⓔ B18.J18 ⓔ NUMBER⌀OF ➤ ➤UNIT ➤BOOK ➤MARKET ➤MARKET ➤"%⌀OF ➤ ➤ANNUAL ⓔ

>A19 ⓔ /FR /R ⓔ B19.J19 ⓔ SHARES ➤SECURITY ➤COST ➤VALUE ➤PRICE ➤VALUE ➤TOTAL ➤DIVIDEND ➤INCOME ➤YIELD ⓔ

>A20 ⓔ /-- ⓔ /R ⓔ B20.J20 ▼ ▼ SECURITY ▼ ▼ /FL

>D24 ⓔ +A24*C24 ➤.00001 ➤+A24*E24 ➤(F24/F30)*100 ➤0 ➤+H24*A24 ➤(H24/E24)*100 ⓔ

>A25 ⓔ /-- ⓔ /R ⓔ B25.J25 ▼ TOTAL ➤STOCKS ➤ ➤@SUM(D20.D25) ➤ ➤@SUM(F20.F25) ➤@SUM(G20.G25) ➤ ➤@SUM(I20.I25) ⓔ

>A27 ⓔ /-- ⓔ /R ⓔ B27.J27 ▼ ▼ /-= ⓔ /R ⓔ B29.J29 ⓔ

>A30 ⓔ PORTFOLIO ➤TOTALS ➤ ➤+D11+D26 ➤ ➤+F11+F26 ➤+G11+G26 ➤ ➤+I11+I26 ⓔ

/GF$ /GC10 Ⓔ

TRANS

>C1 Ⓔ /FRSECURITY ➤/FRTRANS ➤/FLACTION ➤/FLRECORD Ⓔ

>C2 Ⓔ /-* Ⓔ /R Ⓔ D2.F2 Ⓔ

>C6 Ⓔ /FR /R Ⓔ E6.L6 Ⓔ AMOUNT ➤ ➤AMOUNT ➤ ➤SHARES ➤AVERAGE ➤L/S? ➤L.TERM ➤S.TERM ➤NET Ⓔ

>B7 Ⓔ /FR /R Ⓔ C7.L7 Ⓔ DATE ➤BOUGHT ➤PRICE ➤SOLD ➤PRICE ➤HELD ➤COST ➤"(1/0) ➤GAIN/LOSS ➤GAIN/LOSS ➤GAIN/LOSS Ⓔ

>A8 Ⓔ /-- Ⓔ /R Ⓔ B8.L8 ▼ SECURITY Ⓔ

>B10 Ⓔ /FR ➤/FI .00001 ➤ ➤ /FI ➤ ➤/FI+G9+C10–E10 ➤((G9*H9)+(C10*D10))/(E10+G10) ➤/FI ➤+I10*(F10–H10)*E10 ➤(1–I10)*E10*(F10–H10) ➤+L9+J10+K10 Ⓔ

>A11 Ⓔ /-- Ⓔ /R Ⓔ B11.L11 ▼ TOTALS ➤ ➤ @SUM(C8.C11)/FI ➤ ➤@SUM(E8.E11)/FI Ⓔ

>J12 Ⓔ @SUM(J8.J11) ➤@SUM(K8.K11) Ⓔ

>A13 Ⓔ /-- Ⓔ /R Ⓔ B13.L13 Ⓔ

>A16 Ⓔ /R BS A6.L6:A16 Ⓔ /R BS A7.L7:A17 Ⓔ

>A18 Ⓔ /-- Ⓔ /R Ⓔ B18.L18 Ⓔ ▼ SECURITY Ⓔ /R BS A10.L10:A20 Ⓔ (20 R'S)

>A21 Ⓔ /-- Ⓔ /R Ⓔ B21.L21 Ⓔ /R BS A12.L12:A22 Ⓔ RRRRRRRR

>A23 Ⓔ /-- Ⓔ /R Ⓔ B23.L23 Ⓔ

/GF$ /GC10 Ⓔ

PORTFLOW

>A1 Ⓔ /FRPORTRTBF ➤/FL"PORTRIRO ➤/FRPBRPOBJB ➤/FLEBCBTB ERD ➤/FRIBNBCRO ➤/FL"BMBE Ⓔ

Appendix 271

>A3 Ⓔ SECURITY ►/FR /R Ⓔ C3.N3 Ⓔ JAN ►FEB ►MAR ►APR ►MAY ►JUN ►JUL ►AUG ►SEPT ►OCT ►NOV ►DEC ►ANNUAL Ⓔ

>A4 Ⓔ /-- Ⓔ /R Ⓔ B4.N4 Ⓔ

>N5 Ⓔ @SUM(B5.M5) Ⓔ

>A6 Ⓔ /-- Ⓔ /R Ⓔ B6.N6 ▼ /-= Ⓔ /R Ⓔ B7.N7 ▼ MONTHLY ▼ TOTAL ►@SUM(B4.B6) Ⓔ /R Ⓔ C9.M9 Ⓔ RR

>A10 Ⓔ /-= Ⓔ /R Ⓔ B10.N10 ▼ CUM. ▼ TOTAL ►+B9 ►+B12+C9 Ⓔ /R Ⓔ D12.M12 Ⓔ RR

>A13 Ⓔ /-= Ⓔ /R Ⓔ B13.N13 Ⓔ

/GF$

DIVRECS

>B1 Ⓔ /FRINCOME ►"ƀRECORD Ⓔ

>B2 Ⓔ /-* ►/-* Ⓔ

>D4 Ⓔ /FRINTEREST/ Ⓔ

>A5 Ⓔ /FR /R Ⓔ B5.F5 Ⓔ SECURITY ►DATE ►AMOUNT ►DIVIDEND ►TIMES ►TOTAL Ⓔ

>A6 Ⓔ /-= Ⓔ /R Ⓔ B6.F6 Ⓔ

>B7 Ⓔ /FR ►/FI ►/FG ►/FI ►/F$(C7*D7)/E7 Ⓔ

>A8 Ⓔ /-= Ⓔ /R Ⓔ B8.F8 ▼ TOTAL INCOME ►/-= Ⓔ /R Ⓔ C9.E9 ► ► ► ►@SUM(F6.F8) Ⓔ

>A10 Ⓔ /-= Ⓔ /R Ⓔ B10.F10 Ⓔ

Index

Accounts receivable turnover ratio, 129
Adjusted net income method, 202-206
   model, 213-215
Administrative budget, 177-178
Aged account analysis, 99
Apple, 7-9, 11, 13
Asset coverage ratio, 127-128
Asterisk (*), 37
   multiplication, 44
   labels beginning with, 136
@ (at) symbol, 48
Automatic recalculation, 29, 78
Average collection period, 98-99

/B command (see BLANK Command)
Backspace key, 8
   in replicate command, 50
Bad debt ratio, 99
BLANK command, 59-60
Bonds, 221
Border rows,
   adding, 59
   using to define starting and ending range of functions, 63-64
Budgets,
   requirements for success, 172-173, 183-184
   types of,
      manufacturing, 174-178

Budgets, (Contd.)
      models, 185-189
      retail, 178-184
      models, 189-198
Built-in functions, 48

/C command (see Clear screen command)
Cash flow,
   cycle, 201-203
   examples, 42-52
   models, 84-85
Cash flow method, 203
Cell locations, identification of, 19
Cell references, in formulas, 28-29
Checkbook balancing, 25-30
Clear screen command, 20, 36
Colon (:), 43
Columns,
   adjusting width, 70-72
   deleting, 62, 158
   inserting, 64
   replicating, 42-43
Common stock, 219-220
Compound interest, 57-59
Conference Board in Canada, 154
Control panel, 19
Credit, cost of offering, 101, 108
Credit cards, 100-101

Index

Credit management, 94-99
  model, 103-111
Current assets, 97
Current liabilities, 97
Cursor movement, 19-20
Customer credit history, 101
  model, 111-116
Customer inquiry system, 155

/D command (see DELETE Command)
Debentures, 221-222
Debt equity ratio, 125-127
DELETE command, 62
Direct cursor movement, 21-22
Directional indicator, 11, 17-18
Directional keys, 7-8
  Apple, 11
  IBM, 11, 15
  Radio Shack TRS-80 Model II, 9
  Radio Shack TRS-80 Model III, 11
Direct versus indirect costs, 176-177
Discount register, 180
  model of, 192-194
Diversification, 226-227
Dollars and cents format, 33-35
Domino rows, 46-47
Dummy rows, 87-89
Dun and Bradstreet, 99

Earnings per share, 131-132
Econometric indicators, 155
Edit line, 19
Efficiency ratios, 128-130
Electronic sheet,
  defined, 4
  size, 19-21
Ellipsis, 43
Enter key, 8, 22
Entry contents line, 19, 20
  displays entire contents of cell, 27
  displays actual contents of cell, 34
@ERROR, 62-63

/F Command (see FORMAT Command)
Financial ratios (see Ratios, financial)
Financial statements, 120-122
  Tandy Corporation, 140-143
Financing,
  debt, 126
  equity, 126
Fixing titles, 72-73
Float, 207
Forecasting cash needs, 201-208
  models, 209-215

Forecasting sales, 152-156
  model, 158-162
Forecasting the income statement, 156
  model, 162-169
FORMAT command, 33-38
  /FD (default), 35
  /FG (general), 37-38
  /FI (integer), 34
  /FL (left justification), 36
  /FR (right justification), 36
  /F$ (dollars and cents), 34-36
  /F* (bar graph), 37
Formatting a single cell, 34-36

/G command (see GLOBAL Command)
General and administrative budget, 177-178
GLOBAL command, 35
  /GC (column), 70-72
  /GF (format), 35
  /GO (order of recalculation), 35
  /GR (recalculation), 78
GO TO command, 21-22
Gross profit margin:
  budget, 182
  model of, 196-198
  controlling, 178-184
Gross profit margin ratio, 130
Growth stocks, 222-224

/I command (see INSERT command)
IBM Personal Computer, 7-9, 11, 14-15
Income stocks, 224-225
INSERT command, 64
Interest earned calculation, 57
Inventory, opening, 181
Inventory tally sheet, 180-181
  model of, 194-196
Inventory turnover ratio, 128-129

Jury of executive opinion (JEO), 153-154

Keyboards, 10, 12-14

Labels, 25-26
  justification, 38
  numeric entries as labels, 42
Labor budget, 176-177
  model, 187-189
Liquidity ratios, 121-125 (see also Working capital ratio, Quick asset ratio)
Loading the electronic sheet, 31

Index 275

Long-term solvency ratios, 125-128

Materials budget, 175
  models, 185-187
Materials requirement estimate, 174-175
Memory indicator, 18-19
Models,
  loading, 30-31
  packed format, 84-86
  saving, 30-31
Models, packed,
  adjusted net income forecast, 213-215
  credit analysis, 103-111
  credit record, 111-116
  discount register, 192-194
  financial statement analysis, 133-149
  forecasting the income statement, 162-169
  gross margin budget, 196-198
  income Record Model, 244-246
  inventory tally sheet, 194-196
  labor budget, 187-189
  materials budget, 185-189
  portfolio cash flow, 242-244
  receipts and disbursements Cash Forecast, 209-213
  receiving journal, 189-192
  sales force inquiry model, 157-162
  the portfolio, 229-237
  transactions, 237-242
/M command (see MOVE command)
MOVE command, 79

Net profit margin ratio, 130-131

Overflow condition, 60, 71

/P command (see PRINT command)
Packed format, 84, 87, 88-89
Passell, Peter, 217
Plus (+) sign, 29
Portfolios,
  aggressive, 218-222
  defensive, 218-222
  model of composition, 229-237
  model of income received, 244-246
  model of projected cash flow, 242-244
  model of transactions, 237-242
Preferred stock, 220-221
Price earnings ratio, 132-133
PRINT command, 79
Profitability ratios, 130-133
Projected average collection period, 107

Prompt line, 19, 21-22

Quick asset ratio, 98, 124-125
Quotation mark ("), 42

/R command (see REPLICATE command)
Radio Shack TRS-80:
  Model II, 7-9, 9-10
  Model III, 7-9, 11-12
Ratios, financial,
  efficiency, 128-130
  liquidity, 121-125
  long-term solvency, 125-128
  model using, 133-149
  profitability, 130-133
Recalculation,
  automatic, 29, 78
  manual, 78
  order of, 18
Receipts and disbursements method, 202-205
  model, 209-213
Receiving journal, 179
  model of, 189-192
Repeat key, 9
  Apple, 11
  IBM, 15
  Radio Shack TRS-80 Model II, 9, 11
  Radio Shack TRS-80 Model III, 11
REPEATING LABEL command, 70
Repeating rows, 87-89
REPLICATE command, 43-47
  copying formulas with variables, 47-49
  no change option, 47
  relative option, 49
  replicating repeating lines, 87-88
  source range, 43
  target range, 43
Return key (see Enter key)
Return on common equity ratio, 131
Robert Morris Associates, 99
Rows,
  deleting, 62
  domino rows, 46-47
  inserting, 64
  repeating, 87-89
  replicating, 87-88

/S command (see STORAGE command)
Sales, conversion from retail to cost basis, 194
Sales force inquiry method (SFI), 154-155
  model using, 157-162
Sales projections,

Sales projections, *(Contd.)*
  benefits of accurate, 153
  types of, 153-157
Sales to working capital ratio, 129
Saving the electronic sheet, 30-31
Screen widths, 8
  comparing different widths to illustrations, 21
Scrolling, 20
Securities,
  selecting, 218-219
  types of, 219-226
Seneca, 151
Slash (/) key, 33
Source and application of funds method, 202-206
Standard and Poor's Industry Guide, 145
Standard industry code (SIC), 145
STORAGE command, 79
@SUM function, 48-49, 62-63

/T command (see TITLES command)
Time series analysis, 155
Times interest earned, 127
TITLES command, 72-73
  /TB (Both), 73
  /TH (Horizontal), 72-73
  /TN (None), 72, 73
  /TV (Vertical), 72

Values, 27
  cell locations as values, 29
  display of, 71
  justification, 38
Variance, 211

/W command (see WINDOW command)
Warrants, 222
WINDOW command, 73-77
  /WH (Horizontal), 77
  /WV (Vertical), 73-74
  /W1 (One window), 75
    format in effect when reverting to one window, 76
  /WS (Synchronized), 77
  /WU (Unsynchronized), 77
  with different global formats, 75
Working capital ratio, 96-97, 121-124